I0880112

IN SEARCH OF FIRST-CENTURY CHRISTIANITY

In Search of First-Century Christianity contends that Christianity in the first century had no founder but rather evolved as a convergence of many forces: political disillusionment, cultural mutations, religious and theological motifs, psychosocial losses and new expectations. Following an examination of the foundations of historical and literary criticism in the Renaissance, and a detailed study of two writers in antiquity, Thucydides and Chariton, to examine writings in the period between Plato and the Gospel of Mark, the authors explore the writing of Paul and the stories told in the Gospels. With the early Christians drawing from both Greek and Hebrew sources, Barnhart and Kraeger propose that, like Plato, Paul and other Christians generated an 'anti-tragic theatre' gospel with the Jesus figure being the creation of a culture steeped in an anthropomorphic, metaphysical view of the world.

Focusing on Paul's letters and other Christian writings, and the political, intellectual, moral and emotional conflicts they faced, and their formulation of early views of Christ in relation to the roles of Augustus and Caligula, this book explores the difficult question of whether Jesus was an historical figure or an image who first emerged within developing communities of visionaries. Through an exploration into how Christology developed in the early first century, the authors seek to show that Christianity's emerging theology was a venture in human problem solving and that both Paul and the Gospels sought to relate a story in which goodness would ultimately triumph, in the person of Christ.

Joe E. Barnhart is Professor of Philosophy and Religious Studies at the University of North Texas, USA; Linda T. Kraeger is Lecturer in the Department of Literature and Language at Grayson County College, USA.

This book is dedicated to six-year-old Victoria,
a living poem, a dancing rainbow

ASHGATE NEW CRITICAL THINKING IN THEOLOGY & BIBLICAL STUDIES

Ashgate New Critical Thinking in Theology & Biblical Studies presents an open-ended series of quality research drawn from an international field of scholarship. The series aims to bring monograph publishing back into focus for authors, the international library market, and student, academic and research readers. Headed by an international editorial advisory board of acclaimed scholars, this series presents cutting-edge research from established as well as exciting new authors in the field. With specialist focus, yet clear contextual presentation, books in the series aim to take theological and biblical research into new directions; opening the field to new critical debate within the traditions, into areas of related study, and into important topics for contemporary society.

In Search of First-Century Christianity

JOE E. BARNHART
University of North Texas

LINDA T. KRAEGER
Grayson County College, Denison, Texas

Routledge
Taylor & Francis Group
LONDON AND NEW YORK

First published 2000 by Ashgate Publishing

Reissued 2019 by Routledge
2 Park Square, Milton Park, Abingdon, Oxon, OX14 4RN
52 Vanderbilt Avenue, New York, NY 10017

Routledge is an imprint of the Taylor & Francis Group, an informa business

A Library of Congress record exists under LC control number:

ISBN 13: 978-1-138-71611-7 (hbk)
ISBN 13: 978-1-138-71609-4 (pbk)
ISBN 13: 978-1-315-19718-0 (ebk)

Contents

Acknowledgements

The Society of Biblical Literature and the American Academy of Religion have made a lasting impact on us. Pursuing better models and hypotheses, biblical scholars and literary critics have debated the issues, thus creating a remarkable combination of tough-mindedness and openness to both criticism and the exploration of rival hypotheses. The new freedom of exchange and publication in biblical studies that has developed over the past three decades must receive credit if our modest efforts prove to contribute toward a better understanding of early Christianity's emergence. The risks taken in these chapters are by the grace, work and encouragement of others bolder than we. Of course, we carry alone the burden of the many shortcomings of our sixteen chapters.

As any researcher knows, no one can possibly be aware of even half the sources that have fed into his or her thinking over the decades. There is no way to thank all those living and dead who have challenged us to think new thoughts. Personal thanks, nevertheless, go to the following who helped directly with this book:

1) Professor Joseph Stamey for his careful reading of an earlier draft of our manuscript and providing exceedingly useful recommendations for improvements.
2) The Reverend Dr. Donald Fielding and Professor Daryl Schmidt for books, insights, and ideas they almost casually planted in our minds.
3) The University of North Texas for a paid faculty-development leave to do research on this book.
4) Classicist Anthony Damico for patiently fielding some of our questions of etymology and word study.
5) Professor Eugene Hargrove, Chair of the Department of Philosophy and Religion Studies, University of North Texas, for working hard to create a strong academic climate conducive to research and writing.
6) Mary Ann Barnhart for her editorial and culinary skills in making possible the completion of this work.
7) Duane Kraeger for his invaluable proofreading and suggestions.
8) Our departmental colleagues for their goodwill, encouragement, and contribution to an intellectually stimulating environment.
9) The University of North Texas library staff, especially Lou Ann Bradley and Dr. Gary Sanders, without whose help this book might have remained an embryo.
10) Jo Ann Luksich of Data Entry for typing the very first draft of our manuscript.

11) The Fall 1999 UNT Epistemology class for working through the manuscript's third version and raising critical questions that deserved thoughtful responses.
12) Grayson County College's Spring 1999 World Literature class for raising important questions regarding religion in literature.
13) Our good friend Kay Prewitt, who typed and edited several professional papers and journal articles that foreshadowed much of this book.

1 Introduction

During the last quarter of the twentieth century, historical inquiry into the emergence of first-century Christianity resurrected a fresh search for the historical Jesus. A parallel quest shadowing the primary inquiry surfaced in one question. How did Christianity with its elaborate Gospels and theological doctrines about "Jesus Christ the Son of God" come into being?

At the heart of the debate among biblical scholars stands the problem of the bridge between the earthly Jesus and the cosmic Son of God. The Jesus Seminar has worked from the perspective that the canonical Gospels and other early Gospels contain invaluable leads. If properly mined and connected with other relevant materials, they will allow researchers to reconstruct not a full biography, but a reliable account of the earthly Jesus. The scholarly task, therefore, is to cross the bridge that will return us to this Jesus before he became the captive of the theological mythmakers.

Three camps have thus emerged, one portraying Jesus as essentially the originator of a social and religious revolution more profound than any political revolution. The second camp portrays a Jesus possessed with an eschatological if not apocalyptic vision that, simply stated, did not materialize as expected. According to the third camp, one cannot realistically separate the earthly Jesus from the theological claims made about him. Except for those who hold to some theory of biblical inerrancy, the scholars of this camp continue to engage in rigorous historical and literary inquiry into the original Jesus. They think this Jesus not only existed, but also was the special presence of deity in human flesh. Those embracing this position may differ regarding the degree and nature of Jesus' divine incarnation. They, nevertheless, are convinced that only the assumption of the divine incarnation can explain the emergence of the Church with its mission, martyrs, and theological formulations.

In writing this book, we have been constantly aware that the same data can support rival explanatory theories. We have appropriated for our theory much of the evidence used by the models of the first two camps. We believe the third camp is correct in one respect but mistaken in another. The two images of Jesus, we acknowledge, belong together and cannot be separated. At the same time, our working model does not require the conjecture that Jesus Christ was in fact a supernatural incarnation in human history. According to our thesis, Jesus Christ is more accurately viewed as a cultural emergent. Literary critic Harold Bloom is, we suggest, on the right course when he writes that Jesus Christ the Son of God portrayed in Mark's Gospel was a literary creation. "Hamlet is *beyond* us, beyond everyone else in Shakespeare or in literature, unless indeed you agree with me in finding the Yahweh of the J Writer and the Jesus of the Gospel of Mark to be literary characters" (Bloom, 1998, p. 422). At the same time, we submit that neither Mark nor anyone else of the first century set out to invent a Jesus to be solely a literary personage. Rather, like the Egyptians and ancient Greeks, the early Christians believed in their divinities. From the beginning, the Jesus figure was the creation of a culture steeped in a special metaphysical view of the world that was anthropomorphic through and through. Jesus Christ as a stunning cultural mutation and elaboration emerged because Paul as well as other religious thinkers before and after him sought to *solve specific problems.* These problems grew out of the universal human condition of finitude and tragedy within a special Greco-Roman political setting. Furthermore, the problems were formulated in the theological and religious language inherited largely from the Hebrew tradition, including the complex narratives of the Second Temple period (van Buren, 1998, pp. 71-82). As instructors in the humanities, we have an abiding interest in better understanding how first-century Christianity fits into the rich theological and narrative tradition that took millennia to build. We come as a part of that developing human enterprise and as heirs of other, perhaps competing, traditions. This fact alone tends to generate reflection, leading us to become both insiders and outsiders to the worldview that we now call first-century Christianity (Larue, 1996, pp. 3-10, 193-230). This book thus speaks to us as much as to our readers.

Christianity in the first century did not appear from the blue. Fortunately, for the past several decades, biblical scholarship has progressed by astounding leaps and bounds. In this book, we hope to contribute a small part to the continuing quest for a fuller account of Christianity's origin. Progress in biblical studies often comes by crossing borders and making sustained contact with other fields of discipline. New Testament scholars have crossed borders because they had big and difficult problems to confront. They have engaged historians, literary critics, classicists, archaeologists, philosophers, social scientists, linguists, and theologians.

Contrary to what some might claim, no one stands on Mount Neutral to peer down in detachment. All committed scholars are down in the trenches, arriving from their special backgrounds, but concerned to share in the rigorous exchange of ideas. As academicians, we have buried a few of our biases and have seen others endure serious revision. Letting some biases die for us sets us free to cultivate new ones that, we hope, will prove fruitful. In Chapter 2, we offer the conjecture that the Renaissance in Europe was the great womb that gave birth to both historical and literary criticism. Chapter 3 focuses on two writers of antiquity, one a Greek historian and the other a Greek-speaking novelist. We intend to give our readers a "feel" for the way stories were sometimes told in the period between Plato and the Gospel of Mark. We believe this chapter will help set the stage for approaching the stories told in the Gospels.

Chapters 4 through 8 proceed on the assumption that the Apostle Paul's letters provide one of the earliest records of Christian thinking. Paul was striving to solve problems that had become severe crises in the complex worldview he had inherited. As a missionary to the Gentiles, he confronted challenges that sometimes threw him into political, intellectual, moral, and emotional conflict with other apostles presumed to be agents of the gospel. No one could read Paul's letters without sensing that his thinking was not one steady stream flowing untroubled into the sea. Rather, it was several streams rushing into one another to create such swirling eddies as to force him to deal with threatening crises. Strange as it may seem, science too is largely a process of major theories and hypotheses facing severe crises.

Chapter 9 in particular explores the fruitful hypothesis that the earliest Christians envisioned a Christ who was the opposite of Gaius Caesar Germanicus, nicknamed Caligula. According to this hypothesis, the Lord Jesus Christ, although possessing deity, assumed earthly, human form. By contrast, Caligula, though a mere mortal, became increasingly obsessed with self-deification. It is noteworthy that Caligula ruled the Roman Empire at about the time the Apostle Paul underwent transforming experiences and received what he regarded as special revelations from the resurrected Savior and Lord. Augustus' and Caligula's roles in the formation of early views of Christ Jesus will surface in Chapter 12.

Chapters 10, 11, and 13 explore the difficult question of whether Jesus was a historical figure whose followers somehow both preserved and systematically distorted his mission, message, and person. Or, to the contrary, did the image of a cosmic Jesus Christ first emerge within developing communities of visionaries? Did the putative "details" of Christ Jesus' earthly life subsequently evolve and, in some cases, converge eventually to become the warp and woof of the Gospels?

In Chapters 14 through 16, we develop our thesis that, like Plato's dialogues, Paul's epistles and the four Gospels are strongly "anti-tragic theater." Theodicy, the problem of suffering and evil, shadowed the ancient Greek dramatists, who left their audiences shuddering at "the fragility of goodness." Both Paul and the Gospels, we try to show, sought a story in which goodness would ultimately triumph in the person of Christ.

2 The Renaissance and the Bible

The Two Western Canons

The giants among creative writers rewrite endlessly. Dostoevsky, the great Russian novelist, kept reworking a handful of crucial themes from novel to novel, drawing from the superlative narratives of his predecessors and recasting their characters (Fanger, 1965; MacPike, 1981; Weisgerber, 1968). Literary giants rewrite perpetually, borrowing and transforming. "Greatness recognizes greatness and is shadowed by it" (Bloom, 1994, p. 10). The towering canon of literature called the Bible represents centuries of revising and retelling. For example, the authors of Ruth and Jonah could not permit Ezra's account to stand uncorrected. Similarly, Job refused to permit the theology of Proverbs to sail unchallenged.

Harold Bloom wisely places Shakespeare at the center of the secular Western Canon. "Shakespeare *is* the secular canon, or even the secular scripture...." (Bloom, 1994, p. 24). This judgment contains a double irony. First, in myriad ways, Shakespeare learned constantly from the West's religious canon and used it stunningly throughout his career (Shaheen, 1987 and 1989). Even Falstaff partially represents an explosive mutant of Alice, the wife of Bath, around whom Chaucer created a daring commentary on the Apostle Paul's counsel regarding marriage and virginity (1 Cor. 7).[1]

A few sentences can explain the second irony found in the way that the secular canon intersects the religious canon. As a voice of the Renaissance, Shakespeare compelled his contemporaries to ponder in a new light the historical claims of the Bible. His history plays probed until the audience could not escape wondering about the reliability of the meandering story called history. Today, some scholars insist that Shakespeare was a defender of monarchy. Perhaps so. Still, who more than he and the writers of 1 and 2 Samuel and 1 and 2 Kings has cast a shadow of doubt over the institution of monarchy itself? Who has surpassed Shakespeare in relentlessly exposing the fraudulent claims, flaws, and foul deeds of various occupants of the throne? Furthermore, if Shakespeare could raise questions about the claims of England's political foundations, would not questions inevitably rise regarding the head of the Church of England, who happened to be England's monarch, beginning with Henry VIII? Thus, the question of a religion's very foundation naturally arose in the modern history play, which was almost Shakespeare's invention. During the Renaissance, new questions emerged regarding authoritative claims either found in the Bible or imposed upon it.

William Shakespeare, born under the reign of Henry's daughter Elizabeth, died while James I was still posing as an enthroned God on earth. Addressing Parliament, James asserted, "Kings are justly called gods for they exercise a manner or resemblance of divine power upon earth.... [K]ings make and unmake their subjects...." (Martinich, 1992, pp. 46-47). As we will argue in Chapter 12, a presumed effluence from celestial deity to earthly rulers has been a heavy motif in human history since the ancient Egyptian monarchy. The Hebrew tradition developed ambivalence toward the claims and presumptions of mortal kings. First Samuel sets forth the position that the very idea of an earthly king over Israel came not from Yahweh, but from a people weak in faith and eager to emulate neighboring kingdoms. In Chapters 9 and 12, we suggest that early Christianity represents a creative attempt to reformulate the God-Emperor motif. While seeking to maintain the Jesus' humanity, Christians portrayed him as free of the flaws so manifest in Roman emperors and their predecessors, the Seleucid rulers.

New Challenging Kingdoms

Before James' arrival in England to receive the crown, Shakespeare and other Renaissance thinkers had initiated two kingdoms of their own: literary criticism and historical criticism. Although separate disciplines today, the two thriving kingdoms land on each other's shores to exchange thorny questions and fruitful insights. Centuries prior to Shakespeare, the Hebrew tradition generated something akin to literary criticism for both those with eyes to see the subtleties of the multi-layered Hebrew Bible and those with ears to hear its many voices. Many factors, however, helped retard historical criticism for centuries until eventually the humanists of Europe grew thirsty to learn from the ancient Hebrew, Greek, and Latin texts.

The Donation of Constantine

In the fifteenth century, the discovery that the Donation of Constantine was a crude forgery blew the lid off the ecclesiastical pot. For over six-hundred years, many clergymen and scholars who knew about the document believed it the work of the fourth-century Pope Sylvester I. The document purported to give him and his successors temporal power over Italy. Actually written over three centuries after Sylvester's death, it purports to give an authentic account of Emperor Constantine's conversion and baptism. As Professor Phyllis Rackin has pointed out, a critical reading of the texts was the exception until the Renaissance. Lorenzo Valla (1405-1457) not only exposed the falsity of the document, but also doubted that the apostles had composed the Apostles' Creed. Valla also helped lay the foundation for modern New Testament studies by comparing the Latin Vulgate with the Greek manuscripts.

During the Renaissance, more people began to realize that human history was not like pieces appearing simultaneously in a medieval tapestry. Rather, history's unfolding story required real time so that what appeared at one period might have been impossible at another. Renaissance scholars began to see more clearly the need to reconstruct reliable representations, which would require enormous discipline. They gained a glimpse of some crucial differences between people separated by several centuries.

Eventually, some persistent students of the Bible came to perceive the text as not really one voice or one message, but a *process* containing many voices speaking at very different times (Rackin, 1990, pp. 9-12). Furthermore, Renaissance scholars reasoned that various biblical texts must have been composed under strikingly different circumstances and for perhaps different purposes. In short, scholars could not take Holy Writ as a "given" immaculately conceived.

The Christian Humanists and the Text

Erasmus, Luther, Calvin, and other Christian humanists sought to make a distinction between the scriptures and the interpretations that had developed around them over the centuries. Erasmus in particular could no longer view historical truths, records, facts, and witnesses as pieces in a perfect mosaic. Luther had serious doubts about the Epistle of James. Calvin elected not to publish a commentary on the troublesome New Testament Apocalypse. Erasmus had found it necessary to sift through various manuscripts and documents to arrive at what he judged to be the more likely approximation of the original texts. The existence of variant versions eventually created new questions about every version of the Bible.

Catholic apologists often charged that by translating the Bible into readable German, Luther sowed the seeds of skepticism and unbelief throughout all Germany. Thomas More believed Luther had not only turned the moral world upside down, but also threatened to remove all meaning from the universe (Marius, 1985, p. 271). According to historian Richard Marius, Luther proved to be "perhaps the most brilliant wordsmith European civilization produced between Dante and Shakespeare.... [W]hen Luther spoke, people all over Europe repeated what he said" (Marius, 1985, p. 269). Few writers have equaled Dr. Luther in grasping the enormous power of words to create both doubt and belief.

Around September 1514, Martin van Dorp, a University of Louvain lecturer, sent a disturbing letter to Erasmus. In it, he hinted that the faculty might openly condemn Erasmus if he published notes on a thousand New Testament passages or amended the Latin Bible, the Vulgate that the Church had used for centuries. Erasmus' threat profoundly disturbed Dorp. What would the faithful think if they learned that the Church's great doctors and councils had based many doctrines on a flawed Vulgate? If the integrity of the biblical text came under question, would not questions emerge about the Church's teachings and her trustworthiness (Marius, 1985, pp. 145-146)? What then could one say of a God who permitted errors to creep into his sacred Word and his Holy Church?

The Renaissance with its movable type not only made Holy Writ available to vast numbers of believers in England and on the Continent, but also raised gnawing questions for devout humanist scholars themselves. Most people in the pews never learned of questions about textual criticism, just as today most church members remain unaware of the astounding transformation in biblical studies that flourished during the second half of the twentieth century. The Renaissance scholars can perhaps be forgiven for shielding the people from the disturbing questions. They themselves had no ready answers. How indeed could they readily explain the corrupted texts of Scripture and the error-riddled texts of Church fathers (Marius, 1985, pp. 67-69, 146)?

With the translation of Scripture into various languages came the text's increasingly wider distribution. Placing it into the hands of the people was itself revolutionary, even without giving them information about textual corruption. Once the political climate shifted even slightly, new questions and doubts about the Church's interpretations sprang up. Defenders of the old way made dire predictions that new sects would soon spawn in every village if the people gained direct access to Holy Writ. The predictions came true with a vengeance. In England, Thomas Nashe and Francis Bacon complained bitterly that the numerous sects and schisms had pushed many toward atheism. Fulke Greville feared that the "many-headed separation" would stain religion's reputation (Elton, 1988, pp. 45-46).

Censorship of many varieties persisted, which unquestionably prevented the publication of significant elements of Renaissance thought. Nashe went so far as to denounce the superabundance of wit as the maker of atheists. The more heated the debates became, the more frequently people hurled charges of atheism at believers who possessed views contrary to the accusers' definitions of the faith. They also threw the charge "blasphemer" about with abandon (Elton, 1988, pp. 45, 50).

A Poet's Power

Although the Renaissance was too complex to have had one founder,[2] one of the earliest and most provocative forerunners of the Renaissance (and the Reformation) was the Italian poet Dante (1265-1321). What would the Renaissance have been without him? More than two centuries before Dr. Luther translated Scripture into German, Dante wrote *Divine Comedy* in his people's language. The work abounds with such breathtaking power and astounding scenarios that no one has surpassed him as an uncannily bold poet. Perhaps it should come as no surprise that the Renaissance should have begun in Italy. In *Denison Monarchia*, Dante raises serious questions regarding the effluence from celestial deity to earthly rulers. Rather than doubt the effluence itself, he questions the distribution of the flowing power and criticizes both the State and the Papacy for their self-aggrandizement. In particular, he denounces the Papacy's greed for temporal and political power as rooted in the ill-conceived Donation of Constantine. His voice may be one of the earliest to call clearly for some kind of separation of Church and State and for accessible public education (MacAllister,

1982, p. xxiii.) Far from casting Thomas Aquinas' theology into poetry (itself a magnificent achievement), Dante adorned the roles of shaman, poet, prophet, theologian, and bold adventurer to create a wedding of philosophical imagery and poetry that thrust human language into the stratosphere. Thanks to both the incomparable Luther and Dante, the educated of the West were becoming increasingly word-conscious and text-conscience. Once believers understood that translations had come into being, some began to understand that sacred original texts themselves had come into being over long periods.

History as Accurate Accounts

If the Renaissance could begin with unprecedented poetry that soar into highest Heaven and journey through lowest Hell, it could also in time create a new discipline that required the service of uncompromising prose. The writing of history would never again be what it had been for centuries. In *Fact or Fiction: The Dilemma of the Renaissance Storyteller*, William Miller shows that the historians of Shakespeare's time faced anew the problem of sorting out accurate representations of the past from events and speeches the authors invented (Miller, 1973, pp. 105-109). Truth for truth's sake became as powerful a concern as art for art's sake or morality for morality's sake. Dante writes as if Virgil's *Aeneid* is actual history rather than a fiction within fiction (Lindskoog, 1977, p. 32 n.3). The new historical inquiry demanded that truth not serve as handmaiden to art, morality, politics, or religion. Previously, historians had often invented speeches and orations for heroes and villains. Now new standards must prevail. Arguably, the problems raised in Shakespeare's history plays helped create history as a relatively autonomous discipline. The Reformation doubtless did its part, too, as the Reformers fought to root their faith in authoritative texts of Scripture rather than in papal bulls and priestly proclamations (Conklin, 1949, pp. 10, 30-35).

> Rhyme gave way to reason, verse to prose, as the new historians banished the legendary material and the invented speeches that had adorned their predecessors' works to the distinct province of poetry. Even the arrangement of incidents was strictly regulated. Thomas Blunderville's *The true order and Method of wryting and reading Hystories* (1574) flatly stated, "An Hystorye ought to declare the thyngs in suche order, as they were done." (Rackin, 1990, p. 19)

Accurately Reporting Providence

How do historians accurately report or discover the supernatural finger of providence? Sir Thomas More, a Catholic, ridiculed the Protestants for the lack of miracles and supernatural wonders to authenticate their religion. In reply, Protestants scorned the Catholic proliferation of relics entwined with superstitions. In his *Leviathan,* Thomas Hobbes allowed for miracles in biblical times only. After the apostolic age, all new miracles became "counterfeit miracles," a phrase B. B. Warfield later used to title a book in which he attacked the claims of Pentecostals, faith healers, and Christian Science practitioners (Warfield, 1918).

The Renaissance gave birth to a detailed critique of claims involving spirits and witches. Reginald Scot's *Discovery of Witchcraft* (1584), to which he appended a *Discourse upon Devils and Spirits*, was one of Shakespeare's major sources. Perhaps the boldest aspect of Scot's thesis was his attempt to explain away apparitions in Holy Writ, like that of En-Dor (1 Sam. 28:3-25). As a Christian, Scot argued that apparitions were either the illusions of melancholic minds or the knavery of rogues. Because of the political climate in Scot's time, few defended his views publicly. Before assuming the crown, King James I (James VI of Scotland) wrote *Daemonology* to denounce Scot's "damnable opinions." After James became enthroned in England, the state's hangman burned Scot's book. Ironically, James dissociated himself from those who believed in angelic apparitions, since miracles had ceased at the close of the apostolic age (Wilson, J., 1959, p. 62; Hankins, 1941, pp. 134-171; Roland, 1984; Thomas, K., 1971). Apparently deeming himself both a theologian and Head of the Church of England, King James could more readily abide the existence of demons and witches than that of ministering angels.

Erasmus, who had spent some time in More's England, did not grow skeptical of all Catholic miracles. He did, however, find fault with the credulity of the masses. In *Dialogue Concerning Heresies*, More professed to have witnessed the cure of the demon-possessed Anne Wentworth. In *Answers to Thomas More's Dialogue*, William Tyndale pointed out that More had been favorably disposed toward Elizabeth Barton, the Nun of Kent who, like Wentworth, prophesied in trance. Several miracle stories had circulated around both women. Therefore, Tyndale challenged More to set forth the criterion used to discern the difference between those filled with divine inspiration and those possessed of demons. As one contemporary historian notes, More's ambivalence toward the Nun of Kent stemmed partially from a tension in his own faith. Though a medieval man in many ways, he had "absorbed too much of the skepticism of classical culture to believe in the miracles he wanted to believe in (Marius, 1985, pp. 446-452). Today, biblical scholars face the similar problem of how much credence to give to biblical miracle stories.

Had More truly believed that miraculous invention had discovered John the Baptist's head and St. Stephen's body? Where did he draw the line? Tyndale wanted to know. Did More himself know where he would draw it? Tyndale, perhaps the demythologizing Rudolf Bultmann of his time, believed that the Christian faith could better shine in its own light if stripped of papal myths and fanciful tales that insulted the intelligence of the creature made in God's image.

Thomas Hobbes and a host of Protestants before and after him eliminated all miracles after the apostolic age. Hume took arguments that Protestants had successfully leveled at Catholic miracles and turned them against the miracles of Holy Writ. In short, why should people build a wall around the Bible? Spinoza, a Jew in Holland, had earlier raised questions about the Hebrew Bible, questions of a literary and philosophical nature that the rabbis did not wish repeated in the synagogues. In some respects, one may view Spinoza (1632-1677) as the John the Baptist of what later became known among biblical scholars as "higher criticism."[3]

In Quest of the Historical Aeneas and Romulus

Cicero pronounced as an invention or a *fabula ficta* the friendship of the Greek heroes Theseus and Pirithous and their descent into Hell. He did not believe that Castor and Pollux really appeared to a certain Vatienus on a road outside Rome. Yet, this same Cicero fully admitted the historicity of Aeneas, the hero of Virgil's *Aeneid*, who was believed to have escaped from ruined Troy. Not until the nineteenth century did historians conclude that Aeneas was a *fabula ficta* (Veyne, 1988, pp. 50-53).

For centuries, people viewed Romulus as the founder of Rome. Many Romans believed he and his twin brother Remus had been abandoned as infants and suckled by a she-wolf. According to popular belief, Romulus was the son of Mars, just as Aeneas was the son of Venus. According to Cicero, virtually all the details about the lives of these ancient characters were empty tales. Yet, he believed the characters existed. Virtually no one questioned the existence of

Romulus and Aeneas until well into the nineteenth century. Cicero peeled away the mythology and fabrications that had grown around the characters, leaving, he believed, the true kernel of bare existence, a historical reality clothed in virtually nothing (Veyne, 1988, p. 50).

New Testament Scholars in Search of the Real Jesus

Was there a Jesus who existed in the first century? If so, what warranted statements can be made about him? Did he enter a room to greet his disciples even though the doors were closed (Jn. 20:19)? Did he make the long speech of John 13:31-17:26, or did the author compose it in the way many other ancient authors composed speeches for their protagonists? Did Jesus predict the imminent end of the old age and the supernatural establishment of a new kingdom of God on earth (Mt. 24)? Was he crucified? At the hour of his death, did rocks split and tombs open, allowing bodies of many holy people to emerge a few days later and enter the holy city of Jerusalem to appear before the masses? More than likely, if this amazing event had happened, people would have reported it far and wide. Only the Gospel of Matthew mentions it. Some scholars prefer an alternative interpretation: a few days after their graves had opened, many resurrected bodies entered the celestial Jerusalem (not the earthly city) where many saw them in heaven. This interpretation, advanced by some conservative scholars, emerged in the attempt to draw the line between credulity and incredulity.

This later interpretation explains the virtual silence about the event of resurrected bodies entering the earthly Jerusalem, where presumably many witnesses saw them. Even then, a problem remains. What did the resurrected bodies do between their resurrection and their putative removal from earth a few days later? New Testament scholar Robert Gundry conjectures that the risen saints patiently waited inside their tombs for a few days (Gundry, 1982, pp. 576-577).

Many biblical scholars conjecture that Matthew was not reporting an event actually witnessed. Rather, he drew from several Old Testament passages that, he sincerely believed, provided data with which to weave a narrative.[4] Catholic biblical scholar John Dominic Crossan has concluded that among the early Christians, Christ's passion narrative arose from prophecy, not actual history. The putative prophecies were treated as history (Crossan, 1994c, p. 149). Professor Arnold Rothstein sees the New Testament accounts of Jesus as theography, not history. "Apologists 'demonstrated' the truth of Christ-ology not by contemporary evidence, but by textual casuistry; references were made to the Psalms and prophetic writings, which transformed the 'Old' Testament into a prologue of the 'New.' To achieve this transformation, the interpreters relied on symbolism, allegory, allusion, and theosophy..." (Rothstein, 1993, p. 21).

Truth in Narrative Fiction and Poetry

R. Alan Culpepper, versed in historical criticism, has written a watershed book on the Fourth Gospel, the most poetic book among the New Testament Gospels and Epistles. Knowing well the difference between primarily empirical narratives and fictional narratives, Culpepper throws down the gauntlet. Can there be truth in biblical fiction? Can biblical texts be true if they are not undiluted, clear-cut history? As a student of Frank Kermode, Culpepper wishes to show how it is possible to glean profound truth from the history of fictional narratives and poetry. He suggests that in rethinking the relationship between art and history, between fiction and truth, we can eventually read the Gospel as the author's audience read it. However, it remains doubtful that a contemporary reader can ever fully take it as the original audience did.

At the *Anatomy of the Fourth Gospel*'s close, Culpepper agrees with Brian Wicker's challenge:

> Perhaps it is only now, as a result of our long experience of reading novels, that is, narratives that once again combine the empirical and the fictional in a mode of narration more complex than either of these can be by itself, are we able to recover the true narratives that were written before the split occurred. (Culpepper, 1983, p. 237, quoting Wicker, 1975, p. 105)

Certainly, recovering "the true narrative" is one idealized goal; but Culpepper has already warned that no one can possibly repeal the Renaissance's insights and the Enlightenment's advances.

Understanding the biblical texts could not advance beyond a certain point until the split between the empirical and the fictional took place. Without the split, the astounding achievements of recent and contemporary biblical scholarship would never have occurred. A new day has truly come.

> Historians today...are impelled by a cultural and intellectual revolution that forces us to reevaluate the nature of history.... New historicism has taught

> literary scholars to reconceive literary texts that were silenced and [to] recapture the details of ordinary life that were erased by traditional historiographic sources. (Rackin, 1990, p. 34)

Novelist Carlos Fuentes supposedly wondered aloud if literature was what history conceals, forgets, or mutilates. Both historical works and fictional works condense, each in their own way. Nevertheless, the two disciplines have much to teach one another. William Faulkner's "historical shudderings" render revealing tales with such profound historical sympathies and affinities that no historian of the South can afford to ignore them. In other words, "The House of History contains many mansions" (Aaron, 1992, p. 62). If dramatists and fiction writers can sometimes capture vital facts of human life and condense them into powerful poetics, historians may invite them in, not as infallible oracles, but as collaborators. Historian G. W. Bowersock in *Fiction as History: Nero to Julian* (1994) has accepted the challenge. Earlier, Richard I. Pervo had broken fresh ground, deeply penetrating the problem of the Acts of the Apostles' literary genre (Pervo, 1987).

Quotation Marks and Red Letters

In *New Atlantis*, Sir Francis Bacon, one of Shakespeare's contemporaries, employs a narrative form that lies somewhere between direct and indirect speech. Used regularly in oral storytelling, this form so blends the narrator's voice with the characters' voices that the reader has no certain way to separate them. The fused voices already contain the narrator's interpretations and contributions to the presumed "original" words. The Fourth Gospel's author uses this technique with exceptional skill.

Quotation marks were not invented until Shakespeare's day. Even then, writers used them rather unsystematically for over two centuries to indicate mostly classic texts. In Lawrence Sterne's five-hundred-page English novel *Tristram Shandy* (1760 CE), quotation marks rarely occur. Even then, they do not serve the purpose precisely as do quotation marks in contemporary novels. "Until the end of the eighteenth century the speeches of fictional characters were normally unmarked, or (as in *New Atlantis* or *Pilgrim's Progress*) sometimes set in italic type" (Rée, 1987, p. 88).

By having some understanding of the literary forms, techniques and genres *not* available to early Christian writers, we can perhaps better know what *not* to expect of them in our search for "original Christianity" and its reputed founder or founders.

On the other hand, by increasing our understanding of the way first-century Christian writers employed literary forms and techniques available to them, we appreciate better their subtleties and artistic skills. For example, when the Apostle Paul writes, "I know a person in Christ who fourteen years ago was caught up to the third heaven" (2 Cor. 12:2), to whom is he referring? Himself? He says he does not know whether this man was inside the body or outside. Is this Paul's special literary device? Can a writer quote himself indirectly by writing as though referring to another person's experience?

In the famous Roman 7:14-25 passage, Paul discloses his own personal struggle with temptation and sin. However, is he referring to himself as he once was? Or is he using a literary technique to prevent his readers from answering that question? Is he purporting to describe his past self to obscure the truth that he is actually describing his present self (also)? Alternatively, not knowing the answer, might he actually be striving to discover where he is in his own spiritual journey? He says at the passage's beginning, "I do not know for what I am working" (or "what I am doing" or "I do not understand my own behavior").

Contemporary historians who seek an accurate representation of the historical Jesus will render themselves obsolete if they ignore the recent advances made in literary criticism as applied to Scripture. Regardless of how we classify the four canonical Gospels, they are literary creations, not mere chronicles. Even though some publishing houses use red letters to designate the words that various editors have presumed to be Jesus' authentic words, the Gospel writers themselves employed no such device, including quotation marks or italics. They used, instead, various forms, including free indirect speech. According to some biblical scholars, the Gospel writers could not precisely present the stories and sayings of Jesus. Rather, the Gospels were necessarily a fusion of what Jesus said and what his words meant (theologically and in other ways) to the writers themselves and their special first-century audiences.

Questions naturally arise. By dissecting the Gospel events and sayings, can historians distinguish the original content from the narrators' coloring and shaping? Can historians work back through the literature to reconstruct the actual words and deeds of Jesus? This is another way of asking about the Gospel writers' use of literary and theological license in producing their works. Might the writers have invented sayings and events and attributed them to a real or fictional Jesus to spell out not only what they thought Jesus himself meant, but also what others thought his life and death implied? How can we be certain that the added meanings and interpretations do not tell us far more about the writers than about Jesus?

Later, we will examine the thesis that in good faith, the Gospel writers could either invent or borrow sayings and incidents not originally a part of Jesus' earthly life. We will probe the supplementary hypothesis that the Gospel writers nevertheless believed sincerely that they were faithfully representing the truth about Jesus. To accomplish this, however, we must enter the writers' world and look at *their* way of telling stories. In the process, we can compare their way with the way contemporary historians tell their stories and carry out their discipline.

Notes

1 Unless noted otherwise, all biblical references come from the New Revised Standard Version (NRSV).

2 Later in this book, the question will emerge as to whether so complex a movement as first-century Christianity could have had a single founder.

3 Just when the phrase "higher criticism" seemed to have slipped into disuse, a new journal appeared in the fall of 1994, titled "Journal of Higher Criticism." It listed an array of first-rate biblical scholars as the board of advisors and contributing editors. The editor, Robert M. Price, had been a Baptist minister with deep evangelical roots.

4 The Old Testament passages are Ezek. 37:7, 12-13; Dan. 12:2; Zech. 14:4. See also Rev. 11:17-19; 1 Pet. 3:19.

3 Thucydides' History and Chariton's Novel

Even a cursory reading of Thucydides' fifth-century BCE *History of the Peloponnesian War* reveals how it differs strikingly from the four New Testament Gospels. One conspicuous difference is Thucydides' practice of seeing at least two sides of complex issues. His intellectual equivalent of counterpoint stemmed largely from his roots in Greek tragedy, the mild sophist Protagoras' influence, and a broad philosophical heritage.

By contrast, the Gospels as well as the Apostle Paul's epistles have deep roots in apocalyptic models of the world. Even the Gospel of John has apocalyptic roots, although its author thoroughly reworks the tradition. Thucydides the historian projects no supernatural messianic figure into either past or future history. He expects no apocalyptic interruption of history's flow and no cosmic transformations brought about by supernatural power.

At the same time, he does refer to the gods as being of help or hindrance in battle. Some Athenians of his time apparently believed that the gods could be of help in fighting diseases or could inflict a population with diseases. In the case of a devastating plague taking many lives, Thucydides notes, the people concluded that worshiping the gods made no difference, "seeing they all perished alike" (Thucydides, 1993, p. 50).

In discussing the role of power in human history, Thucydides seems to allow that the gods play a role in human affairs. At the same time, he also allows his Athenians to comment that the favor of the gods is on one side as much the other. "So as far as the favor of the gods is concerned," the Athenians say to the Malians, "we have no reason to fear that we will do worse than you" (Thucydides, 1993, p. 106).

Thucydides, like the author of the Gospel of John, likes to include long speeches in his writing. Although not word-for-word accounts of what the speakers actually said, most of the speeches probably do represent what Thucydides thought they actually believed. He "reports" a speech by Nicias, an Athenian politician and general who considers the possibility that his men have offended some of the gods and were sufficiently punished for their offense.

Nicias adds that he has "reason to hope for milder treatment from the gods, since we have come to deserve their pity more than their anger" (Thucydides, 1993, p. 146).

Thucydides favors piety (*eusebeia*), which includes justice and the virtues in which ancient Greeks thought the gods took special interest. Thucydides has no explicit theology, and he certainly does not attempt to describe the gods' activity or to write as if viewing historical events from their standpoint. *History*'s implied author does not view putative miracles as having a special place or meaning. Nor does he discern possible "signs" of providence at work in human history. Though he employs a notion of necessity (*ananke*), it equates to neither fate nor divine providence (Thucydides, 1993, p. ix).

Thucydides was the contemporary of Socrates and Plato. Like Plato, he developed a style of prose to fit his high purpose. Roughly four and a half centuries later, Chariton, a Greek-speaking citizen of Aphrodisia (in southwest Turkey), developed a way of telling stories, not in epic poetry, but in narrative fiction prose. Chariton, secretary to the lawyer Athenagoras, wrote his novel *Chaereas and Callirhoe* at roughly the time the Gospel of Mark was composed. Some date the novel as early as the first century BCE; others as late as the end of the first century CE. Classics Professor and translator of the novel, B. P. Reardon suggests 50 CE, about the time Paul was composing his letter to the Corinthian and Galatian churches (Reardon, 1989, p. 17).

Like the Book of Acts, Chariton's novel is adventurous, highly entertaining, imaginative, creative, and ever alert to dramatic possibilities (Chariton, 1989, pp. 17-124). Unlike the Gospels and the Book of Acts, the early novels of the first century and especially the second century CE are more or less love-and-adventure romances. The line between history and fiction in some works is not always easy to draw, especially when fiction writers consciously set out to give their stories the ring of reality.

> Some Greek historians and biographers…embroider their themes, for purposes as close to the novelist's as to the historian's. At what point does history become fiction…? At what point does hagiography—which is ideologically directed biography—become fiction? (Reardon, 1989, "Introduction," p. 3)

In a later chapter, we will raise the question of whether ancient writers could have created fictional narratives while believing them to be more than fictions. This question opens the door to a fruitful field of research in social psychology. Did the nineteenth-century Joseph Smith, for example, write a novel called the *Book of Mormon*? Did he believe it was a novel?

Although Chariton evidently did not consider his novel an account of actual lives, we find the third book of his story useful in studying popular, first-century religious motifs. In this third book, Chaereas arrives at the tomb of his beloved Callirhoe, the heroine, to offer libations and wreaths. To his amazement, he finds the stones removed and the entrance open. But where is Callirhoe? Rejecting the hypothesis of tomb robbers, Chaereas embraces the conclusion that a God has carried her away, just as Dionysius took Ariadne, or Zeus took Semele. Convinced now that divine power brought her back to life, he vows to search for her on land and sea, and even in the sky if possible.

In studying the Gospels and the Apostle Paul's letters, biblical scholars are becoming increasingly aware that both *borrowing* and *inventing* are essential to virtually all writing. For example, scholars have to invent, articulate, and test hypotheses about past events as best they can. In physics, invention is essential. Thucydides' contemporary, the philosopher Democritus, invented the theory of atoms. Eventually, it became a part of the scientific canon. At the same time, Democritus probably could not have invented his new theory or model had he not thought long and hard about the theories of Pythagoras and Parmenides. He built his marvelous theory on their genius. Similarly, even if the canonical Gospels were new literary inventions, the earliest of them (whether Mark or Matthew) was not immaculately conceived. It had many literary predecessors, both Greek and Hebrew.

Plato constructed several fictions at the end of his major dialogues (the myth of Er in *Republic* 10, for example). He constructed them not merely to entertain, but to communicate what he believed were vital *truths*. As perhaps the supreme epistemologist among philosophers, Plato created fictions and myths because he understood the power of poetry and fictional writing to open the mind. Even when decrying the poets, Plato became one because he needed to. If it turns out that the four Gospels have much in common with the literary form of the ancient novel, biblical scholars and others will explore this conclusion's wider implications and possibilities (Perry, 1967, p. 47; Hock, et al, 1999). In some ways, one can study Paul's "story" of the cosmic Christ as theater or drama. Specifically, the Pauline plot as well as the plots of the four Gospels are "anti-tragic theater." Chapters 15 and 16 will explore this lead in some detail.

4 Paul the Apostle: Problems in the Paradigm

Introduction

For two reasons, we devote five consecutive chapters to understanding the Apostle Paul against the background of his theological heritage. A major figure in shaping both the direction and content of early Christianity, Paul more than any New Testament writer left behind invaluable clues to his thinking process as it emerged within his theological heritage. Each of the five chapters proceeds on the conviction that Paul, a highly creative thinker, did not operate outside a thick web of beliefs. In this inherited web, he encountered severe crises that he felt demanded resolution.

At first, it may seem odd to say that Paul was doing what philosophers John Dewey (1955) and Karl Popper (1989, pp. 72-74) contend that all thinkers strive to do, namely, to solve perceived problems, crises, or challenges. Paul was not the first or last creative mind to believe his solutions came from supernatural sources. Nor was he the first or last to seek a supernatural guarantee of their truth and power. In each of the five chapters, we try to spell out the crucial problems that plagued Paul. Only then can we more fully appreciate his genius and discover some of the strengths and weaknesses of his governing paradigm.

Biblical scholars generally agree that the apostle played a major role in shaping the Christian doctrine. But what thinking process led Paul to leave one view of reality and to embrace what appears to be a strikingly different one? Any attempt to answer this question will start with the observation that Paul's conversion was *not* a paradigm shift in his thinking. T. S. Kuhn's second edition of *The Structure of Scientific Revolutions* (1971) distinguishes a model from a paradigm. One may see Paul's revolution as a shift in the central model within an *anthropomorphic paradigm* that includes a ruling deity as well as subordinate supernatural beings. Paul believed many of these beings to be in revolt against the ruling deity and Creator, namely, God the Father.

According to such philosophers of science as Imre Lakatos and Gary Gutting, a scientific *model* serves to apply and extend in concrete detail the home paradigm's program. Though not a scientist, Paul did in some ways think as scientists do when working through *metaphysical* implications and presuppositions of their theories. Of course, Paul did not design any research program for testing his theories under strict controls open for public observation and possible falsification. Yet, he may have come to believe that certain elements of his metaphysics had been falsified. More of this later.

Before his conversion, Paul was, he insisted, a zealous participant in the tradition of the Pharisees, a branch of Judaism that treated Torah or the Law (*nomos*) as the central model within the paradigm of ethical monotheism. To be sure, Hyam Maccoby in his book *Paul and Hellenism* contends that Paul was not deeply rooted in the Hebrew tradition of the prophets and the Old Testament. Despite the fact that Paul claimed to have been brought up as a Pharisee, Maccoby contends that he misrepresented himself to give his scheme of salvation a "Jewish clothing" (Maccoby, 1991, pp. 130-133, 137). Paul van Buren strongly contests this in his book *According to the Scriptures: the Origin of the Gospel and of the Church's Old Testament* (van Buren, 1998).

After noting similarities the Jesus of the Gospels has with rabbinic idioms and style of argument, Maccoby concludes that Paul's use of the Torah "ignores every canon of rabbinic interpretation." Furthermore, Paul "garbles" Hebrew Scripture.

> A rabbi might depart from the plain meaning of a biblical text in his interpretation. He might even resort to an outrageous pun on a word in a text, in order to extract a meaning not there. But what he would never do is misquote the text deliberately in the first place. (Maccoby, 1991, p. 151)

Maccoby's most serious complaint against Paul is that he misrepresents Judaism by presenting it at its most primitive level while ignoring the reforms it underwent over the centuries. "Paul responds to the Hebrew Bible, which he reads in the Greek of the Septuagint, by reading back into it attitudes which it had outgrown but vestiges of which remained in the text" (Maccoby, 1991, p. 69).

A more generous interpretation is that Paul, while receiving some training as a Pharisee, did not succeed in understanding the depths of its central model, the Law, the Torah. Paul, of course, thinking he understood it more profoundly than did any of his contemporaries, found it inadequate at best. No longer able to embrace the old model, he came upon a new one, thanks in part to divine revelations he believed he had been privileged to receive.

In Philippians, he claimed he was circumcised on the eighth day, born of Israel, a Hebrew of the tribe of Benjamin, and a trained Pharisee (Phil. 3:5). In his epistle to the Galatians, he made strong claims about his accomplishments as a Pharisee. Luke, the Acts of the Apostles author, portrays Paul as a Jew born in Tarsus yet raised in Jerusalem by the noted rabbi Gamaliel, who trained him in every point of his ancestral law. Paul zealously received his training, says Luke (Acts 22:3). Luke has Paul asserting the following before King Agrippa:

> All the Jews know my way of life from my youth, a life spent from the beginning among my own people and in Jerusalem. They have known for a long time, if they are willing to testify, that I have belonged to the strictest sect of our religion and lived as a Pharisee.... Indeed, I myself was convinced that I ought to do many things against the name of Jesus of Nazareth. And that is what I did in Jerusalem; with authority received from the chief priests, I not only locked up many of the saints in prison, but I also cast my vote against them when they were being condemned to death. By punishing them often in all the synagogues I tried to force them to blaspheme; and since I was so furiously enraged at them, I pursued them even to foreign cities. (Acts 26:4-5, 9-11)

Luke then has Paul tell about a "heavenly vision" on his way to Damascus. "After that, King Agrippa, I was not disobedient to the heavenly vision, but declared first to those in Damascus..." (Acts 26:19).

Some of Paul's own words support Luke's version of Paul's life, but many scholars hold that Luke sometimes rearranged the facts and invented material to serve his own thematic interests. Indeed, Episcopal clergyman Richard I. Pervo has argued in considerable detail that the Acts of the Apostles was composed as an adventure novel weaving together threads of history with threads of fiction (Pervo, 1987).

Problem Solving

According to the noted philosopher of science Karl Popper, the human species is a problem solver. Or, stated more accurately, because we as a species perpetually encounter problems to overcome, we can better understand one another if we uncover the distinctive problems we are trying to solve. The Apostle Paul is no exception; for he, too, was trying to solve problems. One may see his theological conjectures as attempts to solve specific problems that he believes affect the destiny of the whole cosmos and every creature in it.

Within the individual stirs a restless search for new liberties, new possibilities. All organisms fully occupy themselves with problem solving, including the search for better living conditions, greater freedom, and a better environment (Popper, 1992, pp. 12-13). This does not mean that organisms succeed in overcoming all the obstacles encountered. Rather, we as human beings understand others and ourselves better if we can locate the problems we are working on. Popper wisely notes that human problem solving and invention do not always occur at the fully conscious level. Maccoby fails to deal adequately with the central fact that the Apostle Paul was wrestling with what he clearly thought were critical difficulties created by the Torah. It seems clear also that he believed he had come upon a multifaceted solution that gave him astonishing liberty previously unknown to him. The esteemed sociologist Max Weber calls attention to the "overpowering joy" radiating from Paul's letters, the joy of one who believed himself liberated from enslavement. In Paul's case, says Weber, it was the "slave law" that failed to provide the sense of salvation and that kept its devotees locked into "the fate of pariah status" suffered by Jews at that time (Weber, 1965, p. 260). According to Weber, Paul's shift to a new model gave him unparalleled freedom. Christ set them free, the apostle wrote to the churches at Galatia, so that they should remain free. "Stand firm, therefore, and do not submit again to a yoke of slavery" (Gal. 5:1). He believed that Christ had set him free. But is Weber correct in suggesting that Paul's basic perplexity was his feeling trapped in pariah status? Why would he need a cosmic Christ to resolve that problem? Perhaps studying Paul's view of Christ can bring insight into his fundamental perplexity. If Christ is, for Paul, the solution, then at least a preliminary look at Christ as the apostle characterized him will likely throw light on the problem(s). Admittedly, shuttling between conjectured problems to proposed solutions equates to the method of trial and error. Nevertheless, all other promising methods seem to manifest this process.

Paul's Christ

More than one New Testament scholar has called attention to the glaring fact that Paul seemed virtually uninterested in the details of the earthly Jesus. His letters abound with references to Jesus, calling him Lord, Christ, the Second Adam, and even the Wisdom of God. Paul quotes from none of the parables attributed to Jesus in the Gospels. He offers no clear-cut evidence to suggest that he knew anything about either the so-called Sermon on the Mount or the supposed trial that Jesus underwent in Jerusalem.

It is imperative to keep in mind that the four Gospels—Matthew, Mark, Luke, and John—were written after Paul's literary career had ended presumably before Titus destroyed the Second Temple. For Paul, Christ was fundamentally a cosmic figure who for a short time left Heaven, took on human form, suffered, died as a sacrifice, was resurrected, and would return soon. Despite Morton Smith's claim that Paul had known the earthly Jesus, most scholars hold that Paul had never met him in the flesh. Indeed, the question remains as to what Paul did or did not know about the Jesus who allegedly grew up in Nazareth and preached in Galilee. Paul apparently had no interest in learning from either Peter or James any details about Jesus' earthly life. This is indeed curious. In his books on the theme of the earthly Jesus, G. A. Wells suggests one clear reason for Paul's lack of interest. He knew that Peter and James possessed no knowledge of a historical Jesus. It is sufficient at this point to understand that for Paul, Christ was a cosmic Savior with the power to resolve problems that the law recognized but could not resolve (Wells, 1975, pp. 129-132, 136-137).

The Law

If Christ replaced the law as the central model of Paul's paradigm, it will prove useful to ask what the law meant to Paul. Apparently, most rabbis of the time would have agreed that the Creator had given the law as reliable instruction and guidance. According to this model, those who lived by the Torah's or law's precepts and requirements could be counted among the righteous inheritors of salvation. Nevertheless, Paul came to view the law as limited at best and an enslaving curse at worst.

According to his letter to the Galatians, he believed that the law required circumcision of males who wished to obtain salvation. However, Paul found that this requirement kept some Gentiles from converting to ethical monotheism.

Evidently, missionaries who visited the churches of Galatia convinced some members that they could combine devotion to the law with devotion to Christ. This upset Paul so much that he wrote a heated letter to the churches, refuting "those from the circumcision [group]." He warned:

> Listen! I, Paul, am telling you that if you let yourselves be circumcised, Christ will be of no benefit to you. Once again I testify to every man who lets himself be circumcised that he is obliged to obey the entire law. You who want to be justified by the law have cut yourselves off from Christ; you have fallen away from grace. (Gal. 5:2-4)

In this epistle to the Galatians, Paul rebukes, denounces, cajoles, appeals, and uses various other rhetorical devices to draw his readers back into the circle of freedom. Sparing no words in castigating his opponents—those of the circumcision group—he vehemently expresses his wish that those enemies who had unsettled the churches would go the whole way and cut themselves off, that is, emasculate themselves (Gal. 5:12).

Paul used harsh language in this letter because he was on the defense. The heart of the gospel as he interpreted it had come under severe attack, as had his own authority as an apostle. From the very beginning of the letter, he tried to solve two critical problems. He had to defend not only his gospel, but also his right to call himself an apostle. The opening context has to do with a meeting that took place in Antioch in which Paul and Peter came into open conflict. Astoundingly, nowhere did either Paul or Peter, or anyone else involved in the conflict, attempt to quote the earthly Jesus to settle their dispute. Are we to assume that no preacher, deacon, apostle, or prophet at that church conference in Antioch thought to quote Jesus' authoritative words to settle the heated controversy among them? Paul's account offers no quotation from Jesus, and neither does Luke's account in the fifteenth chapter of Acts.

The Problem of Paul's Authority

In both Galatians and 1 Corinthians, Paul responds to an apparent challenge to his standing as Christ's spokesman. In 1 Cor. 15:5, he seems to think Cephas (or

Peter) held distinction because he witnessed the resurrected Christ first. Later, the resurrected Christ appeared to the Twelve, to over five hundred brothers at once, to James, and afterwards to all the apostles (15:6-7). The identity of "the Twelve" and those included among the apostles is unclear. Was the Apostle Apollos connected with the Twelve?

In his insightful book *The Sayings of Jesus in the Churches of Paul*, David L. Dungan presents one clear reason for Paul's failure to quote or even allude to Jesus' sayings on the Law (Torah). None was on his side. "[A]ll the sayings of Jesus on the Torah, or related to this issue, probably were in the possession of his opponents among the Jerusalem circle." In short, unlike Paul, "Jesus never had radically overthrown the Torah at all" (see Gal. 4:4; Rom. 15:8). Dungan acknowledges that this conclusion complicates his own hypothesis that Paul and his readers possessed a common tradition or collection of Jesus' sayings. It becomes further complicated when Dungan seemingly denies the existence of the putative Q document conjectured to contain a number of Jesus' teachings and sayings (Dungan, 1971, pp. 144-145, 150).

Dungan's careful nuances evolve into a complex position. He regards as romantic the claim that a fixed, sacred code of Jesus' teachings existed in Paul's time. He insists that Paul invoked his own general, all-inclusive principle that allowed him to alter and even "relativize the entire tradition of the sayings of the Lord [Jesus]." At the same time, he seems to hold that Paul "treated the tradition very carefully, while the gospel editors changed it around to suit their aims..."(Dungan, 1971, p. 144). To the editors of the four canonical Gospels, Dungan attributes great creative powers. He refers to their freedom in "inventing, altering, rearranging, omitting, and combining...on an astonishingly massive scale..." (Dungan, 1971, p. 142). As a leading scholar on the Synoptic problem, Dungan certainly understands the difficulty, if not impossibility, of using the Synoptic Gospels to reconstruct a coherent body of Jesus' sayings. Still, he persists in writing as if the Palestinian Christians had at least a loose collection of such sayings. Dungan's painstaking work fits readily with the thesis that no first-century, earthly Jesus uttered a bulk of sayings and teachings that made their way into the New Testament. G. A. Wells contends that Paul needed no tradition containing details about an earthly Jesus so long as he could believe himself the recipient of direct revelations from a resurrected Christ (Wells, 1996, p.29). Historian Gilbert Murray notes, "The Greek bards always owe, not only what we should call their inspiration, but their *actual knowledge of facts* to the Muses. The Muses 'are present and know all things'" (Murray, 1924, p. 96, Italics added).

Presumably, Apollos is numbered among the apostles (1 Cor. 1:12; 3:22; 4:6; 16:12) even though in 1 Corinthians 15 Paul does not specifically refer to him by name. The Gospels do not mention him. Paul designates himself as the least among the apostles because he persecuted the church of God. He says Christ appeared to him last of all (15:8-9).

Evidently, at Corinth someone or some group had cast aspersion on Paul's authority. He reaffirmed that he was truly an apostle by pointing out that he was a witness to the risen Lord and had founded the church at Corinth (1 Cor. 9:1-2). In Galatia, a group had evidently stirred up considerable controversy regarding both Paul's credentials and gospel. Beginning with the first line of his epistle to the Galatians, he replies to the criticisms and charges. First of all, he calls himself an apostle whose commission did not come by any human authority or human act (1:1). In the second place, he seeks no human approval and thinks he would be no servant of Christ if he should seek it (1:10). Apparently, wanting no reader to misunderstand, he repeats his point. "For I want you to know, brothers and sisters, that the gospel that was proclaimed by me is not of human origin; for I did not receive it from a human source, nor was I taught it" (Gal. 1:11-12).

If an earthly Jesus existed who had selected Cephas and others as his disciples and traveling companions, would Paul not have asked them about Jesus? Would he not have entreated them to answer his many questions about what Jesus said and did in their presence? Would he not have gone to other believers—both men and women—to seek information and to hear the wondrous stories? Indeed, they would have been instructing him, rather than he them, in the details of Jesus' ministry. Strange as it seems, however, Paul says that the gospel he preached to the Galatians came by way of divine revelation *to him* (1:12).

After this putative revelation took place "in and through" Paul, he went immediately to Arabia without consulting a single person or going to Jerusalem to consult with those known to be apostles before his conversion (1:16-17). Three years elapsed before he journeyed to Jerusalem to become acquainted with Cephas, whom he stayed with for two weeks. He saw no other apostle except James (1:18-19). Then he adds the rather strange comment: "What I write is plain truth; God knows I am not lying" (1:20).

Ordinarily, we feel no need to assert our veracity until someone overtly challenges it. Unless Paul is being melodramatic, he is responding to actual accusations against him. The issue, of course, involves his authority. In chapter 2 of Galatians, he claims to have waited fourteen years before returning to Jerusalem. Even then, he went, not because Cephas and James had summoned him, but because he believed God had given him a revelation (2:1-2). From verses 2 through 9 of the second chapter, he uses the term "seeming" (or a version of it) to refer to those viewed as leaders in the Jerusalem church. He refers to James, Cephas, and John as the reputed or seeming *pillars*. In Galatians 2:6, Paul approaches sarcasm: "And from those who were supposed [seeming] to be acknowledged leaders (what they actually were makes no difference to me; God shows no partiality)—those leaders contributed nothing to me." Paul not only attempts to establish independence from the Jerusalem leaders regarding his calling and gospel, but also denies that God established their position as pillars! The distinction in Jerusalem is only a human one, an external appearance.

Later, the Gospel of Matthew will bestow on Peter the position of prominence (16:18). Paul, however, will take second place to no human mortal on the question of authority. At the Antioch church meeting sometime after his visit to Jerusalem, he confronts Peter before the entire congregation, accusing him of acting falsely regarding the gospel. They quarrel over whether Gentile Christians should be required to undergo circumcision. Cephas, contradicting his previous action, has refused to sit at the table to eat with uncircumcised Gentile believers. Addressing Cephas, Paul asks, "If you, though a Jew, live like a Gentile and not like a Jew, how can you compel the Gentiles to live like Jews" (Gal. 2:14)? Paul uses the strong word hypocrisy (*hypokrisei*) to describe Cephas' behavior, a term used later by Matthew's Jesus to denounce scribes and Pharisees.

5 Paul, the Hellenistic Jew

The Law or Christ

Excellent biblical scholars have disagreed among themselves regarding the depth of Paul's roots in Judaism. Admittedly, some passages suggest that Paul suffered ambivalence regarding the Torah or Law. W. D. Davies in *Paul and Rabbinic Judaism* contends that Paul remained a Pharisee all his life and never forsook "his devotion to the Law" (Davies, 1955, pp. 70-71, 74). But even Davies softens his claim by suggesting that Paul, like Jesus, remained loyal to the Torah by preaching a *new* Torah that reframed the old (Davies, 1955, p. 74). To what extent, however, is this like telling a Protestant or Catholic that Mormonism with its new Scripture improves upon the Christian Bible? Davies wrestles with the question of Paul's reason for observing the law's requirements. Did the need to maintain rapport with other rabbis and faithful Jews motivate Paul (Davies, 1955, p. 74)? Regarding the Jesus of the Gospels, many contemporary scholars hold that Matthew's Jesus most certainly observes the Jewish law—or most of it. By contrast, the Jesus of the Gospel of John bitterly opposes "the Jews," portrayed as eager to kill him because he breaks the Sabbath and makes himself equal with God. Indeed, the Gospel of John's prologue asserts unequivocally that, first, Jesus is the divine *logos* who was with God from the beginning and, second, through the *logos* God created the world.

Clearly, in this Gospel, the real issue revolves around the question of the locus of revelation—Jesus or the law (Culpepper, 1983, pp. 91, 114). Repeatedly the Jesus of this Fourth Gospel emphasizes that the law is *their law*, not Jesus' (Jn. 7:19; 8:17; 10:34; 15:25). The narrator portrays Nicodemus, a ruler of the Jews, as one who cannot comprehend divine truth even though he is a teacher of Israel. He comes to Jesus at night, and apparently the narrator wants the readers to believe that Nicodemus remained in the dark as "one of them" (Jn. 7:50). Later, we will say more about the Jesus of this Fourth Gospel, who reflects the intense hostility between Christians and Jews near the first-century's close.

Paul's Hellenism

Hyam Maccoby seeks to demonstrate that Paul had roots in Hellenistic religion. He attempts to show that Paul's view of the cosmic Christ was fundamentally pagan in origin. He even accuses Paul of setting in motion a process that eventually developed into anti-Semitism. A combination of mystery religion and a mild dosage of Gnosticism allowed Paul to reinterpret the Greek translation of the Hebrew Bible. He projected a divine figure who suffered violence on the cross and mystically became the Savior for all who would accept his sacrifice as atonement for their sin (Maccoby, 1991, pp. 84-89). Maccoby contends:

> Pauline baptism is a mystical and even magical sacrament by which the passion and resurrection of Christ is appropriated by the believer for his own salvation.... While the Eucharist corresponds to the regular communion meal of the mystery cults, Pauline baptism is the analogue of the *taurobolion* in the cults of Mithras and Attis, and is essentially a once-for-all rite of initiation into a mystery. (Maccoby, 1991, pp. 127-128)

Rather than view Paul as a deceiver pretending to be a Jew, we think he was a Hellenized Jew whose writings show signs of Hellenistic education. His epistles abound with the Hellenistic writing style, reasoning, and arguing. He calls himself Paul, the Greek equivalent to the Hebrew name Saul. Many of his metaphors come from the Greco-Roman world of sports and military life, but that in no way entails that the mystery cults profoundly influenced him. We contend, rather, that Greek ideas, stories, and images pervaded the culture that Paul inhabited. They "played" in his thinking like musical motifs or movie scenes today pervade American culture. Adaptations and mutations abounded then as today. Just as the song "I'm Always Chasing Rainbows," for example, is an offshoot of Chopin's "Fantasy-Impromptu," so early Christianity is a highly creative mutation of its Jewish, Greek, Roman, and even Egyptian legacies.

Christ as the Conquering Trojan Horse

The ancient Trojan horse story thrived as part of the Greco-Roman popular culture into which Paul was born in Tarsus. Quite possibly, this story more than the mystery religions strongly influenced his view of the cosmic Savior. In his letter to the Philippians, Paul portrayed Christ as one who, while being in the form of God, emptied himself to take the form of a slave. As a human slave, he became human in every way, even to the point of humbling himself to accept death on a cross (2:6-8). Most important, the Jewish Messiah (Christ) was ordinarily not expected to arrive as a slave who would eventually find himself hanging from a cross (Bellinger and Farmer, 1998).

Something quite surprising was at play in Paul's notion of a crucified Messiah. Clearly, Paul was obsessed with the idea that *power* came out of the crucified Messiah who had arrived on earth in humility. Like the Trojan horse, the divine Messiah's human form contained hidden power. According to 1 Corinthians 2:8, none of the "rulers of this age" recognized what was taking place. They did not see that behind the apparent weakness of the Messiah destined for crucifixion was incomparable power! If the rulers had recognized it, Paul wrote, they would not have crucified the Messiah, who, it turned out, was none other than "the Lord of glory."

Now, this preordained drama began in disguise—in secret (1 Cor. 2:7). In 1 Corinthians 15, Paul pictures Christ as eventually not only destroying every principality, ruling force, and power, but as placing all his enemies under him (15:24-25). All things will be put in subjection under God's feet because of Christ's death and resurrection (15:27). Just as the soldiers inside the Trojan horse overpowered the city, so Christ on the cross "disarmed the rulers and authorities and made a public example of them, triumphing over them in it." (The *Oxford Study Bible* gives the translation "cosmic powers and authorities.") This last quote, Colossians 2:15, possibly comes from, not Paul, but someone writing in his name and representing much of his thought. In Romans, Paul himself speaks of the cosmic Christ as controlling the realm of spirits and superhuman powers (Rom. 8:38-39).

Christ as Bait

In the first two chapters of 1 Corinthians, Paul places weakness and foolishness on one side. On the other, he places power and wisdom. Elsewhere he has identified himself with weakness (2 Cor. 12). In 1 Corinthians 1, he says that whereas the Jews demanded miracles and the Greeks looked for wisdom, he did not meet their expectations but, rather, preached "a crucified Christ." Paul's whole point is that despite appearances, the *humiliated Messiah's crucifixion brought real power and wisdom into being.* According to the ancient tradition, the leaders of Troy brought the gigantic wooden horse into their walled city, not knowing that their conquerors had concealed themselves inside the horse's belly. Similarly, the rulers of the age took Jesus to the cross, not knowing that in crucifying him they would release a cosmic force which would conquer them.

In the early centuries of Christianity, various believers embraced the *mousetrap* or *fishhook* theory of Christ's atonement. They portrayed the cross as a clever device to deceive and trap the devil. "Tawdry imagination developed the fishhook and mousetrap plays, in which the hungry devil seizes the bait of Christ's humanity only to be caught by the hidden power of deity and so destroyed" (Wolf, 1957, p. 99).

The Problem of Weakness

Paul was highly conscious of something about himself that he classified under "weakness." It seems likely that he became preoccupied with the model or image of a cosmic being who becomes a slave and appears so weak and powerless as to die in shame and humility on a cross. The thought that enormous authority erupted from absolute weakness apparently captured Paul's imagination. He wanted to identify himself somehow with this Christ crucified. Why? Evidently, he came to view this transformation or new creation as the only way to receive sufficient control over the weaknesses that plagued him. "I have been crucified with Christ; and it is no longer I who live, but it is Christ who lives in me..." (Gal. 2:19f). To the church at Corinth, he explained, "He [Christ] was crucified in *weakness*, but lives by the *power* of God. For we are *weak* in him, but in dealing with you we will live with him by the *power* of God" (2 Cor. 13:4 Italics added). Earlier in this same letter, he wrote that the Lord's grace rendered power perfect through Paul's weakness (2 Cor. 12:9).

Sociologists might find Paul's audience in Corinth considerably interesting. Who were the Corinthian church members? Paul has given a brief description. Few were wise according to worldly standards. Few possessed power, that is, political and economic influence. Few were of noble birth (1 Cor. 1:26). First Corinthians 1:27-28, opens a door that allows the careful reader to gain insight into both Paul's self-image and his image of those he addressed at Corinth.

> But God chose what is foolish in the world to shame the wise; God chose what is weak in the world to shame the strong; God chose what is low and despised in the world, things that are not…. (1 Cor. 1:27-28)

Paul sounds like someone who felt alienated from much of his society and perhaps from himself. He portrays himself and the Corinthian Christians as outsiders in need of a way to gain cosmic status and power. Paul thought he had found a way to gain power and wisdom, if not in society at large, then in a realm that he considered more real than his present society and age. Some might charge that Paul journeyed into a make-believe world that promised to give him the status, wisdom, and power previously denied him. Notably, in the very passage discussing his weakness and the external challenge to his status as an apostle, he partially discloses the subjective process by which he received what he deemed as divine revelations about another world or realm, "the third heaven" (1 Cor. 12:1-12).

The Wisdom of God

Very likely, Philo in Alexandria and Paul in Corinth found it necessary to compete with virtuoso orators called sophists. In both these cities, sophists belonged to a professional guild of speakers with public followings from families of wealth and status. Paul apparently could not measure up to the sophists either as an orator with rhetorical prowess or as a person with physical attractiveness. His bodily presence was "weak" (2 Cor. 10:10), and his message—indeed his gospel—focused on a Jesus Christ who was crucified (Winter, 1997, *Philo and Paul among the Sophists*, p. 217).

If the sophists glowed in wealth, status and rhetorical power, Paul countered that God's power worked through human weakness, faith, and the cross. Philo the Alexandrian Jew, by appealing to the Books of Moses, set up standards by which he measured the sophists and found them morally deficient. With a touch of irony, he countered the sophists with Sophia, divine wisdom. Some scholars think the Apostle Paul might have borrowed from his older contemporary Philo, who died about 50 CE. Paul referred to Christ as the power of God and wisdom of God. It is an open question as to whether Philo in his own mind identified Wisdom with the Logos (the Word), the highest of God's powers. Proverbs 8:22-31; 8:1-36:9:1-6 personify Wisdom. As a supernatural personage at God's side, Wisdom participated in the creation of the world. Job 28 eulogizes Wisdom. The Greek Bible contains the Book of Baruch, which was written a century before Paul wrote Galatians. Baruch's Wisdom poem (3:9-4:4) clearly identifies the Law with Wisdom. In Ecclesiasticus or the Wisdom of Jesus Ben Sirach, dated about 180 BCE, Wisdom again appears as a personified being, identified with the Word spoken by the Most High.

> I came forth from the mouth of the Most High, and covered the earth like a mist. I dwelt in the highest heavens, and my throne was in a pillar of cloud. Alone I compassed the vault of heaven and traversed the depths of the abyss. Over waves of the sea, over all the earth, and over every people and nation I have held sway. Among all these I sought a resting place; in whose territory should I abide? Then the Creator of all things gave me a command, and my Creator chose the place for my tent. He said, "Make your dwelling in Jacob, and in Israel receive your inheritance." Before the ages, in the beginning, he created me, and for all the ages I shall not cease to be.... I took root in an honored people, in the portion of the Lord, his heritage. (Ecclus. 24:3-12, Edgar J. Goodspeed, trans.)

In 1 Corinthians 8:6, Paul refers to one Lord, Christ Jesus, as a similar cosmic figure serving as God's agent in creating and sustaining life. Paul reveals little interest in the details of Jesus' earthly life beyond his coming to earth as a slave, having a special meal with a group, obeying unto death on the cross, rising from the grave as the triumphant sacrifice-redeemer-Lord, making appearances of some sort, and now standing on the brink of returning to gather up the faithful. A later chapter will deal with Paul's view of the Lord's Supper.

Prometheus and Wisdom

The Pre-Socratic philosophers and Plato wrestled with the problem of the one-and-the many. Entwined with it was the problem of substance and change. How could something change and yet be the same substance? Before Tales (the first philosopher in the West), the Greeks struggled with dubious success to keep a consistent account of their Gods. One writer might attribute to Zeus actions or qualities that another attributed to a different God. According to Simone Weil, although Zeus the God of Wisdom is above every God, the dramatist Aeschylus in *Prometheus Bound* strongly implies that Prometheus is the Wisdom of Zeus (Weil, 1976, p. 68). So, in what sense were the two Gods one? Was the conflict between Zeus and Prometheus the inner conflict of one God? Or did the Greeks think of them as two distinct deities?

Furthermore, did the Greeks have a fully consistent account of the relationship between the gods? As deities, did they conduct themselves according to stable principles or standards not subject to every God's changing whim or purpose? The problem intensified as the gods became increasingly involved in human affairs, sometimes appearing themselves as human beings.

The God Prometheus became an arbiter at a contest between Gods and human mortals (Hesiod, *Theogony*, 535). In the tragedy *Prometheus Bound*, Aeschylus portrays Prometheus as enduring affliction because of his compassion for humanity. Zeus in anger has him chained and nailed, "held by a hook," to punish his compassion, for which he refuses to repent. Having taken a personal and caring interest in human mortals, Prometheus endows them with mind and wisdom, including knowledge. Like Jesus' disciples, however, the recipients of such love and wisdom hear but do not always comprehend.

Since Prometheus exemplifies divine intelligence and wisdom, he is the very source of human wisdom and all the arts and skills. When Zeus and the Titans prepared for war with one another, Prometheus offered his wise counsel to Cronus, who ignored the counsel. Because Zeus accepted it, Cronus suffered defeat. It was because of his wisdom that Prometheus could also generate compassion for the human race.

When Zeus, Father of the gods, resolved to destroy all human beings, Prometheus persuaded him to spare them. In saving humanity from the deepest black of Hades, however, Prometheus sacrificed his own happiness. In his wrath, Zeus had him chained to a jagged rock and impaled or nailed. Aeschylus closes his play with Prometheus, amid earthquake and thunder, sinking into the endless abyss. As the God of wisdom, Prometheus became humanity's savior with the foreknowledge that he would suffer torment.

The Gift of Fire

Prometheus' love for human mortals was manifest in another way. Despite Zeus's objection, Prometheus sent the mortals the gift of fire. With that and the many other gifts (e.g., skills, arts, knowledge, and expertise), human life rose above mere animal existence. Prometheus' love for humanity made him a tremendous, though tragic, hero. His great "crime" was his undying love for humanity and his steadfast refusal to regard his love as a moral flaw.

Fire, of course, originally descended from the heavens in the form of storms. Although spiritualized in the New Testament, fire is still regarded as a wondrous visitation from heaven. According to the Acts of the Apostles, on the day of Pentecost (the Harvest Festival), the apostles were meeting, when all at once from the sky came a violent sound like a blast of wind, filling the whole house. They saw tongues like flames separating and settling on each of them. Soon they were speaking in tongues or languages whatever the Spirit prompted them to say (2:3-4). In the Hebrew tradition, fire often signified the manifestation of God's presence. Perhaps the most memorable example is the burning bush from which God spoke to Moses. An angel or messenger of Yahweh appeared in a flame of fire (Ex. 3:2-6). Later in the Exodus story, smoke envelopes Mount Sinai, Yahweh having descended in fire. Like Zeus, Yahweh speaks in thunder (Ex. 19:18f.). In the Gospel of Mark, John the Baptist tells the crowd that whereas he baptizes with water, the one to come (Jesus) will baptize with the Holy Spirit. Matthew and Luke add "and with fire" (Mk. 1:8; Mt. 3:11; Lk. 3:16). Clearly, in both his Gospel and Acts, Luke associates fire with the Holy Spirit, who like Prometheus bestows gifts and skills upon mortals.

Justice and Justification

The Greeks bequeathed to the West a preoccupation with the problem of justice and the problem of discerning the meaning of human life. The tragedies raised the question of cosmic justice. Were the gods just in their dealings with humanity? Is justice a standard by which even the gods stand judged, or does it shift with the will or whim of this or that god? In short, is justice whatever the gods say it is at any given time?

The Apostle Paul, far from inventing the problem of skewed justice, inherited it from both the Greeks and the Hebrews. In Romans 9:11-33, he advances the position that justice is whatever God wills. God's electing some to become the recipients of his mercy and others to receive his wrath is entirely just since no independent standard of justice exists beyond God's activities.

For Paul, the real problem then was that the sinful human race stood under fully deserved divine judgment and wrath. Rather than God's having a need to justify his acts, human beings needed to be justified before God. Was there, however, a Prometheus-like figure who could so love the human race (or at least the elect) as to provide a way for them to escape divine judgment and endless wrath? Instead of regarding divine Wisdom as a standard or principle relatively independent of God's unconditional will, Paul personifies Wisdom as the Messiah (Christ Jesus) and views him as totally and meekly submissive to God's will even unto death.

Plato's Problem and Solution

Plato disliked the tragedies for their portrayal of the gods as immoral and, in some cases, as tragic figures. In the conflict between Zeus and Prometheus, the former appears more like a vindictive tyrant than the wise king of the gods. In *Theatetus* (176b.c.), Socrates states plainly that in the divine life there can be no shadow of unrighteousness. Plato does not mean that God's acts can be classified as good irrespective of what they are. Rather, Plato makes the fundamental point that there is a standard of goodness itself which God always fulfills to the supreme degree. The unchanging pattern of divine happiness partakes of goodness, without which God could not be happy and could not be God (*Theatetus*, 176e).

Plato knew of the Egyptians' Sun-God, and he knew what he was doing when he described "the good itself" by analogy with the sun. Far from defining the good merely as the actions of the Egyptian God Ra, he was reforming every version of God by envisioning deity as always partaking of the good. The life-bestowing good contains its own dignity and power, is the source of truth, the cause of knowledge, and the governor of the intelligible order (*Republic*, VI, 509 a-d).

In a bold and eloquent passage, Plato argues that it is misleading to portray the gods as quarreling and making war on one another and creating plots of revenge. Although Homer was something of a sacred text to Athenians, Plato insists that Homer's tales about the shameful deeds of the gods have no place in the city. He asks, "Is God not always good? Should he not always be represented as such?" Furthermore, one must characterize God as the cause of good, never of evil and never as a wizard changing shapes (*Republic* II, 378 b-381c).

The Child of the Good

In a poetic passage, Plato speaks of the child or offspring of the good, begotten (*egennesen*) in the likeness of the good. In the same passage, he refers to the relationship between the good and reason (*Republic*, VI, 508b-c), which raises the question of the relationship between God and Wisdom. Wisdom is of supreme beauty; and since Love desires beauty, he desires Wisdom. Love may even be described as the lover of Wisdom, a philosopher, who mediates ignorance and Wisdom (*Symposium*, 204). Plato then raises the question of whether the beautiful and the good are identical (329). The Gospel of John represents Jesus as saying, "The Father and I are one." (Jn. 10:30), a proposition that generated a number of thematic arrangements and elaborate theological formulas for subsequent centuries of Church history. Although Plato does not himself personify the "offspring of the good," it is easy to see how his more anthropomorphic readers might. Later, the Apostle Paul will boldly write of God's Son existing in God's likeness or form.

Whereas the Hebrew tradition could speak of human life as created in the Creator's image, Plato contends that God created the entire world in the divine likeness. The World Soul and World Body are as one in the divine image. As God's only begotten (*monogene*), it is the incarnation of divine order and reason. (*Timaeus*, 30c-31a).

Divine Reason and Love

In the Republic, Plato openly opposed the notion that the gods quarrel and make war on one another. In the *Timaeus* (47e-48e), he advances the view that the world is the result of combining Necessity and Reason. By "Necessity," he means something like random space, matter, or energy. If it could exist in itself, it would be purposeless disorder. Divine Reason operates on this bare condition to bring about a world. Since divine Reason does not resort to force, however, persuasion is its way of operating. This is a radical break with the ancient Gods who often intruded into the world and human life with acts of violence or caprice. This vision of divine Reason at work resembles Plato's version of Love in the *Symposium*.

Both Paul and the Gospel of John elaborate on the thesis of divine love. According to Paul, it is poured out into human hearts through the Holy Spirit

(Rom. 5:5), who generates not by force, but by joy, peace, patience, kindness, generosity, faithfulness, gentleness, and self-control (Gal. 5:22). According to John 3:16, it was out of love that God gave his only begotten (*monogene*). Those who disobey the only begotten, however, will receive divine wrath (3:36). The First Epistle of John states categorically that God is love, and those who abide in love abide in God, and God in them (1 Jn. 4:16). This love of God entails love of fellow believers.

Love's Qualities

Before the New Testament, Plato and others attempted to describe love. In the *Symposium*, Plato speaks of the tenderness of Love "in the hearts and souls of both Gods and men.... [I]n them he walks and dwells and makes his home" (195). Agathon, a speaker in the *Symposium*, contends that because Love is the youngest of the Gods, the older Gods of whom Hesiod and Parmenides wrote acted out of Necessity, that is, without an orderly, creative purpose. If Love had existed then, no God would have chained or mutilated another (195). Plato sometimes allows Love, Reason, and Wisdom to blend. According to Agathon, divine Love exemplifies such qualities as courage, temperance, beauty, sweetness, justice, and grace. "As a proof of Love's flexibility and symmetry of form is his grace, which is universally admitted to be in an especial manner the attribute of Love" (*Symposium* 196). Perhaps Jesus' resurrected body's entering a locked room graphically illustrates the belief in Love's flexibility (Jn. 20:19).

Plato allows Agathon to characterize Love as in some sense the Creator. "Who will deny that the creation of animals is his doing?" (196). Love is a poet, and his creations are the poetic works of wisdom. This implies that he is also the inspirer of poetry. Like Prometheus working through Wisdom, the God Love is the source of human skills, gifts, and talents (196-197). In 1 Corinthians 12:4-11, Paul lists varied gifts and activities: the utterance of wisdom, the utterance of knowledge, faith, healing, working of miracles, prophecy, various tongues, and the interpretation of tongues. The one and same Holy Spirit activates all of these for the common good. Just as Plato emphasized Love's harmony or symmetry, so Paul stresses that all the spiritual gifts are like the various members of the body working in harmony, each contributing to the work and honor of the others (12:12-26). Of course, the greatest gift is Love (1 Cor. 13:13).

Paul's famous 1 Corinthians 13 description of love reads like a redaction of a passage from the *Symposium*. In it, Love gives kindness and never unkindness, gives regard to good rather that evil, ranks the fairest in everything, fills mortals with affection, sends courtesy, and fosters grace and delicacy. Plato goes so far as to portray Love as savior, pilot, comrade, helper, leader, and the glory of Gods and mortals. Those whom Love touches do not walk in darkness (197). This last description reverberates in Luke 1:78-79: "By the tender mercy of our God, the dawn from on high will break upon us, to give light to those who sit in darkness and in the shadow of death, to guide our feet in the way of peace."

In some respects, the Synoptic Gospels contain a narrative expansion of a line of poetry quoted in the *Symposium*. It is the God Love who "gives peace on earth and calms the stormy deep, who stills the wind and bids the sufferer sleep" (197).

Love's Poverty

In a rather surprising passage, Plato permits another speaker, Diotima, to portray Love as the offspring of Resource (or Plenty) and Poverty. In virtue of having Poverty as his mother, Love is always poor and is in a situation not in the least tender and fair. Love must live outdoors, under the heavens, having no house or shoes, and no permanent place to rest (*Symposium* 203). The Synoptic Gospels portray Jesus in a similar light. "Foxes have holes, and the birds of the air have nests; but the Son of Man has nowhere to lay his head" (Lk. 9:58). The description of Love that Diotima offers does not square fully with that given by Agathon. Later, the early Christians wrestled with the same problem. How could the divine Love become a suffering mortal involved in human flesh? Diotima goes so far as to say that Love in his position between Wisdom and ignorance is in constant distress and even plots against the fair and good (*Symposium* 203). Centuries later, the Christians of the Docetic strain denied that God could become truly human flesh. They wanted to protect the divine Christ from not only the frailties of human flesh, but also the sin that inevitably issued from such embodiment. Like the Pythagoreans of the sixth century BCE, they regarded the body as the soul's prison. Paul pictures a Christ who suffers mortal imprisonment and yet breaks the bonds, including the bonds of death.

Paul's Vision

Paul boldly asserts that God sent "his own Son in the likeness of sinful flesh" (Rom. 8:3). Presumably, this is more than an external appearance of being human. Drawing in part from his Hebrew tradition, Paul envisions the Christ coming to earth in the flesh to be the Second Adam. Unlike the First Adam, the Second succeeds in dealing with sin through unfailing obedience. The First Adam presumably did not suffer the disadvantage of having to begin his earthy life in *sinful* flesh. The Second Adam, despite having to deal with this enormous disadvantage, succeeded in condemning sin in the flesh. The law's requirements were fully met through perfect love (Rom. 13:10), thus liberating believers from the law of sin and of death (Rom. 8:2; 1 Cor. 15:46-47).

Paul claims to have received revelations from the resurrected Christ (Gal. 1:12); and he goes so far as to claim that before his birth, he was divinely set apart so that God could reveal his Son to him (Gal. 1:15-16). While quite willing to acknowledge that Paul believed these claims about himself, we join those who focus on the earthly sources of his thinking and visions. No serious student of Shakespeare today can deny the bard's unsurpassed creative powers. Yet, A. L. Rowse's *What Shakespeare Read—and Thought* shows that Shakespeare borrowed from a variety of sources. In a chapter titled "From *Leir* to *Lear*," Shakespeare scholar William R. Elton shows how the playwright took a hundred-year-old chronicle play and transformed it into one of the greatest tragedies ever written (Elton, 1988, pp.63-71). In "*Hamlet* and the Art of Grafting" and "The Genealogy of Ideals: *Troylus and Cressida,*" Graham Bradshaw indicates how Shakespeare strengthened his ability to think and write by standing on the shoulders of his intellectual and artistic predecessors (Bradshaw, 1987b, pp. 95-125; Bradshaw, 1987a, pp. 126-163).

Our calling attention to critical passages from Plato does not diminish the creative genius of the Apostle Paul and other first-century Christians. Rather, our goal is to present Paul as a thinker who made creative use of various themes, images, theological scenarios, and problems that existed in both the Greek tradition and the Hebrew tradition centuries before his birth. Creative brilliance does not take place in a vacuum. While Philo the Jew consciously borrowed from Plato, Paul more than likely did not. Rather, he drew from an entire culture—or cross-cultures—that had already absorbed many ideas, arguments, themes, and images that Plato and the Greek playwrights expressed with great literary power.[1] First-century Christianity could not have emerged without deep roots in rich Hebrew and Greek legacies. Just as science and music must create from their legacies, so must religions develop their mutants and variations from their multi-layered antecedents. We have explored in this chapter only a fraction of the insights that Simone Weil offers in *Intimations of Christianity among the Ancient Greeks*. She discovers among the ancient Greeks so many themes playing in the New Testament that she feels compelled to write, "They can in no case serve as arguments against the historical character of the Gospels" (Weil, 1976, p. 71). We, by contrast, offer the conjecture that the Gospels were in fact literary creations that came not from eyewitnesses centered on one particular Jesus of the first century. Rather, they grew from theological themes, folk stories, sayings, problems, key images (Farrar, 1948, pp. 36-39, 57), and the various other sources and genres that Form Criticism has sorted out over the decades. Far from detracting from the literary power and skill of the Gospel narratives, we stress that the authors and redactors enjoyed ancient literary, philosophical, and theological roots. Paul and the other first-century Christian writers encountered and deeply felt critical *problems* both in their legacies and in their sociopolitical settings. The *solutions* they believed they found came largely by inventing and recasting characters and creatively reformulating themes, images, stories, and visions from their Greek, Roman, and Hebrew traditions.

The Perennial Problems

The Greek and Hebrew traditions teem with new variations stimulated by the emergence of either new external crises or problems in their legacies perceived in new ways. Second Isaiah, for example, developed a theme in the Hebrew tradition with such intellectual subtlety, literary boldness, and moral power that one should understand it as a new creation or invention. Paul in turn, probing Second Isaiah's theme of the suffering servant, helped generate a new version of a cosmic suffering servant, proclaiming his death as the redemptive event unprecedented in human history.

The question naturally emerges: "Why have Isaiah, Paul, and others of the Hebrew tradition soared into such grand and sweeping realms?" A part of the answer is that they could not help reflecting on the three hoary problems of a species that had discovered its own drive to talk about itself. The three problems pervade the Greek tragedies and enrich Near Eastern writings. First, what is the meaning of this world that mortals are living in with its many conflicts, demands, intoxicating possibilities, and seeming contradictions? Second, how do these mortals relate to Gods, spirits, demons, and other extraordinary beings so that they may be on good terms with them and gain their favor? Third, how do mortals relate to one another while trying to negotiate with the extraordinary beings and the forces of earth and sky? These three questions appear perpetually because of a paradox: although human finitude has yet to be conquered, the torch of human ingenuity continues to pass from generation to generation.

Note

1 First Corinthians 13 is possibly a poetic "arrangement" of passages from *Symposium*. Paul either composed or adopted it.

6 Paul and Two Jews of Alexandria

The Wisdom of Solomon

The Wisdom of Solomon was composed probably in the second half of the first century BCE. The author, an Alexandrian Jew, personifies Wisdom (Sophia), who is described as "a reflection of eternal light, a spotless mirror of the working of God, and an image of his goodness" (7:26). Furthermore, Wisdom "reaches mightily from one end of the earth to the other, and she orders all things well" (8:1). The Lord of all has taken Wisdom as his collaborator. Living with God, Wisdom serves as his agent in the creation of all things (8:3-4).

In *The Wisdom of Solomon*, readers can find Platonic and other Greek concepts and apparent Hellenistic influences. Evidence suggests that Paul, a Hellenistic Jew, applied descriptions of Wisdom from *The Wisdom of Solomon* to the supernatural, cosmic being whom he called Lord Jesus Christ. According to this document, Wisdom is the divine guardian and presence that successfully guided the Israelites through many tribulations, including the crisis at the Red Sea. Wisdom inspired Moses, defended the Israelites against enemies, and quenched their thirst in the desert (*The Wisdom of Solomon* 10-11).

Paul did not hesitate to identify the activity of this personified Wisdom with that of a pre-existent Christ. At various points in Israel's history, therefore, God manifested his power and presence through the pre-existent Christ. Legend had it that a rock with a spring of water followed the Israelites in their desert travels. Paul identified the rock as Christ. "For they drank from the spiritual rock that followed them, and the rock was Christ" (1 Cor. 10:4). New Testament scholar A. T. Hanson argues that Paul advanced the view that what Moses saw in the tabernacle was really the Christ-God in the form of a man (Hanson, 1955, pp. 108-111; Ex. 34; 2 Cor. 3:7-18). If Hanson is correct, the implication is striking: Paul did not need to go consciously outside the Jewish tradition to find a divine being appearing in human form. Before Paul, in fact, Greek and Hebrew motifs had already interacted in many Jewish writings.

Paul appears to have systematically selected Wisdom passages from *The Wisdom of Solomon* and interpreted them as references to the Lord Messiah whom he called *Jesus*, the Greek translation of the name *Joshua*. The name means "Yahweh delivers (or saves)." According to the Pentateuch, Joshua succeeded Moses and led the Israelites into the Promised Land. The Jewish Wisdom teacher (author of *Ecclesiasticus*) is named Jesus. The alternate title of this 180 BCE book is *The Wisdom of Jesus Son of Sirach*. In his book, Jesus identifies the personified Wisdom with the personified utterance coming from the mouth of the Most High. Furthermore, Wisdom leaves her dwelling place in high heaven to dwell in the land of Jacob or Israel (24:4,8). The Apostle Paul, however, seems to have borrowed most from the pseudonymous *Wisdom of Solomon*. According to this first-century BCE book, Wisdom sits beside God's throne. The author refers to himself as God's servant or slave and as weak (9:4,5). Later, Paul will refer to himself as weak and as the servant or slave of Christ (Rom. 1:1, Gal. 1:10).

Of perhaps more importance, however, is the description of personified Wisdom as the revealer of God's purposes (*Wisdom of Solomon* 9:17). In this same passage, she is God's holy Spirit sent from heaven to earth. In the eleventh chapter, the author, while continuing his description of Wisdom's performance of mighty deeds in Israel's history, seems to refer to Wisdom as *Lord*! "For when they [i.e., Israel's enemies] heard that through their own punishments the righteous had received benefit, they perceived it was the Lord's doing" (11:13). This same Chapter 11 describes the divine being as one whose almighty hand created the world out of formless matter (11:17). The Hebrew writer uses a Platonic model of formless matter. For Plato, the demiurge (or divine architect) created the world out of formless matter. Paul's older contemporary, Philo Judaeus of Alexandria, appropriated some of Plato's cosmology and metaphysics. Before looking into Philo's attempt to harmonize Hebrew theology with Greek philosophy, we may note the clear deification of the Wisdom-Lord figure of *The Wisdom of Solomon*. "For it is always in your power to show great strength, and who can withstand the might of your arm? Because the whole world before you is like a speck that tips the scales..." (11:21-22).

It is noteworthy that while the author of *The Wisdom of Solomon* does not identify Wisdom as God Elohim, he does appear to blend her with the God Yahweh. In the Septuagint (LXX) the Greek translation of the Hebrew Yahweh is *kurios*, which is translated *Lord*. Wisdom is subtly identified as Lord in the eleventh chapter. Similarly, although the Apostle Paul never referred to Jesus

Christ as God, he frequently identified this cosmic being as Lord (*kurios*). Evidently, Paul wished to avoid being accused of forsaking Hebrew monotheism. Yet, at the same time, to solve the sweeping and momentous problems generated by his paradigm, he needed a Savior who possessed divine power and status. In his mind, the death of a mere human mortal on the cross would not suffice as atonement for the universal sin of the human race. Nor would it solve the other major problems generated by his paradigm. We will examine those problems later. We turn now to Philo Judaeus.

Philo Judaeus and the Logos

Philo flourished between 20 BCE and 40 or 50 CE in Alexandria, where he wrote on a variety of topics. The Jewish community of Alexandria sent him as their delegate to appeal to Emperor Caligula. The main bulk of his works attempts to read scriptural teachings in light of Greek philosophy and to revise Greek philosophy in light of scriptural traditions. He spoke of "heart circumcision" (*SpecLeg* 1:4-7), a concept employed later by Paul (Rom. 2:29).

According to Greek and Egyptian tradition, Plato had visited Egypt and had learned from the priests of Pharaoh. In Philo's Alexandria, intellectuals had received Platonic philosophy well. In Plato's *Timaeus*, both God and an eternal array of ideas coexist from eternity. However, since strict Judaism prevented Philo from accepting the ideas as coeternal with God, he revised Plato by endowing them with a twofold stage of existence. First, he placed them inside God's mind as divine thoughts from eternity. Then before creating the world, Philo's God created his ideas or thoughts as real beings. Centuries earlier, Plato had somewhat vaguely referred to the ideas as "an intelligible world." Philo came to believe that these more-or-less autonomous ideas existed within a more-or-less autonomous mind to which he gave the name *Logos*. This Greek term Logos can be translated as *Word*, *Thought*, or perhaps even *Reason*. Logos and the divine Wisdom (Sophia) seem strikingly similar, especially when Philo describes the cyclical changes in human history as under the guidance of "the divine Logos." Included within the divine Logos' repertoire of ideas is the eternal plan for the world and for those in it.

The prologue to the Gospel of John asserts that the Logos is the divine Son of God, the pre-existing Jesus Christ, who became flesh on earth. Paul preferred to designate his pre-existing Messiah (Christ) as the Wisdom of God, the

Second Adam, Son of God, Lord, and Savior. Like Philo, Paul drew from, and elaborated upon, the reputed prophecies of Isaiah. According to Hyam Maccoby, however, the underlying theory of Paul's Christ has its deepest roots in a combination of Hellenistic Gnosticism and the mystery religions of antiquity. G. A. Wells in *The Jesus of the Early Christians* (Wells, 1971). his first book on Jesus, argued that the mystery religions had greatly influenced the early Christians' thinking about a supernatural redeemer. Four years later, however, in the first edition of *Did Jesus Exist?* Wells argued that the Jewish antecedents must have exerted far greater influence (Wells, 1975). He appears to agree with Walter Burkert that the similarities between early Christianity and the mystery religions are greatly exaggerated. The mysteries were never mutually exclusive religions in the sense that Judaism, Christianity, and Islam became (Burkert, 1987, pp. 3f).

Perhaps one can resolve the difference between Wells and Maccoby by pointing out that the pagan and Jewish traditions were not hermetically sealed off from one another in the Mediterranean world of the first century BCE and the following century. Perpetual cross-fertilization of ideas and beliefs occurred. The Alexandrian Jew who wrote *The Wisdom of Solomon*, for example, found it necessary to denounce the Jewish skeptics of his day who had experienced the impact of the mystery religions, various philosophical views, and the general Hellenization of northern Egypt and Palestine. This same author nevertheless had to use the Greek translation of the Bible (the Septuagint) and to write in Greek although he was well versed in his Jewish tradition. Like the Pharisees of Paul's day, the author came also to adopt an unequivocal doctrine of life after death, along with its postmortem punishments and rewards. The ancient Hebrews remained quite equivocal about the doctrine. The Sadducees flatly denied immortality. Regarding life after death, the Acts of the Apostles portrays Paul as siding with the Pharisees against the Sadducees. The author of *The Wisdom of Solomon* became perhaps more Hellenized than he realized. He embraced the Platonic distinction between body and soul as well as Greek theories of providence (6:7; 4:3), conscience (17:11), and the cardinal virtues (8:7). He used a synthesis of Greek and Hebrew thought to appeal to his pagan readers. He even identified Wisdom with the traditional Hebrew concept of the Spirit of the Lord (Suggs, et al, 1992, p. 1099).

He also wrote eloquently of the righteous person. Although made in the image of eternal God, the righteous person will suffer torment and death at the hands of his enemies. In due time, however, he will sit in judgment against them

(2:20; 29; 5:1-5). Later, Paul will elaborate on this theme by making Christ the model righteous one. After suffering persecution and death, Christ will be resurrected in such glory "that at the name of Jesus every knee should bend, in heaven and on earth and under the earth, and every tongue should confess that Jesus Christ is Lord, to the glory of God the Father" (Phil. 2:10-11).

G. A. Wells calls attention to a passage in the late Jewish writing 4 Maccabees that appears to advance the theory that Jewish martyrs can serve as a vicarious atonement for the sins of others. "[T]hey having become, as it were, a ransom [*antipsuchon*] for the sin of our nation. And through the blood of those devout ones and their death as an atoning [*hilasterion*] sacrifice, divine Providence preserved [rescued] Israel that previously had been mistreated" (4 Macc. 17:21-22; 6:20-29; Wells, 1996, p. xxvi; Dowd, 1990, p. 537). Later, Paul will argue that the death of the Second Adam who came from heaven will remove the sin of all who believe in his name or authority.

But is the passage from 4 Maccabees typical of Judaism? Did Paul, the author of the Gospel of Mark, the author of the Epistle to the Hebrews, and other Christians take their view of Christ's vicarious atonement from the Hebrew tradition? Or did they draw more heavily from the Gnostics and mystery religions?

7 Paul and 2 Esdras

Adam's Curse

A fruitful hypothesis is that the supposed mystery religion motifs in Paul's Christianity stem largely from Jewish thought of the Second Temple period. In light of this hypothesis, we probe a work by a Jewish writer who, like Paul, had an apocalyptic outlook and wrestled with what he presumed to be Adam's curse. Second Esdras (Vulgate 4 Esdras), composed late in the first century CE, throws light on the Apostle Paul because the author was struggling with the problem that had plagued Paul, namely, *universal human evil*. In examining this problem, we can gain some insight into both Paul's creative genius and his amendment of Pharisaic Judaism as he understood it. In tracking Paul's struggle, we can also gain insight into his sharp disagreement with some of his fellow Christians, notably, the Christian branch represented in the Epistle of James.

Whether we operate within an anthropomorphic paradigm or a more scientific one,[1] the fact of widespread human violence and evil poses a critical two-pronged problem:

1) How and why did human evil emerge and spread?
2) How can evil be restrained in general and in ourselves individually?

Paul and the Jewish author of 2 Esdras often embrace the same (or a similar) explanation of human evil's emergence. Their heritage has given them the hypothesis of an original man, Adam, who served more or less as the unelected federal head and representative of the human race. In 2 Esdras 3:21-22, the protagonist addresses the Most High:

> [T]he first Adam, burdened with an evil heart [because of his prior disobedience 3:7], transgressed and was overcome, as were also all who were descended from him. Thus the disease became permanent; the law was in the hearts of the people along with the evil root; but what was good departed, and the evil remained.

Now, rabbinical thought had earlier spawned the explanatory hypothesis of the "evil inclination" (evil *yeser*) and the "good inclination" (good *yeser*). Although God eventually gave Israel the law, the evil disposition remained deeply rooted.

The author of 2 Esdras has discovered both theoretical and practical difficulties near the center of his paradigm. He wants to know why the earth produced Adam in the first place. Alternatively, if Adam had to be, why had God not restrained him from sinning (7:46)?

> For what good is it to all that they live in sorrow now and expect punishment after death? O Adam, what have you done? For though it was you who sinned, the fall was not yours alone, but ours also who are your descendants. For what good is it to us, if an immortal time has been promised to us, but we have done deeds that bring death? And what good is it that an everlasting hope has been promised to us, but we have miserably failed? (2 Esd. 7:117-120 [7:47-50])

> He [the angel] answered and said, "This is the significance of the contest that all who are born on earth shall wage: if they are defeated they shall suffer what you have said, but if they are victorious they shall receive what I have said. For this is the way of which Moses, while he was alive, spoke to the people, saying, 'Choose life for yourself, so that you may live!' But they did not believe him or the prophets after him, or even myself who have spoken to them. Therefore there shall not be grief at their destruction, so much as joy over those to whom salvation is assured." (2 Esd. 7:127-131 [57-61])

We must not overlook the power and subtlety of this strand of Jewish literature. With a certain tenacity, the author exposes what seems to him a glaring contradiction. The Creator has gone to great lengths to bring the human race into existence and to keep it going. Most of the race will, nevertheless, end up suffering damnation (8:4-19a). "But if you should lightly destroy what was fashioned by your command with so much labor, to what purpose was it created?" (8:14).

The Angel Who Is More Than an Angel

The exceedingly subtle author is arguing with a being designated as "the angel." Both of them refer to "The Most High." At the same time, however, the author (or his literary protagonist Ezra) addresses the angel as "Lord." Indeed, he even says, "Oh Lord above, if I may be allowed to approach you in prayer, implant a seed in our hearts and minds, and make it grow until it bears fruit, so that fallen men may obtain life. For you alone are God..." (8:6-7).

Here we have a case of an angel addressed as Lord and apparently identified with God. Not only that, the protagonist is challenging a fundamental element of his inherited paradigm. Like a modern theoretical physicist, he wants to revise the theory by using an auxiliary hypothesis to overcome the apparent contradiction or anomaly.

As noted earlier, Paul did not designate his cosmic Christ as God (*theos*), but he did call him Lord (*kurios*) and elevated him far above the angels. Furthermore, Paul makes it clear that he receives direct revelations from this Lord Christ Jesus. The author of 2 Esdras is, of course, raising questions and receiving answers from his own literary creation, the angel or Lord. One major literary difference between Paul's own epistles and 2 Esdras is that the latter does not reveal his own name but rather purports to be Ezra, who lived almost half a millennium earlier than the author.

The Problem of Widespread Sin and Damnation

Profoundly struck by his own sinfulness and the sinfulness of humanity at large, the author speaks through his character Ezra (8:15, 32). "The truth is no one was ever born who did not sin, no one alive is innocent of offense" (8:35). Then in a rather audacious argument, Ezra informs the Lord that it is because human beings have sinned and have no fund of good deeds to their name that the Lord becomes known as just and merciful (8:31, 37).

In reply, the angel (the Lord) points out that while farmers sow many seeds and plant many plants, not all take root. To this, Ezra asks the Lord if he really wants to compare human beings, the creature fashioned in his image, with seed sown by a farmer (8:44). Ezra does not want to make the Lord angry, but he thinks he has made a point worthy of a divine response.

The Lord answers rather testily and bluntly, "It is not possible for you to love my creation with a love greater than mine—far from it!" (8:47). Instead of answering Ezra's question, however, the Lord tells him to inquire no more about the lost sinners. They enjoyed freedom. Of course, the Lord had not wanted anyone destroyed or tormented, but sinners brought their end on themselves (8:55-60).

Ironically, when Ezra shows sufficient humility and modesty by ranking himself among the unrighteous, the Most High promotes him. From now on, Ezra is to avoid ranking himself among the unrighteous. In addition, the Most High commanded him to give up thinking about the lost so that he may focus on the glory that waits those from whom the root of evil had been cut off. "[F]or your disease is at an end and death abolished, hell is gone, and the corruption of the grave blotted out" (8:47-55).

The Path to Salvation

Eventually, a critical question will emerge in the theistic paradigm of people like Paul and the author of 2 Esdras. How may a person receive justification before the righteous Creator and gain redemption's benefits? The author of 2 Esdras points to the path of Moses and the prophets, which stipulates that the individual must lead a righteous life. Unfortunately, this terribly vague answer seems unfit, given the presumably high stakes. Human beings ought to have a more precise way of knowing when they are leading the kind of life that guarantees salvation rather than damnation. Possibly, 2 Esdras offers two paths:

1) the way of good works
2) the way of faith.

> All who come safely through and escape destruction, thanks to their good works or the faith they have shown, will survive the dangers I have foretold and [will] witness the salvation I shall bring to my land, the territory I have set apart from all eternity as my own. (9:7-8)

The protagonist Ezra has indeed posed a difficult problem for his paradigm. In trying to deal with it, he comes at it from an angle. Instead of precisely spelling out the requirements essential to salvation, he spells out those factors that will *exclude* one from salvation. Presumably, those who do not qualify for perdition will qualify for salvation. Among the damned will be those who have "utter contempt" for the Lord's ways, those who fail to acknowledge the Lord despite the benefits he has bestowed, and all who disdained the Lord's law and scornfully dismissed penitence while the way was still open (9:9-11). Penitence does not mean adding up points or piling up good deeds to impress the Lord. Rather, it has more to do with humility and modesty while striving to live by the law. Penitence, the opposite of contempt and ingratitude, includes acknowledging one's sins to the Lord rather than denying them. Second Esdras concludes, "Abandon your sins, and have done with your wicked deeds forever! Then God will set you free from all distress" (16:67).

But can *all* sins be abandoned? The author seems to realize that he has not resolved the critical problem within his paradigm, the problem of indivdiuals' gaining salvation as long as they are finite, imperfect mortals. In the end, 2 Esdras fails to resolve the problem that will not be swept under the rug: "the lost outnumber the saved as a wave exceeds a drop of water" (9:15-16). Earth, the mother of humanity, mourns. "In the beginning, all sprang from her, and there are more still to come; yet almost all her children go to perdition..." (10:10, 14).

Paul's Good News

Paul very likely agonized over this very problem before becoming convinced he had received a divine revelation to become the bearer of the good news of salvation to the Gentiles! Salvation was not for the Jews only. Paul believed he was going far beyond "those of the circumcision (group)," who would shackle the Gentiles with unnecessary requirements, thus closing the door of salvation to the majority of the human race. Furthermore, Paul believed the way of salvation was faith, not works (Gal. 2:15-16). According to Galatians, Cephas (Peter) agreed with Paul on this even if occasionally he played the hypocrite to please the circumcision group.

In the Epistle to the Romans, Paul dares to raise the question of Israel's salvation. If, as conjectured above, Paul did agonize over the conclusion that almost all human beings end in perdition, then we can understand his puzzling comment that "all Israel shall be saved" (Rom. 11:26). It involves a wider problem troubling many Pharisees and other first-century Jewish thinkers. Paul even advances an auxiliary hypothesis as to why Israel has not (yet) turned to Christ. Even Israel's rebellion is made to be a part of divine providence to open the door of salvation to the Gentiles (Rom: 11:11-12, 25).

The Law and the Servant

Scholarly treatises on Paul's thought cannot escape noting Paul's hostility toward the law, the Torah. At the same time, he reveals ambivalence toward it. Perhaps an analogy can throw light on the apostle's mixed feelings. (Some would say *contradictory* feelings.) Let us imagine that we live at a time when families employed household servants. In a particular family, one special servant functions somewhat as a family member. He fulfills his assignments well, let us say, to help raise the children. He gives them sound counsel and sees that they avoid bad company, take care of their health, arrive at school on time, and show proper respect for their parents and others. Though not their schoolteacher, he helps them understand that they need the teachers' guidance, instruction, and training. When they misbehave, he helps discipline them.

Eventually, however, the servant forgets his place. He begins to act as if the children belong to him and exist to serve *him*. He lays down regulations and restrictions that have little to do with their maturation, safety, and well-being. He behaves as if he were the primary reason for the children's existence. Furthermore, he sets up obstacles to their schoolwork and seems jealous of their schoolteacher, who clearly can introduce them to a world the servant scarcely knows. Clearly, the servant cannot teach the children all they need to know for later enjoying wider freedom and the accompanying responsibilities.

The children grow up. Looking back, they can see that the servant has done much for them. Though grateful, they resent his interference and intrusiveness. They resent also his attempt to bring them back under his control. In short, he wants to keep them as children. The person who once worked toward their maturity and freedom seeks now to ensure their dependency and essentially enslave them.

Now grown, the children cannot permit him to dominate their lives. They must free themselves from his controlling ways. While profoundly appreciating the values he imparted, they as adults seek the freedom to appropriate the values for themselves. In setting their own guidelines and laws, they realize that much of their servant's teachings have become a part of them. Nevertheless, they must see everything in the perspective of their higher law, their mature way. They, of course, feel ambivalent toward the old servant. Although he has meant much to them and still does, he evidently can no longer understand them. Nor can he appreciate their right to live as free men and women under the new law by which they guide their lives. Despite their gratitude, they must oppose him without compromise when he tries to steal into their homes, intending to undermine them and their children.

For the Apostle Paul, Christ is the new law. Rather than absorb the old uncritically, believers in Christ must see its value and usefulness as the way of the beloved servant who escorted the children to the school of Christ. When believers entered Christ's school, they cannot forget everything their servant did to help them over the years. They cannot denigrate all his ways. The servant—the law—helped them see their extreme need for true righteousness and their lack of it. Still, the law in itself could not give them that righteousness. In a source other than themselves, they must find the full righteousness required to permit them to stand in fellowship with the righteous and holy God. That source, Paul came to think, was the Lord, the Son of God himself, who came as Messiah (Christ) in the form of the slave Jesus.

In his insightful 1995 article "Spheres of Influence: A Possible Solution to the Problem of Paul and the Law," Professor Klyne Snodgrass points out that for Paul, the Law of Moses tends to become the law of works rather than faith. This results in evil because the law becomes an end in itself, turning into a self-serving tyrant. The individual caught up in the works of the law begins to boast in his own achievements. This, in turn, cuts the individual off from life in the Spirit, a life of trust in God's mercy and righteousness imparted to the believer as a gift. By taking the law as a means of boasting in one's own works, the individual, in effect, pursues the way of the flesh. By flesh, Paul means pride, arrogance, lust, and exclusiveness. Those who become boastful and proud in their own works and achievements tend to be exclusive. They would deny God's life and Spirit to those who do not adhere to circumcision, dietary regulations, and certain other works of the law that Paul believed have nothing to do with righteousness or life in the Spirit. The law seen in the spirit of boastfulness brings spiritual death and invites sin into the heart. Boasting is very much the issue, Snodgrass points out. The law is something positive when brought into its proper sphere, namely, love and faith or trust in divine grace. "Any boasting that is done in the sphere of faith is not boasting in self, but is boasting in the Lord" (Snodgrass, 1995, p. 166).

Paul in Personal Conflict—Romans 7:7-25

Earlier references to Paul's preoccupation with the theme of weakness and power relate directly to the puzzling Romans 7:14-16 passage regarding the law.

> We know that the law is spiritual; but I am unspiritual, sold as a slave to sin. I do not understand what I do. For what I want to do, I do not do; but what I hate I do. And if I do what I do not want to do, I agree that the law is good.

Earlier in this same chapter, Paul had made an even more puzzling comment: "But sin, seizing the opportunity afforded by the [tenth] commandment [against covetousness], produced in me every kind of covetous desire.... I found that the very commandment that was intended to bring life brought death" (7:8, 10).

Paul's experience proves universal even when we cast it in a paradigm not his own. To be human is to have conflicting desires. Paul classifies some of his as belonging to the law of sin, which is at work in the members of his body. By contrast, his mind serves God's law (the law of the spirit) in the war against the flesh and its law.

As noted earlier, the Jewish author of 2 Esdras struggled with the depressing conviction that most human beings lose in the personal battle for righteousness and salvation. Most of the human race ends in torment and perdition. Despite the Law of Moses and other elements of goodness in both the world and individuals, righteousness usually lacks the power to thwart evil. This baleful human predicament must have plagued Paul. It became an all-consuming problem that threatened to eat the heart out of the anthropomorphic paradigm. If our earlier analysis of Paul's thinking comes close to the mark, we may conjecture that the problem (with its terrifying implications) drove Paul to make a major change at the heart of his paradigm. He replaced the law (Torah) with Christ.

For him, Christ exemplified weakness, humiliation, and slavery (Phil. 2:7-8). What could manifest weakness more than taking on the nature of a slave and obediently dying in agony on a cross? *Yet, it is out of this utter weakness that God fully demonstrates his power.* The event of the Israelite slaves' escaping across the Sea of Reeds was God's deliverance of his people, Joshua eventually taking the former slaves into the Promised Land. However, for Paul, nothing can compare with the event of the cross. He believes that through Christ crucified, the liberation of the elect among both Jews and Gentiles has become possible. The new Joshua (Jesus) will lead the believers into the very presence of God and the spiritual territory of redeeming grace.

Note

1 Science's major impact on metaphysics is not the destruction of the cognitive role of metaphysics (the logical positivists' mistake). Rather, science has drastically reduced the number of conscious, purposive agents (whether benevolent or malevolent) presumably controlling the universe. We emphasize reduction, rather than elimination, of purposive agents; for science combined with technology has, in some ways, increased the role of human agents. Science has also given us reason to think that inorganic elements as well as unconscious living agents such as microorganisms play a more significant role on earth than the ancients imagined.

8 Paul on Sinful Desires and Divine Providence

The Law and Sinful Desires

Evidently, Paul had given a great deal of thought to the role of the law in coming to terms with his own weakness that drove him to both the heights and the depths. At the heights, he could boldly proclaim himself an apostle of the Lord Messiah, God's Son, so that not even Cephas or James could challenge his authority. At the same time, despite professing to have personally received the risen Christ's commission, Paul felt driven to despair. "I do not understand what I do. For I do, not what I want, but what I hate" (Rom 7:15 our translation).

In this now-famous Romans 7 passage, Paul focuses on the Tenth Commandment for a reason. More than any other, it locates the source of human weakness in the conflict of desires. Attempting to discover the pattern of human collective violence, René Girard examines the relationship between desire and its objects (Girard, 1977; Girard, 1987). Dostoevsky earlier developed the idea of what might be called original conflict rather than original sin (Kraeger and Barnhart, 1992, p. 59). Paul believes that some desires conflict and simply cannot be harmonized. On this point, he shares insights with Buddhism, Platonic psychology, and Stoicism. He has discovered that some human desires must suffer defeat. The "law is spiritual" in that it exposes the desires of the flesh as evil or sinful. This same law, Paul believes, had made him conscious of the sinful nature within him. His mind, his inner being, allies with the spiritual law that makes him hate satisfying his sinful desires (Rom. 7:8, 15-20).

Perverting the Law

Even the law, however, can be perverted and made to serve evil desires. Centuries later, another Jew, Sigmund Freud, conjectured that the id with its passions and cravings has an unconscious intelligence of its own (a law to itself?) that seeks to manipulate conscience and the superego, using them for its own purposes. Paul had a similar insight into the cunning of the fleshly desires and their power not only to pervert even the law of righteousness, but also to use it for evil.

> For in my inner being I delight in God's law; but I see another law at work in my members, warring against the law of my mind and making me a prisoner of the law of sin at work in my members. What a wretched man I am! Who will deliver me from this body of death? (7:22-24)

For Paul, the law in itself is not sinful, but spiritual. In the service of the flesh and its sophisticated manifestation in pride and boasting, however, the law becomes a curse. Furthermore, it becomes semi-autonomous by generating its own desires and demands. The person who identifies with these special cravings of the perverted law will become self-righteous and grow contemptuous of outsiders. However, even those who do not fully identify with it may feel its power to enslave. It becomes a tyrant creating demands impossible to satisfy. It will even spawn new laws (circumcision, for one) that substitute self-righteousness for genuine righteousness before the holy God.

We can then understand Paul's ambivalence toward the law. On the one hand, it entails respect for the way of Christ and the Spirit. On the other hand, it breeds hostility, kills the spirit, perverts the divine intent of the law itself, and nullifies Christ's death. In Chapter 13, we will draw from the insights of René Girard and others to spell out a social and political view of the "law of sin."

Apostle to the Gentiles

Professor Krister Stendahl notes the great weight Paul gave to his call to serve as apostle to the Gentiles (Stendahl, 1976, pp. 7-14). Whatever readers make of Paul's conversion, it must include a profound sense of this calling. Like the author of 2 Esdras, Paul apparently agonized over the conclusion that everlasting destruction awaited most Gentiles. If he could find a way for the Gentiles to share in the blessing that God had bestowed on Abraham and his seed, that would indeed be gospel or good news (*euangelion*). If Paul's account of his meeting with John, Cephas, and James is reasonably accurate, we may surmise that the "pillars" of the Jerusalem church had shown no strong inclination to preach their Christ to the Gentiles. In the Acts of the Apostles, however, Luke portrays the two apostles as in full theological agreement. Even James is made to say to a gathering of apostles and elders, "[W]e should not make it difficult for the Gentiles who are turning to God" (Acts 15:19). Yet, Luke cannot deny that some Christians had insisted that Gentile converts "be circumcised and required to obey the Law of Moses" (Acts 15:5b). Those making this demand were, according to Luke, "of the party of the Pharisees" (15:5a). In his epistles, however, Paul ignores the Pharisees' role regarding this specific controversy and leaves the distinct impression that James made the demand (Gal. 2:12). The point is, Paul saw himself as the most committed apostle to the Gentiles.

It requires no stretch of the imagination to see that his drive to bring salvation to the Gentiles helped him see the need to remove every obstacle to winning Gentile converts. This concern required his judging not only the law's *function* in divine providence, but also its essential *content*. Already, Pharisees had sought proselytes or converts from among the Gentiles. Since the Pharisees had developed the oral law (i.e., interpretations and applications of the biblical law) for the Jews, nothing prevented them from helping Gentiles convert to share in the Hebrew faith's true essence.

Paul stepped over the line that his fellow Pharisees presumably had drawn. He practiced a type of anthropological gerrymandering by drawing the religious map with different boundaries. The significant boundary no longer lay between those within the law and those outside, but between those within Christ and those outside. In Christ, there was neither Jew nor Greek (or Gentile), neither slave nor freeman, neither male nor female. All were one—in Christ (Gal. 3:28-29). For Paul, the line was still drawn hard and fast. He simply changed the location of the boundaries.

Paul believed that in times past, being a Jew brought genuine spiritual advantages. In the new age, however, the advantages no longer held, since God has opened the door to the elect among all nations and peoples. Faith or trust in the grace of God manifested in the crucified and resurrected Christ Jesus is the doorway to redemption (Gal. 3:13-14, 26; Rom. 4:16; 8:1-4). The promised son of Abraham was not Isaac, but Jesus so that all who enter Christ receive the promise to Abraham (Gal. 3:16, 26).

Professor Jon D. Levenson correctly concludes that in his allegory of Hagar and Sarah (with their sons Ishmael and Isaac [Gal. 4:21-5:1]), Paul sought to establish the Church's claim to the patrimony of Israel. The old community's inheritance is bestowed upon the new as though the Christian churches become

Jacob, taking both blessing and birthright from Esau (Levenson, 1993, p. 229.) The last shall be first. Yet, in Romans 11, Paul advances the hypothesis that Israel's rejection of the gospel will lead to the reconciliation of the world. That, in turn, will arouse envy or jealousy in Paul's own people, the Jews. So, out of envy, at least some of Israel will become believers in Christ and be saved (Rom. 11:13-15). Although some interpretations might regard this extended auxiliary hypothesis as an ad hoc addition, we regard it as central to the problem Paul is working on, now that he has developed a new model within his inherited paradigm.

The Jews and Divine Providence

Clearly, in Romans 9-11, Paul tries to work out his own theory of divine providence and the role of both Israel and the Gentiles in the grand scheme of things. Evidently, he does not follow the free-will argument that the author of 2 Esdras advances. As seen above, divine *power* is central to Paul's thought. For him, God must control both nations and individuals, not in general, but in each specific or detail. Hence, he can bring himself to write that while Jacob and Esau were still in the womb and before they had done anything good or bad, God loved Jacob and hated Esau (Rom. 9-11-13).

It does not follow, however, that Paul propagated the doctrine that God hated Israel. As Levenson notes:

> For all his fulminations against the observance of Jewish law, Paul never blames the Jews for the death of Jesus or ascribes the founding of the Church to God's wrath against the people of the old covenant. Indeed, he does not attribute Jesus' demise to the Jews at all—an extraordinary datum in light of the reports of the trial and execution of Jesus in the canonical Gospels. (Levenson, 1993, p. 230)

The Gospel of Matthew shows extreme hostility toward the Pharisees, denouncing them as blind guides, hypocrites, whitewashed sepulchers, serpents, murderers, and a brood of vipers doomed to hell (Mt. 23). By contrast, Paul did not attack the Pharisees although he knew how to engage in invectives when doing so suited his purpose. When in Philippians 3:5 he called himself a Pharisee as to the law, Paul did not even suggest that he had been hypocritical.

Rather, as a Pharisee, he asserted his own sincerity in striving to fulfill the law (Beare, 1973, pp. 107-108).

Ironically, according to most New Testament scholars, a Christian inserted into one of Paul's letters the bitter, anti-Semitic passage of 1 Thessalonians 2:14-16:

> For you, brothers, have become imitators of the churches of God that are in Judea in Christ Jesus. For you suffer the same things from your compatriots as they did from the Jews, who killed both the Lord Jesus and the prophets and persecuted us; they do not please God, and are opposed to everyone, trying to prevent us from speaking to the Gentiles that they may be saved, thus constantly filling up the measure of their sins. But the wrath of God has finally begun to come upon them. (*New American Bible*)

G. A. Wells contends that the passage is not typical of Paul, but of Christian writings later in the first century, namely, the Gospels and Acts (Wells, 1982, pp. 24-25). While most scholars consider the passage an interpolator's view and not Paul's, some regard it as something like Paul's dark side erupting in an unguarded moment of anger (Ewert, 1989, pp. 1075).[1]

Thirty to forty years after Paul wrote his earlier epistles, the author of the Gospel of Matthew expressed undeniable hostility. He went so far as to portray the chief priests, the elders, and the Jewish people of Jerusalem as responsible for Christ's death. When Pilate washed his hands, the evangelist portrayed the people as answering, "His blood be on us and on our children" (Mt. 27:25)!

Both the Gospel of Matthew and the Gospel of John appear to have more than a theological disagreement with Judaism and the Jews who did not convert to Christianity. The Jesus of the Gospel of John goes out of his way to antagonize and alienate "the Jews," whose rather useful and intelligent questions receive disrespect. "[I]t is not hard to understand why he [i.e., the Jesus of the Gospel of John] provokes hostility" (Culpepper, 1983, p. 112). The Gospel of John portrays the Jews as symbolizing unbelief, darkness, and spiritual blindness (Culpepper,1983, pp. 128-132, 135). In a later chapter, we will examine the Fourth Gospel's portrayal of Jesus and his attitude toward the Jews.

Paul could not follow those Gnostics who felt the Jews could be dismissed as insignificant because they completely failed to comprehend higher spiritual matters. His theory of divine providence and heavenly control of all earthly affairs assigns a role for Israel in the mystery of God. Even Israel's temporary blindness serves as an essential element in salvation's total pattern. Paul must explain God's preoccupation with Israel. He cannot dismiss the scriptures (the Old Testament) as so much idle speculation. Israel, therefore, becomes a necessary link. Israel's putative blindness in rejecting the Messiah Jesus becomes a necessary evil that eventually leads to a great good, namely salvation for the Gentiles (Maccoby, 1991, p. 182).

Paul's theology of providence later led other Christian writers to portray the death of Christ and all events leading to it as foreordained. In the Gospel of Matthew, the Jews become the Judas-nation, whose appalling crime Heaven designed as necessary to humanity's redemption.

Jon D. Levenson comments on this grim story.

> Here again one can reasonably suspect that the betrayal of Jesus by Judas is a midrashic play on the sale of Joseph by Judah, with Judas, as his name suggests, perhaps typifying the Jews as the homicidal opponents of the beloved son of God. The father's gift has been recast as the brothers' crime. (Levenson, 1993, p. 230)

Note

1 According to evangelical scholar David Ewert, Paul himself penned this "outburst" against only those Jews who were "opponents of the gospel," whom Ewert apparently labels as "unbelieving Jews." But who are *they*? Evidently, they are all Jews who did not convert to Christianity. Ewert seems to hold that Paul regarded them as "hostile to all men" (Ewert, 1989, 1075). This, of course, raises the question of whether those influenced by the literary critic René Girard perhaps correctly suggest that some Christians of the last third of the first century tried to make a scapegoat of the Jews (Price, 1993, pp. 294-300). Jesus was the scapegoat whom the Jews killed! Now the Jews and their children must bear the guilt.

> And ...who killed Jesus? They are now the Jews instead of the Romans, thus reflecting the early rivalries forced by the new social formations.... So who are the persecutors writing the Gospels? They are Christians. And who are the victims? They are the Jews. And what is unique about the Gospels? The victims are cast as persecutors of an innocent victim. (Mack, 1985, p. 156)

9 An Apocalyptic Vision of Ultimate Power

Paul's Apocalypticism

Readers certainly cannot label apocalyptic visions as modest. Apocalyptic literature may or may not come in coded and disguised language. One undisguised feature of apocalyptic literature is the writers' sustained interest in sweeping, global, and often cosmic power. A disciple of Nietzsche might describe their literature as the work of people who not only believe they have a rightful place in the grand scheme of things, but also intend to have their place restored and their enemies either punished severely or transformed into believers.

One ingredient of Paul's apocalyptic outlook is his dualistic doctrine of two ages. He senses that he lives on the boundary of two worlds, one dying and the other being born. He expects the last trumpet to sound soon. "Not all of us will fall asleep" (1 Cor. 15:51). While he cannot fix the precise time and date, he assures the believers at Thessalonica that "the Day of the Lord will come like a thief in the night" (1 Thess. 5:2). They should, therefore, prepare themselves (5:4). In a subsequent letter, he writes that, while "the coming of our Lord Jesus Christ" has not yet taken place, events are adding up. "The mystery of iniquity" is already at work and will shortly appear openly to execute an assortment of counterfeit miracles, signs, wonders, and a variety of deceptions for those en route to destruction. Delusions and falsehoods will both flood those who choose to live in darkness and seal their doom (2 Thess. 2:7-12). Eventually, however, the "Lord [Jesus] will destroy him [i.e., the mystery of wickedness] with the breath of his mouth and annihilate him with his glorious appearance at his coming" (2 Thess. 2:8). Believers now suffering hardship because of oppressors will find relief. In the end, the oppressors will suffer hardship "when the Lord Jesus appears from heaven with the angels of power" (2 Thess. 2:7). Though the believers enjoy little power to resist their oppressors, the Lord will return with his agents and their delegated power. "He will come amid flaming fire; he will impose a penalty on those who...refuse to accept the gospel of our Lord Jesus" (2 Thess. 1:8).

Apocalyptic literature often focuses on wrath, judgment, and the Day of the Lord. Infused with his doctrine of the messianic age, Paul expects a supernatural termination of "the present evil age." Like apocalyptic Jewish writers before him, Paul (or whoever wrote 2 Thessalonians) warns the readers of the coming wrath. If they commit to Christ, however, they will, he assures them, escape the wrath and enjoy the new creation (Rom. 8:18-25).

Two Worlds Populated

Paul's paradigm populates the world with, in effect, two worlds or two ages. For him, the present age abounds in evil beings—Satan and powerful elemental spirits inflicting great hardship on the righteous. Ironically, Christ's earlier coming in the form of a slave was perhaps itself a form of deception that disarmed the Great Deceiver. From Paul's perspective, life in the present age is perpetual warfare. Christ in his death and resurrection, however, has defeated two of the most powerful enemies of humanity—death and all the cosmic evil beings, including Satan, "the god of this world" (2 Cor. 4:4; Gal. 4:3; 1 Cor. 2:8; 15:24-28; Rom. 8:37-39). The new age around the corner comes only through supernatural power, bringing a new creation (1 Cor. 7:31; Gal. 6:14; 2 Cor. 5:17) and establishing a divine empire, an age of glory (1 Thess. 2:10-12; 1 Cor. 15:20-28; 2 Cor. 4:17; Rom. 5:2, 21).

The Deification of Earthly Mortals

Apocalyptic literature flourished during a period when Greek and Roman rulers were deified. Grandiose claims were sometimes made also about other significant mortals. The Roman poet Lucretius (94-55 BCE) praised his philosopher-savior Epicurus (c. 340-270 BCE) as a God and referred to his "revelations" and "philosophy" as gospel (*euangelion*) broadcast throughout the empire. People regarded several kings and rulers of the ancient Mediterranean world as manifestations of the gods. Scholars have well established that many Roman emperors were regarded as divine beings. A Roman edict enacted in 9 BCE refers to Augustus Caesar as a savior (*soter*) sent by Providence to "put an end to war and [to] set all things in order." Furthermore, having become a God visible, Caesar now fulfills the hopes of earlier times. Moreover, because the

God Caesar's birthday has brought the gospel (*euangelion*) to the whole world, everyone will reckon a new age (or era) from the date of Augustus Caesar's birth. "Let his birthday mark the beginning of the new year" (Grant, 1957, p. 174).

Around 48 CE, while Paul was perhaps in Ephesus, the Ephesian City Council passed a resolution concerning the Roman Emperor Caligula.

> The Council and the people (of Ephesus and other Greek) cities which dwell in Asia [Minor] and the nations (acknowledge) Gaius Julius, the son of Gaius Caesar as High Priest and Absolute Ruler..., the God Visible who is born of (the gods) Ares and Aphrodite, the shared savior (*soter*) of human life. (Cartlidge and Dungan, 1980, p. 14)

Almost two and a half centuries earlier and in three languages, people proclaimed the divinity of a Greek king of Egypt, Ptolemy V Epiphanes (210-180 BCE). The following inscription about Ptolemy V appear on the now-famous Rosetta Stone:

> In the reign of the young king by inheritance from his father, Lord of the Diadems, great in glory, pacificator of Egypt and pious toward the great Gods, superior over his adversaries, restorer of the life of man...king like the Sun, Great King of the Upper and Lower Lands, child of the gods through the love of the father...*living image of Zeus*, Son of the Sun, Ptolemy the immortal...priest of the (divine) Alexander (the Great) and the Savior Gods and the Brotherly Gods and the Benefactor Gods and the gods of love of the Father, the God visible, for whom thanks be given. (Cartlidge and Dungan, 1980, pp. 14-15, italics added)

Christ as Divine King

A portion of the Jewish population in Paul's time perceived David as the ideal or archetypal king. Paul embraced an apocalyptic expectation that the Messiah would be not only David's descendent, but also the supreme ruler of the world under God (Rom. 1:3; Phil. 2:6-9). Surprisingly, Paul makes very little of Jesus' alleged Davidic ancestry. He allows Jesus to meet the requirement, but immediately drops the matter. The Davidic character serves as scarcely more than support for Paul's theology (Rom. 4:6; 11:9). Clearly, David is in many ways too limited a figure to serve as Christ's archetype. For Paul's sweeping apocalyptic mind, Christ is the archetype, while David is at best the imperfect foreshadow. Paul's Savior Jesus Christ simply will not fit into David's armor. David fought mere earthly enemies whereas Paul's Christ took abuse from both earthly powers and celestial principalities and power. Christ did nevertheless what David could not, namely, defeat the cosmic enemies through his crucifixion and resurrection. David established an earthly kingdom whereas Christ brought about a cosmic transformation that will establish his reign over the many Gods and lords in heaven and on earth (1 Cor. 8:5-6). According to David Seeley of the Institute for Antiquity and Christianity at Claremont Graduate School, at least some early Christians envisioned Christ as Caesar's rival (Seeley, 1994, pp.71-72.).

Rulers against the Temple and the Law of Moses

Not everyone deified the ruler in power. Apocalyptic literature often portrayed tyrants as persecutors whom God will humiliate. Ordinarily, apocalyptic writers are not political insiders. The Seleucid ruler Antiochus IV Epiphanes (Manifestation) graphically expressed his resolve to eliminate Judaism by building a pagan altar in Jerusalem and in 167 BCE permitting a pig (pork) to be sacrificed to Zeus. He had earlier plundered Jewish villages and appointed his own High Priest to tax the Jews. He also forbade Jews either to observe the Sabbath or to practice circumcision. Antiochus' successors fought several battles with the Jewish rebels—the Maccabees or Hasmonaeans—until the Romans took control in 63 BCE.

Ironically, in John 2:19-20, Jesus' resurrected body becomes in some ways the replacement for the destroyed temple in Jerusalem. Although considering himself a Pharisee of the Benjamin tribe, the Apostle Paul declared circumcision as of no further religious or moral value. Astoundingly, Paul's Christ, not a Seleucid ruler, has nullified circumcision (Gal. 5:12, 6:12-13) and possibly the Jewish Sabbath (Col. 2:16). Paul does not set forth his view of the Sabbath explicitly. What is clear and of utmost importance is his view of blood sacrifice. Both Paul and the author of the Epistle to the Hebrews contended that Christ's death on the cross marked the end of *all* blood sacrifices, including those offered in compliance with the Mosaic law. Whereas the Ephesian Council proclaimed Caligula as High Priest, the Epistle to the Hebrews proclaims Christ as High Priest who entered the heavenly sanctuary not built by mortal hands (Heb. 9:11,

24). Since the crucified Christ is the only blood sacrifice wholly acceptable to God, the sacrificial system has no further religious or moral reason to exist.

Before Paul, the Hebrew tradition wrestled with the question of whether Yahweh truly desired blood sacrifice at any time. When childless Hannah begged Yahweh to give her a child, she vowed to give it back to Yahweh. In this subtle story of 1 Samuel 1, Hannah returned to the temple only after weaning her son Samuel. When she did return, she, unlike Abraham and Jephthah, did not consider the sacrifice of her child on an altar to be an option. Rather, she provided Yahweh with a slaughtered bull and kept her vow to Yahweh by giving up her son in *service* to Yahweh and the temple. Literally, not a hair of Samuel's head was touched, for no razor was put to his head to cut his hair. Centuries later, the Apostle Paul implored believers to offer themselves as a *living* sacrifice (Rom. 12:1).

Apocalyptic literature has sometimes speculated on whether the blood of martyrs served as a sacrifice to God. It is fruitful to ask if circumcision was perceived as a substitute sacrifice. In one aspect, all forms of blood sacrifice are substitutionary. Antioch, ironically, was the city where Paul confronted Cephas to his face regarding circumcision (a form of sacrifice to the deity?) and doubtless other matters concerning the Torah. The city was named after Antiochus, father of Seleucus I, the first of the dynasty of Hellenistic kings that at various times ruled Persia, Babylonia, Syria, Bastria and southern Asia Minor from 312 to 63 BCE. Strange as it may seem, Paul furthered the Hellenization of some branches of Judaism by eliminating from his theology certain Jewish practices and beliefs. In addition, he added elements from Jewish Gnosticism, apocalypticism, and reformation motifs that grew out of the Platonic tradition.

Apocalypticism and Government

Paul's real position on government's role remains elusive at best. His apocalypticism seems to regard all governments as under the control of evil powers, so evil that Christ is about to appear and change everything. Paul advances a theology that regards Christ as the only ruler. On the other hand, Romans 13:1-7 states that God established the state's magistrates. "Consequently, he who rebels against the authority is rebelling against what God has instructed..." (13:2). This puzzling passage has raised far more questions for Christians than it has answered because it fails to deal with the most conspicuous two-pronged problem. Are believers to view the government as instituted by God regardless of how it came to power and treated the citizens?[1]

People can read Romans 13:1-7 in two ways: either an early redactor of Paul's letters added the passage or Paul is answering an inquiry as to whether believers awaiting the apocalyptic end should obey pagan magistrates. In this Romans 13 passage, he perhaps considers it pointless to reform any government, since the new age with Christ's return would soon change everything. A strong pro-government hand might have added the passage later, although no external manuscript evidence exists to buttress this supposition.

Caligula's Grasp for Divinity

The first Roman Empire emperors perhaps did not aspire to the title Lord (Cuss, 1974, p. 54). Initially, Augustus Caesar discouraged using the title for himself or his family members (Cuss, 1974, pp. 55-56, referring to Suetonius, *Augustus 53:1-2*). The masses, however, longed to infuse their rulers with divinity, especially admired rulers like an Antony or Augustus. In the forties BCE,

> Mark Antony, Caesar's true political heir, entered Ephesus behind a procession of Bacchantes, Pans and Satyrs, to the sound of Pan-pipes and flutes: he was acclaimed as a New Dionysus, "bringer of joy and source of peace." (Turcan, 1992, p. 307, citing Plutarch's *Antony* 24:4)

In or around Palestine, many cities and fortresses received the names of emperors and other rulers: Caesarea, Tiberius, Caesarea Philippi, Archelais, Ptolemais, Antioch, Seleucia, Herodium and Alexandrium. Although most people of the Roman empire saw only busts or statues of their emperor, rulers felt the pressure to appear in splendor and pomp. Josephus reports Agrippa's grand entrance into the festival celebrations at Caesarea, clad in a brilliant garment woven of silver. When the rays of the rising sun reflected off the garment, shouts rang out, proclaiming him a God (*theos*) (Josephus, *Antiquities of the Jews* XIX, 8.2). According to Acts 12:21-22 Herod, wearing his robes of state and seated on his throne, addressed the crowd, which responded, "It is a God speaking, not a man."

Caligula (37-41 CE) took advantage of the masses' longings to advance their emperor as a God. The Jews of Palestine in particular resisted. In

Alexandria, Philo wrote in criticism that when Caligula became emperor, "nothing was to be seen throughout the cities but altars, oblations, sacrifices, men in white robes and crowned with garlands..." (Seeley, 1994, p. 53n28). Augustus repressed the Romanization that took place at the expense of the ancestral worship centers, and Caligula encouraged the spread of Egypt's Isis and various other divinities.

Augustus tried, at least for a while, to hold off the attempts to deify himself. He seemed more content believing that his "victories which gained him the principate" had come through the gods' favor (Fears, 1997, p. 216). By contrast, Caligula, caught up in his own self-aggrandizement, strove to present himself in the form of deity. Professor David Seeley offers the highly fruitful hypothesis that the author of the Philippians 2:6-11 poem consciously set out to portray the Christ figure as the very opposite of the grasping Caligula (Seeley, 1994, pp. 66-68). Suetonius reports that after ordering the most famous and admired statues of Gods to be brought from Greece, Caligula had their heads removed and replaced with his own likeness. He established a temple to his own divinity (Suetonius, *Caligula 22:3-4*). The Jews organized against him, however, when he demanded that statues to his divinity be set up in synagogues and the temple (Seeley, 1994, p. 63). Suetonius charges that Caligula began to lay claim (*adsero*) to divine majesty (*divina maiestas*) (Suetonius, *Caligula 22:2*). Philo accused him of overstepping (*hyperkupto*) the bounds of human nature (*physis* or *phusis*) in his eagerness (*spoudalo*) to be thought of as a God (Philo, *Leg. Gaj.*, 77*)*. Whereas the Greek Gods held each to his or her own honor and did not lay claim (*metapoieo*) to those shared by others, envious and covetous (*phthonos* and *pleonekxia*) Caligula took wholesale possession (*spheterizo*) of all the deities' honors and the deities themselves. This he did by remaking his body into different shapes (*metaschaematizo*). He behaved the opposite of those whose honors he proposed to share as their equal, for he invested himself (*skeuazomai*) with their insignia each in turn (Philo, *Leg. Gaj.*, 80, 98).

It is not difficult to see how emperors and rulers came to regard themselves as divine. Politicians in various Roman towns encouraged using pomp and ceremony to extol the emperor.

> A choir established by the province of Asia sang hymns in honor of [Augustus], and other officials praised the emperor in verse.... [F]estivals included competitions, not only in athletics and music, but also in imperial *encomia*.... We hear of one Coan who "in all the most distinguished cities of

> Asia won competitions in encomia to the founder of the city Sebaston Caesar and the benefactors Tiberius Caesar and Germanicus Caesar and all their house and to all other gods in each city." Contests in praising the emperor in prose and verse were widespread in the Greek world, both at festivals in honor of the emperor and as a part of the festivals of traditional gods. (Seeley, 1994, p. 70n116, citing Price, S. R. F., 1984, p. 90, inner quotation from Robert, 1938, p. 23)

According to Seeley's compelling thesis, while Augustus was an exceptionally wise and moderate leader, those after him set the course for growing disillusionment among the people. Tiberius could be both cruel and severely flawed in judgment. After Caligula, it became difficult to believe that the supreme ruler would sail clear of tyranny or even madness. Judea suffered nothing short of a crisis. In maintaining order, Herod resorted to terror. His heirs did not win confidence, and Jewish resentment against Rome increased. The gap between the ruler and the ruled grew wider as Jews longed for their own independent state with their own monarch, God (Seeley, 1994, p. 71). Luke in his dramatic style shows his contempt for rulers who deify themselves. In Acts 12:23, he writes that as soon as the crowd proclaimed Herod as a God rather than a man, "the Lord's anger struck him down, because he had not given God the glory." Josephus' contempt for such self-deification was no less pronounced than Luke's. He describes in graphic detail Agrippa's apotheosis. "When he had come down from the tribunal, he became food for worms even while he was still alive. And so he died" (Acts 12:23). With literary license, 2 Maccabees 9:4-10 graphically details the hostility toward the Seleucid ruler Antiochus. Writing in biting sarcasm about 124 BCE, the author, speaks of the defeat of the arrogant ruler who "thought in his superhuman boastfulness he could command the waves of the sea [and]...imagined he could weigh mountain peaks in a balance..." (2 Macc. 9:8). Now he finds his eyes teeming with worms and his flesh rotting while he lingers in agonizing pain. The stench of his rotted flesh sickens his own army. "A short while before, he had thought to grasp the stars of the heavens; no one could bring himself to act as his bearer, for the stench was intolerable" (2 Macc. 9:10).

Alternate Visions

Judea spawned alternative ways to confront the miserable circumstances many Jews believed had come upon them during Seleucid and Roman domination. With roots to the Maccabees or Hasmonaeans, the Zealots of Paul's youth and early adulthood fiercely advocated home rule. Their hatred of Herod and the encroachments of Hellenism and Rome led them to violence. They saw themselves as a resistance movement ready to fight the foreign oppressors. Judas the Galilean led a revolt during the census of Quirinus in 6 CE. His violent band regarded it as treason against God and country to pay tribute to Rome. The vision of a restored kingdom of David on earth stirred the Zealots to fight for their cause. With the putative fall of Masada, however, the Zealots never again had the means to challenge Rome's might.

During the Seleucid dynasty and the first century BCE, other Jews embraced an apocalyptic vision of divine intervention on the Jews' behalf. Other cultures, too, had developed ways to come to terms with political systems that seemed either oppressive or corrupt. Four centuries before Caligula and Paul, the Greek philosopher Plato envisioned a society in which neither tyrants, mobs, nor the greedy guided the ship of state. Rather, at the helm stood the philosopher-king, whose vision of beauty and goodness guided his decisions in a society where justice prevailed.

But would the people accept such a philosopher-king? Plato has Socrates tell the parable of a person who, after seeing objects in the sunlight, descends into the cave to visit the chained slaves who can see only shadows moving on the cave wall. Socrates suggests that the slaves would, if they could, kill the very man who has come to release and guide them toward the sunlight (Plato, *The Republic,* VII:515-517).

The author of 2 Maccabees creates a hopeful and fanciful ending to his "account" of Antiochus IV Epiphanes. First of all, pagan Antiochus realizes that "no mortal should aspire to equality with the Godhead" (9:12). Second, he declares Jerusalem a free city. Third, he declares the Jews to have rights equal to the Athenians. Fourth, the sacred vessels and other plundered objects of the temple will be restored many times over. Fifth, from his personal revenue, he would defray the expenses incurred for the sacrifices. Sixth, "to crown all, he would himself turn Jew and visit every inhabited place, proclaiming the power of God" (9:13-17).

Either Paul or another Christian composed a poem with an even more hopeful ending for the Christians. After his crucifixion and resurrection, Christ is raised high and given a name above all names so that everyone everywhere will proclaim Jesus Christ as Lord (Phil. 2:9-11). Seeley offers the plausible conjecture that the entire poem was created to contrast the ideal Lord's behavior with the reprehensible behavior of Caligula. The ideal or model Lord (*kurios*) reflects the highest and noblest expectations of a true and good ruler. Such expectations had been projected over the centuries. Seeley points to some of these royal, noble qualities. The ideal king serves his people and takes no thought for himself. Rather than greedily *grasping* after that which belongs to others, he selflessly labors for others. He manifests wisdom and humility (Seeley, 1994, pp. 64-67). Margaret Morris goes into much greater depth to show that the idealized kings of Egypt and Rome become mythological shepherds to their people and take on the life of humility, becoming in some cases servants or peasants (Morris, 1999).

The Christian hymn of Philippians 2:6-11 takes this exceedingly ancient model of the ideal king and casts the Jesus Christ figure into the role. Examining the hymn, we may consider it in light of Seeley's thesis that the author created it in conscious opposition to the self-aggrandizing ruler who grasped greedily for a divine status he could never possess.

> Let the same mind be in you that was in Christ Jesus, who, though he was in the form of God, did not regard equality with God as something to be exploited, but emptied himself, taking the form of a slave, being born in human likeness. And being found in human form, he humbled himself and became obedient to the point of death—even death on a cross. Therefore God also highly exalted him and gave him the name that is above every name, so that at the name of Jesus every knee should bend, in heaven and on earth and under the earth, and every tongue should confess that Jesus Christ is Lord, to the glory of God the Father. (Phil. 2:5-11)

Seeley suggests that the author composed the hymn in response not only to the religious and political crises exemplified by mad Caligula, but also to the stories of the suffering righteous. Isaiah 45 begins with a reference to Yahweh's anointed one (Messiah, Christ) Cyrus whom Yahweh will use for the benefit of Israel, who has endured much suffering in exile. Near the chapter's end, Yahweh affirms that all shall bend the knee to him and every tongue confess Yahweh's justice and power.

Seeley seems to argue that the need for the Christian hymn in the first century becomes clear when viewed against the historical setting of disillusionment with first-century political life. The literary, cultural, and apocalyptic backgrounds provide the hymn's composer with rich material for developing the theological and political vision of the ideal king or Lord coming from heaven to earth in humility and death only to be resurrected in power over all creation.

Earlier, the Roman poet Ovid had written the following about his beloved ruler Augustus: "Jupiter controls the heights of heaven and kingdoms of the triformed universe; but the earth is under Augustus' sway" (Miller, 1916, 15:858-860, citing Ovid, *Metamorphoses*). The Christian poet took one step beyond Ovid to portray his Lord Jesus Christ as receiving power over everything "in the heavens, on earth, and under the earth" (Phil. 2:10). Unlimited force and unblemished piety joined in one being. Unlike Caligula, the Christ of the Philippians hymn emptied himself of the very possession for which Caligula grasped during all his reign but could never call his own.

Summary or Missing Details?

The Philippians hymn contains virtually no details about the earthly life of the Christ who came and was obedient unto death. It offers the barest sketch of Christ's coming. Did the author not know the empirical details about this heavenly being's visit to earth? How did this cosmic Christ come to die? Did the author have a Judas figure in mind? Was there a trial, or did Christ die at the hands of vigilantes or a single murderer lurking in the dark? Is Burton Mack correct in his view that the early churches in places like Antioch had no desire to develop a narrative embellishment of Jesus' trial or to identify the persecutors? Mack suggests the early Christians wished to avoid pointing a finger at, and thereby antagonizing, either the Romans or the temple establishment (Mack, 1988, p. 111). By contrast, G. A. Wells suggests that Paul believed Christ lived an *obscure life* perhaps more than a century before Paul's own time, so obscure that the apostle knew nothing concrete about that life. The author of Matthew, to the contrary, writes (thirty to forty years after Paul's early epistles) that Christ's *fame spread* throughout all Syria (Mt. 4:24). As the acknowledged leader of the scholarly Jesus Seminar, Robert Funk contends that Jesus was not a divine being, but a human mortal who taught in parables and made a profound impact on his followers. Only later, Funk argues, did people who failed to grasp the depth of Jesus' message turn Jesus into a God. They turned the religion *of* Jesus into a religion *about* Jesus (Funk, 1996, pp. 219-256). At the other end of the pole, G. A. Wells contends that early Christians like Paul *began* with the belief in a cosmic, supernatural Savior-Lord who came to earth, died in obedience, and was resurrected as Lord of all. Only gradually, Wells contends, did the details of his presumed earthly life become filled in by the authors' drawing from texts of Hebrew Scripture and other literary and cultural sources.

Note

1 Shakespeare's history plays probe this question deeply. The Puritan poet and essayist John Milton faced the question headlong, as did some of the early American colonists. Milton went so far as to write a treatise defending a people's right to behead a king who proves to be a tyrant.

10 Versions of the Jesus Story

Harmony of the Gospels

Evangelical Bible teachers used to affirm that the four Gospels of the Christian canon could be harmonized at least in principle. This claim arose from the assumption that the Bible was infallible in its "original autographs." Recent evangelicals have made various necessary qualifications to account for the Gospels' considerable diversity. Professor Darrell L. Bock, a specialist in Luke-Acts, is sensitive to the problem of recovering the precise words Jesus spoke or even of harmonizing all the words of the text. He makes a crucial distinction between the "very words" (*ipsissma verba*) that Jesus presumably spoke and "his very voice" (*ipsissma vox*). The New Testament, Bock argues, contains "his voice," which is what the New Testament Gospel writers in particular were concerned to give. Jesus' "voice" (*vox*) is both a summary of what Jesus taught and the *subsequent interpretation* given by the inspired writers of the Gospels (Bock, 1995, pp. 77-80). Bock's scholarship leads him to face the question of various arrangements and rearrangements of events reported in the Gospels. His treatment of "the multitiered nature of historical meaning and portrayal" is both fascinating and insightful (Bock, 1995, p. 84). Indeed, whatever "harmony of the Gospels" evangelicals today could make after coming to terms with Bock's forthrightness would be considerably different from the older harmonies.

Catholic scholar Luke Timothy Johnson adopts a conclusion somewhat similar to Bock's, but he goes further to give the Christian community or Gospel writers more creativity than Bock would perhaps allow. For Johnson, Jesus himself most likely did not tell the Prodigal Son story, which occurs only in Luke's Gospel. Yet, says Johnson, the parable remains true to Christ's teaching and most certainly represents his view of God and forgiveness.

Coming from the Dutch Reformed tradition, Professor C. J. Den Heyer suggests that any attempt to harmonize the four canonical Gospels is misguided from the start. The different interests and "faces" that the Gospel writers put on Jesus intrigue the professor. Because of the writers' selective and interpretive roles, they cannot collectively give us, strictly speaking, the real Jesus. Himself a writer with considerable talent, C. J. Den Heyer offers an imaginary, but insightful, meeting between Paul and the Gospel writers. The conversation, whirling around the meaning of the Jesus stories, erupts into a rather fierce argument about the role of the Torah in shaping the faith. Agreement seems highly unlikely. Indeed, persuading the participants to listen to one another reflectively would appear to be a major accomplishment. If they could agree at least to listen to the author of *Mark*, they might eventually question him about Jesus' early secrecy regarding his messianic claims. Much of the imaginary conversation seems rather strange to the Fourth Gospel evangelist. In turn, the other evangelists demand to know his sources for so many stories unknown to them: the wedding feast of Cana, the exchange between Jesus and Nicodemus, the conversation with the Samaritan woman at the well, the Bethseda healing, and Lazarus' resurrection. What about the numerous long speeches that the Fourth Gospel attributes to Jesus? Who reported those speeches to the evangelist? Who remembered them in such detail? How did the other evangelists fail to be informed about them (den Heyer, 1997, p. 169)?

Finding stories about Jesus' everyday life to be not of primary interest to him, Paul would, den Heyer suggests, be quite disturbed that the Gospel of John had so little to say about Christ's suffering. The conference would then threaten to come apart the moment the participants opened talk of the "future" as the cacophony of voices contributed to the confusion. Would the author of the Gospel of Thomas think the ensuing debate reprehensible? Since his work focuses almost exclusively on Jesus' words, would the other members regard him as an interloper? He would have to speak, but would they hear him (den Heyer, 1997, p. 170)?

Altered Stories and Invented Sayings

Dale C. Allison argues that a first-century Jesus had disciples who with him expected the world to be utterly and completely changed, bringing redemption and a reversal that would divide humanity irrevocably into two camps. Instead of witnessing the greatest transformation of all time, however, the disciples saw their vision collapse and their messiah suffer execution. Their highest hope became the worst nightmare of their lives. Soon after his death, however, they became convinced he had been resurrected and was alive (Allison, 1998, pp. 70-77).

If formerly they were preaching a message of apocalyptic expectation, what would they now preach? The marvelous event of world transformation had not happened, yet their Messiah had been raised from death. Allison contends that they had to change their preaching, create new events, and emend the stories and teachings to explain the unexpected turn. From Galilee, Lake Tiberias, and other areas, stories and sayings had to be collected. The disciples were desperate to explain to others and to themselves just who this Jesus was. At the same time, they were under pressure to communicate what he and his teachings *meant* for themselves and for the new recipients of their preaching and missionary efforts. When Jesus was with them in the flesh, his teachings and sayings meant one thing, namely, preparing for the apocalyptic end. Now, however, they needed to present his words and actions in a new light. Although not trained historians and epistemologists, the disciples had somehow to deal with miracle stories from the north, folklore, popular tales about Jesus' mentor John the Baptist, and storytellers at markets and elsewhere eager to entertain their audiences (Allison, 1998, pp. 73-74).

In the attempt to preserve old traditions and create new ones, it became necessary to organize the growing material, which included both selecting and rejecting candidates. Allison conjectures that two major traditions eventually emerge, one becoming the Gospel of Mark, the other becoming Q, which is material common to the Gospel of Luke and the Gospel of Matthew. He compares this process to the storytelling process that took place in the United States after Abraham Lincoln died. His life "drew to itself mythological motifs" that in effect turned him into "the first American deity." His martyrdom became the catalyst for two major biographical traditions, the Eastern and the Western. The latter portrayed him as a folk hero with pioneer values and hardiness, the former with innate loftiness devoted to the common good (Allison, 1998, p. 74).

Allison acknowledges the difficulty of organizing the first-century texts now available and constructing from them a plausible account of what actually happened. After reading one scholar's constructed account and the hypothetical stages he went through, Allison thought it made sense. Later, however, doubts assailed him when he encountered a competing and no less plausible "tradition-story" based on the same material and the necessary background information. "But good sense," he forthrightly confesses, "should compel us to admit how fragile and uncertain our hypothetical histories usually are. This includes [John Dominic] Crossan's histories as well as those of everyone else" (Allison, 1998, p. 31).

The Historical Lincoln and the Legendary Lincoln

Don E. Fehenbacher, one of the leading Lincoln scholars alive, cautions readers to beware of the vast apocrypha attributed to Abraham Lincoln, the most quoted figure in American history. For several years, Don and Virginia Fehenbacher have combed through the Lincoln material with critical eyes of historians to produce a trustworthy guide to the authentic words of Lincoln. Each quotation receives a letter grade as a guide to its authenticity, the most authentic receiving the grade of A. The criteria that are used for making the evaluations reflect the Fehenbachers' long experience and training as historians. A quotation about which there is more than average doubt receives a grade of D. An E indicates that the quotation is probably not authentic. This arduous process resembles the Jesus Seminar's evaluation process by which the seminar members carefully study the putative sayings and deeds of the Jesus of the Gospels. After considering various arguments pro and con from diverse sources and after reading relevant scholarly articles and papers, each participant eventually grades each saying and deed that the Gospels attribute to Jesus. The results have been collected, published, and criticized.

In recommending the Fehenbachers' book *Recollected Words of Abraham Lincoln* (592 pages), James M. McPherson notes that the Fehenbachers have given their readers insight into "the perils and pitfalls of Lincoln scholarship" (McPherson, 1996, p. 121). Lincoln scholars have, of course, a distinct advantage over New Testament scholars. Whereas no historical Jesus is known to have written anything, Lincoln wrote numerous letters, speeches and memoranda himself and uttered such in the presence of newspaper stenographers ("phonographers") who transcribed them. Furthermore, auditors either wrote down many of his words or paraphrased them. There remain, nevertheless, large gaps in the Lincoln story, both in his presidential years and in his early life.

The Importance of Inauthentic Sayings and Deeds

The Fehenbachers believe that a careful study of the inauthentic quotations attributed to Lincoln can give scholars a deep understanding of the paths that the creation of myths and legends can take. The most dubious Lincoln quotations are included in the *Recollected Words of Abraham Lincoln* because the legendary Lincoln has had almost as powerful an influence on American culture as has the historical Lincoln. Many biblical scholars appear to think that the legendary Jesus has been as influential as, if not more influential than, the historical Jesus. Numerous stories and sayings grew around Lincoln, and many grew around the Jesus figure.

From Hero to Myth and Legend

A mythology developed quickly around George Washington, who, ironically, lived during the Enlightenment. His journey to New York from Virginia via Philadelphia resembled the triumphal entry of Hellenistic and Roman days. "Triumphal arches were erected, roses strewn in his path by girls dressed in white, and lyrics sung to Handel's 'See the Conquering Hero Come'" (Wecter, 1943, p. 125). Bands, music, firecrackers, cannon fire, church bells, and cheers welcomed Father Washington to the presidency. Later, John Adams noted that if Americans could have had their prayers answered, George Washington would have been placed among the immortals. In fact, in 1800, David Edwin published an elegant engraving of the apotheosis of Washington resting ethereally upon the clouds and being received into heaven by great generals who had ascended to glory before him. A wreath of immortality suspends over his head, and the engraving is entitled *Apotheosis of Washington*. American historian Edwin S. Gaustad suggests that it might more accurately have been called *The Bodily Assumption of the Blessed Hero George* (Gaustad, 1993, p. 81). J. J. Barralet's 1802 engraving blends Washington's heavenly translation with symbolism of Greek mythology, Christian iconography, the new nation's history, and military valor. The religious overtones are manifest, Washington with outstretched arms sitting on a cloud under protective angelic wings while a shaft of celestial light descends upon him. One can almost hear a voice from heaven; "This is my beloved Son." Thus, Washington became perhaps America's first icon. Just as the faces of Roman emperors appeared on Roman coins, so the faces of Washington and Lincoln appear on their nation's coins and bills.

Recently the documentary *Ayn Rand: A Sense of Life* was produced to keep the memory of her alive and to portray her as one of the great heroes of libertarianism. The overall presentation takes liberties with the truth, which is ironic, given that Rand had labeled her philosophy as "objectivism." Although an almost constant depression plagued her during her last twenty-five years of life, her successor Leonard Peikoff presents her as approaching perfect happiness. He shows her as not only the greatest philosopher and greatest novelist of all time, but thoroughly consistent in her thinking at all levels. Instead of revealing Ayn Rand as the interesting, complex woman that she was, the film presents her as virtually faultless. By turning her into St. Rand, the film gives us not biography, but hagiography. With her canonization came the dilution of her humanness (Bradford, 1998, pp. 64-65). Far from wishing to misrepresent Rand, however, the film's producer selected what he and Peikoff took to be the distilled substance of her life. In one respect, they succeeded; for their purpose was to capture the lasting *meaning* of her life for posterity.

Although many New Testament scholars contend that the Gospels, Paul's epistles, and the Epistle to the Hebrews transformed the historical Jesus into a supernatural being, they do not believe the motive was that of misrepresenting Jesus the man. Rather, their devotion and needs rendered them susceptible to hyperbole, extravagance, and embroidery in the service of what they believed to be of profound and eternal significance.

Fabrication for the Kingdom's Sake

One of the Mormon Church's most popular speakers and elders, Paul Dunn, embroidered his own biography. He created events that did not really happen to him and transposed incidents and ingredients from some people's lives to other people's lives. His purpose in making such alterations and inventing various fabrications, he insisted, was to provide his audiences with moving stories that would inspire young Mormons to pursue moral and wholesome lives. In carrying out his goal, he generated stories of his baseball connections with such heroes of the game as Stan Musial, Joe DiMaggio, Ted Williams, Willie Mays, Lou Gehrig, Babe Ruth, and the great pitcher Bob Feller.

Elder Dunn's war stories, too, had the noble end of promoting upright living among the young. Denying any intention of trying to "embellish or rewrite history," he said his purpose was to create interest and to encourage young Mormons in their faith. "Combining war stories is simply putting history in a little, finer package" (Packer, 1991b; Robertson, 1991a, pp. 29, 35).

In one of the war stories, Dunn not only told of being with his friend Harold Brown who was dying in a foxhole in Okinawa, but quoted Brown's last words, which were for the young people of America. Four decades after the war ended, *The Arizona Republic* (February 16, 1991) reported that Harold Brown had not only survived the war, but subsequently exchanged Christmas cards with Dunn. Elder Paul Dunn told other war stories about himself that are at best exaggerations and serious alteration. "The thing I'm trying to say," Dunn later explained, "is that there was a power higher than my own…a wonderful spiritual force out there" (Robertson, 1991a, p. 29).

According to University of Utah Professor Frank Jonas, in the 1950's Utah Congressman Douglas R. Stringfellow created a new format for public address, weaving war stories into his compelling lectures on good and evil. Eventually, his stories were exposed as fabrications rather than simple slips of memory or confusion. Until the congressman's public confession, his administrative assistant Keith H. Jaques had believed the stories were accurate accounts of real events in Stringfellow's war career (Packer, 1991a, p. 40).

Life-Discrediting Tales

People sometimes create or transmit false stories with the evident intent of discrediting the life of someone who has not embraced the speaker's religion or ideology. Instead of embroidering on a life to enhance its reputation, the discrediting tale functions to demean both the ideology and the individual who lives by it. Evangelist Billy Graham apparently believes he is quoting Voltaire's dying words: "I am abandoned by God and man! I shall go to hell! O Christ. O Jesus Christ!" The words are apocryphal, as are the words that Graham attributes to Thomas Paine, another writer the evangelist labels as an infidel (Graham, 1981, pp. 202-203). Perhaps more than any writer in the Bible, the author/redactor of the story of Saul and David succeeds in transcending this ideological tactic. The achievement is all the more remarkable because the redactor has his or her own theological premises. The writers in the New Testament who appear the least able to transcend the tactic of ideological discrediting are perhaps the Gospels of John and the Book of Revelation.

Shifting and Rearranging

Darrell L. Bock, representing the newer generation of Evangelical scholars, raises the question of whether the authors of the four Gospels presented their own rather than Jesus' theology. He concludes that they did not. To account for obvious differences among the Gospel accounts, he acknowledges that the authors have different styles and interests. One writer includes the dialogue while another gives the gist. Bock contends that whereas one Gospel writer tells the story with the tone and ambiguity that the disciples presumably had at the original scene, another Gospel writer retells the story by looking back on earlier events from "a larger context" (Bock, 1995, p. 84).

This euphemism means that in the retelling, the author added material into the story that was not originally there. The writer injected what he or she believed to be "the ultimate intended force" or meaning that could only be made clear by subsequent events. This kind of revisionism may come under the heading of "redaction."

Bock recognizes that for their own purposes, Gospel writers were redactors or editors when they adopted material or changed some of the details and the order–e.g., topical rather than sequential (Bock, 1995, pp. 85-87).

Although one of the best among Evangelical scholars in portraying a Jesus that fits with the orthodox conjecture of a supernatural visitation in the first century,[1] Bock's critique of the Jesus Seminar scholars shows little understanding of the depth of their approach. He perhaps relies too much on the past generation of Evangelical apologists who felt that to expose a model's bias or underlying criterion equated to refuting it.

The issue among contemporary biblical scholars, therefore, is not whether the biblical writers practiced redaction and editing, but whether all the redactors possessed the same image of Jesus and used the same theological premises in composing their narratives. The working hypothesis of redaction criticism is that most of the biblical writers were either weaving a narrative with a plot or saw themselves as operating within a theological narrative. Redaction critics mine the texts in the hope of discovering themes and plots that helped give the biblical authors focus in sifting, selecting, and arranging their material.

One of the greatest practitioners of redaction in English literature was Shakespeare. While his goals were many, he seems never to have forgotten his goal of providing a powerful drama containing such an aesthetic, intellectual, and emotional impact that his audience would gladly return to the theatre. No one who reads the Gospels of Mark or the Acts of the Apostles with a literary eye can fail to conclude the authors had a feel for high drama. The dramatic interest must be factored in with any attempt to understand the composition of the Gospels, the Book of Acts, and, of course, the Book of Revelation. If Bock is right in holding that biblical authors arranged material in light of their various interests and purposes, might the Book of Revelation be read as a seven-act drama rather than as a cryptic outline of future events in real time? In addition, to what extent may the Book of Acts be read as an adventure novel that used various historical facts as well as created stories to serve a religious end?

A Lesson from a Mormon Folklorist

Struggling to come to terms with the exposé of Elder Paul Dunn's embellishments and fabrications, Brigham Young University's Professor of English William A. Wilson raises the question of whether, or in what circumstances, one may "change the truth in order to teach the truth" (Wilson, W., 1991, p. 50).

In attempting to lay hold of slippery historical truth, we should, Wilson contends, pay attention to at least three points. First, one can never fully recover or reconstruct the past. The altered past is "in the final analysis a fiction." He means, not that it is entirely fiction void of every fact, but that historians reconstruct only in part because they see through a glass darkly.

Second, in selecting important dates, historians do not add or drop details in a random fashion. Hunches, clues, changing interests, theories and educated guesses are a part of the selection process. An individual will often remember the same incident differently at different stages in his life. "[T]he construction of memory includes such subjective causes as desires, continuing attention, and interpretation. Emotions and ambitions have much to do with the memory level a person prefers to use" (Bolles, 1988, p. 244).

Remembering is not a passive reception but a creative and constructive process requiring both imagination and critical judgment. It is also exceedingly purposive. As a folklorist, Wilson contends that people do not tell stories exclusively to keep the past alive, but to use the stories in negotiating their way through the present and into the future. The Fourth Gospel's author or redactor says plainly that his purpose in writing was "that you may come to believe that Jesus is the Messiah, the Son of God, and that through believing you may have life in his name" (20:31).

Wilson's third point is that a story's focus and details interact, each absorbing and shaping the other. The speaker or writer, furthermore, responds to the perceived needs of the audience. This requires adjustments for effective communication. New Testament scholars versed in reader and redaction criticism do not always agree on all the sources that went into the composition of the four Gospels. They do, however, agree that, in Wilson's words, "any oral narrative is finally the joint creation of both teller and audience, as both respond dynamically to one another" (Wilson, W., 1991, p. 51). This holds for the written narrative, too, for the audience is in many ways a part of the selective environment.

Having made these three points, however, Wilson must still face the difficult question of what he can believe about Paul Dunn's stories. He has frequently told a very special story about an incident in his own youth. Upon reflection, he writes candidly that he has had to wonder if the incident actually happened the way he tells it, or if he has "embellished it to make an effective point." In response he writes, "I have to answer that I really don't know. I think I am telling the truth, but cannot say absolutely that I am." As a collector of stories, Wilson has heard too many other people relate events that they believed to be true but which later proved not to be (Wilson, W., 1991, p. 51).

Reflective Mormons like Wilson have asked themselves the difficult question of whether Joseph Smith's stories about heavenly visitations really happened. Did an angel guide Smith to a plot of ground where he found literal golden plates containing inscriptions that guided him in translating or writing the Book of Mormon? Did Smith tell the story so often that he came to believe it himself? Did he believe it from the first? Reflective Christians ask similar questions. En route to Emmaus, did the disciples really fail to recognize Jesus when he joined them and talked with them for a considerable while? To explain this oddity, the narrator of the Gospel of Luke says the disciples' eyes were kept from recognizing Jesus (Lk. 24:16). Yet, could they not recognize his voice? Had something happened to the resurrected vocal chords of Jesus that made his voice sound altogether different? Does the narrator perhaps imply that something had happened to the disciples' ears as well as their eyes so that they could not discriminate as they had earlier? Clearly, the author had a point in telling this story, but it raises serious problems of credibility just as do some of Joseph Smith's stories.

Reworking History

Mormon scholar and editor Elbert Eugene Peck recognizes that myths that are factually wrong "can be powerfully true and can guide us through chaos." Yet, he sees what is also on the other side of the fence. He, therefore, asks how the Mormon general authorities can be angry with Elder Dunn for rewriting and recreating his personal history for an inspiring purpose when the Church authorities themselves "demand the same kind of reworking of Church history." Peck points out that the reworking began with Joseph Smith himself. "After all, the four accounts by Joseph Smith of the First Vision shows an evolution and recrafting of the event to make dramatically different points at different times in his life" (Peck, 1991, pp. 12,14). Since Mormons have scholars equivalent to Evangelicalism's Darrell Bock, they can "harmonize" Smith's various accounts. But such a harmony comes with a price, and sometimes the cost is more than would be incurred in acknowledging that the account of the "original event" might contain far more myth than previously realized. Editor Peck's words to fellow Mormon believers are applicable to everyone engaged in biblical studies.

> As much as we need stories to live, we also need historians and journalists to keep our storytelling in touch with the world of fact and experience, to keep it honest. Still, a story has to be more than factually honest to represent the world in which we live. It must also courageously, dramatically, and maybe heroically, portray belief and the delicate task of balancing values and perspectives. Stories must interpret and even prescribe; they must tell the "higher truths." Even so, single, moralistic stories often just don't prepare us for the ambiguities of adult religious life. (Peck, 1991, p. 13)

Note

1 Bock's *Commentary on Luke 1: 1-9:50* (Grand Rapids: Baker, 1994) is a model of clarity that scholars of every school of thought can hold up as an example of professional ethics.

11 Borg's Jesus, Anderson's Christ

Restoration

In antebellum nineteenth-century America, the Christians comprising the Restoration eagerly sought to establish churches as replicas of the first-century New Testament churches. Alexander Campbell and Barton Warren Stone became two major voices of this movement. The Restorationists hoped to bring the various denominations together in common agreement on the form and content of a true New Testament church. Joseph Smith, also disturbed by the bewildering diversity among nineteenth-century believers, thought the problem solvable if the seekers of truth would recognize that he had received a new revelation. He offered the Book of Mormon as a beacon of light to the wandering denomination. Smith felt compelled to restore not only the New Testament model, but also the model set forth, he believed, in the Hebrew Bible. Hence his eagerness to restore the priesthood, the Temple, and polygamy itself.

As a movement, the Restoration failed to unite the fragmented Christians. It succeeded, rather, in creating still more denominations, one of which still declines to classify itself as a denomination. The movement failed for several reasons, chiefly because the believers could not agree on what counted as the New Testament model.

Today, Marcus J. Borg, Professor of Religion and Culture at Oregon State University, has distinguished himself as one of the most thorough and fair-minded members of the committee of published scholars popularly known as the Jesus Seminar. While acknowledging the enormous difficulty of weaving a coherent picture of first-century Christianity, Professor Borg has joined those dedicated to restoring an accurate portrayal of the historical Jesus. Together, they challenge the conclusion that the original Jesus is virtually unknowable. Borg wrote a stimulating article contending that "the mainstream church is rather quiet about the historical Jesus, in part because of the difficulty of adapting the eschatological Jesus to Christian preaching and teaching" (Borg, 1985, pp. 764-767). Borg has a point. Many American and European Christians have never known what to make of Jesus' warnings about the imminent end of the world (eschatology). Indeed, people have made various attempts either to tone down the eschatological message or to deny that its centrality to Christ's teachings about the coming Kingdom of God.

According to Borg, Jesus himself lived virtually free of the eschatological worldview. Either the Synoptic Gospels or earlier believers put end-of-the-world talk into his mouth. Borg contends that, fortunately, the Gospels preserve strong traces of the original Jesus. Although a full biography of Jesus is impossible, a reconstructed portrayal of his ministry and message is possible. For Borg, these traces in the Gospels converge to bring sensitive readers to the threshold of the "primordial tradition" (Borg, 1994a, pp. 56-64).

The Other World

Convinced of the profound historical meaning of Jesus' ministry and message, Borg devoted many years to understanding Jesus. But is he correct in saying that Jesus brought and brings finite human mortals to the primordial tradition? According to Borg, the tradition introduces us to "the other world" that is at least as real as the empirical world. He believes this "other reality" comprises the very foundation of our empirical world (Borg, 1994a, pp. 56). But what is Borg talking about? The Spirit? Finite spirits? For good or ill, he is quite cautious in pinning down his own meaning. With the noted biblical scholar Rudolf Bultmann, he agrees that New Testament imagery cannot always be taken literally. Borg even warns his readers to avoid identifying the primordial tradition exclusively with a particular cultural expression of it. Quite aware of journeying to the realm of myth and metaphor, he writes:

> One does not need to affirm the ontological reality of another world in order to take seriously the fact that people had experiences which they believed to be experiences of another world. (Borg, 1994a, pp. 136-137)

Borg means that a Jesus actually existed and made it possible for his early followers to have very special, profound religious experiences. They interpreted their experiences, however, somewhat according to the culture and time in which they lived. Contemporary readers do not need to adopt those first-century interpretations. Still, Borg implies that contemporary men and women can share in the early Christians' primordial experience. They can simultaneously enter it and interpret and express it in contemporary categories. To encounter the reconstructed portrayal of Jesus, we not only become acquainted somewhat with the real historical Jesus, but also perceive reality in a new and perhaps more profound way than we had hitherto (Borg, 1994a, pp. 136-137).

The Challenge of the Humanities

In some ways, Borg is a contemporary humanist. He reaffirms the liberal arts tradition, which serves to liberate us so that we may enter another tradition or what Wittgenstein called a life-form. We do this in the hope of enriching our lives with new insights, values, and meanings. In essence, the world has more depths and dimensions than we have perhaps realized. Borg's talk of the primordial tradition is vague. Perhaps he wants to keep it vague rather than offer an interpretation or cognitive map of "the other world." He is not urging his readers to expect theophanies (appearances), hierophantic mysteries, or other more-or-less sensual experiences of supernatural beings. Evidently, he has a strong conviction that in encountering a more genuine picture of the historical Jesus and his message, readers will more likely feel and think about life in surprisingly enriching and profound ways. Far from becoming a mere shadow of the supernatural, the natural world itself will be experienced as transforming. Certainly, the world of Albert Einstein, Stephen Hawking, and Charles Darwin's heirs is not supernatural. In what sense, however, is it the same world Homer and Solomon thought existed? The "other world" is always both the same world and yet profoundly another.

New Testament scholar Hans Dieter Betz's observation throws light on Borg's point.

> [I]f you confront great texts from the past in depth, they will change you. If you wrestle with them for a long time, and if you get to the bottom of them, these texts will change you.... I regard it to be part of scholarly objectivity. I would not know what to do with a scholar who works, for instance, on Dostoevsky for twenty years and is not affected by it. (Betz and Schweiker, 1997, p. 26)

A New Version of Biblical Authority

Scholars like Betz and Borg are in effect advancing a new understanding of biblical authority. Instead of approaching the Bible as though it were a repository of inerrant truths delivered once-and-for-all to believers, they approach it with open-ended anticipation. They expect to be challenged intellectually, emotionally, morally, and aesthetically. The Bible becomes an authority in that it continues to attract its readers. Communities of seekers—scholars and laypersons—journey into the worlds of the Bible because the perpetual discoveries fascinate, inspire, puzzle, challenge, inform, and delight them.

The Bible's authority lies not in a system of theological doctrines thought to be implied in the texts, but in its power to attract and challenge. Its power draws both theists and nontheistic naturalists. Theists may interpret their journey in theistic categories. The naturalists will view the Bible as a richly *human* book. Though not participating in what they regard as theistic anthropomorphism, naturalists find in the Bible profound struggles, defeats, and triumphs of fellow human mortals. Both theists and naturalists perpetually discover the Bible to be a challenging inquiry into human nature and the human condition.

For many, a version of Christ has become an "authority" in the sense described above. Walter Wink, despite his postmodernist critique of the Jesus Seminar, joins the members in probing for the "originating impulse" behind the Gospels. They believe some tremendous force gave birth to the parables and to what eventually became the Gospels (Wink, 1997, p. 32). This may be compared with the physicists' discovery of critical "field disturbances" and their subsequent quest for their cause(s). Throughout this book, the following questions persist. Was that "originating impulse" a historical Jesus, or was it a community of emerging believers who became the impulse that gave birth both to the Jesus figure and to first-century Christian literature? Was an earthly Jesus transformed into a cosmic Christ, or was the image of a cosmic Christ the originating impulse that, over the decades, attracted a growing number of earthly details, some finding their way into the Gospels?

The Dialectic Approach

Paul N. Anderson's 1996 book on the Fourth Gospel (John) reads like a highly complex mystery novel (Anderson, 1996). Anderson seeks to determine who wrote this Gospel, why he or she wrote it, and what problems it sets out to solve. Like the Fourth Gospel's author, Anderson has reflected long and hard on the Jesus tradition. He wants to know what it *means*. While convinced that Jesus did in fact exist, Anderson has doubts about various details appearing in the New Testament's four canonical Gospels. Ironically, what specifically Anderson believes the historical Jesus did and said in the early part of the first century remains a mystery. Clearly, however, the professor thinks the Christians at the first-century's middle and end disagreed about the meaning of Jesus' acts and words. He is also quite familiar with the way Gospel writers manipulated deeds and sayings attributed to Jesus. In a revealing passage, he conjectures that the Fourth Gospel's author strongly disagreed with the branch of early Christianity that made Cephas (Peter) the Christian community's institutional head. Anderson does not hesitate to say that the author of John felt the rival branch "distracted from the religion of the historical Jesus *as he understood it*" (Anderson, 1996, p. 134, italics added). Our point is, Anderson recognizes that the early Christians had sometimes profoundly different interpretations of not only what Jesus did and said, but also what he intended and meant.

According to Anderson's analysis, the Fourth Gospel's primary author employed the dialectical technique, deliberately incorporating contradictory views of Christ. He did this for several reasons. First, the churches in the latter part of the first century harbored views about Jesus that they could not harmonize. Second, the author judged that a response of commitment to Jesus was more important than nailing down the precise doctrine about him. This is not to say that they considered the content of the belief or commitment unimportant. Rather, the Gospel author felt content to operate within a range of beliefs without requiring resolution of the cognitive tension. Anderson argues that *retaining the tension* brings a more profound understanding of the historical Jesus. In some respects, the Fourth Gospel's "compromise" compares to Niels Bohr's so-called *principle of complementarity* in subatomic physics, with both its strengths and weaknesses. At least one literary critic has made fruitful use of Niels Bohr's conceptual framework in reading Shakespeare (Rabkin, 1967; Rabkin, 1981, pp. 67, 113-114).[1]

The Encounter

Whereas Marcus Borg extols the primordial tradition, Paul Anderson extols the sacred encounter. His is an *involvement* theory of reading or hearing the text. By journeying into the claims made by the Gospels, the earnest seeker will perhaps become involved with Christ. In short, something important may very well happen to the seeker.

However, Anderson insists also that interpreting the significance of Jesus' ministry is a perpetual activity. What does that imply? He states unequivocally that for the Fourth Gospel, "Christology *never* was a totally-fixed and well-defined set of noncontradictory propositions about who Jesus was and what he came to do" (Anderson, 1996, p. 263). The phrase "living Christology" designated the Gospel writer and later Christian writers in their mode of "groping for new ways to articulate the truth which has been glimpsed through *spiritual encounters* with Jesus" (Anderson, 1996, p. 265, italics added).

Problems

The Fourth Gospel narrative is an attempt to solve problems. If early Christians had expected the second coming of Christ, the Christians toward the end of the century, and even earlier, were beginning to have doubts. The question of miracles also began to surface. If Christ performed miracles and if his followers were supposed to do even greater works of wonder, what happened? What prompted the original miracles? If persecution was now experienced, where was God's deliverance? Other problems emerged in the first century. If Jesus was the Son of God, what was his status regarding the Father? Were they equal? Was the Son subordinate? Anderson contends that the Fourth Gospel author faced this last problem in particular and deliberately set out to deal with it. On the one hand, he tried to make Jesus fully human. Several verses refer to his fleshly existence (Jn. 1:14, 6:51-56, 63). Blood and water flow from his pierced side (19:34). Thomas touches the wound in his hands and side (20:27). In the Fourth Gospel, Jesus suffers pathos and has human emotions. He weeps, is deeply troubled, groans, has thirst, and loves his own. "Nowhere in the canonical scripture is Jesus' *humanity* portrayed more extensively than in John" (Anderson, 1996, p. 267).

On the other hand, the Fourth Gospel makes Jesus one with God the Father, portraying Jesus as having supernatural knowledge. He knows Nathaniel from a distance (1:48f). He reads the human heart (2:24f), foreknows the Samaritan woman (4:39), and knows what will transpire beforehand. (4:1; 6:64; 13:1, 3, 13). Anderson is right: "Nowhere in the canonical scripture is Jesus' *divinity* portrayed more graphically than in John" (Anderson, 1996, p. 266).

But how can someone fully human and walking about in a tiny country on a little globe in one of numerous galaxies be identical with God? Despite his faith in the dialectical method, Anderson ventures beyond it to suggest a resolution to the problem.

The following is at least a resolution posed by the Fourth Gospel. Jesus is God's supreme agent. He speaks for God because he receives the word perfectly from God. His words are therefore God's words. Jesus re-*presents* the Father. Anderson refers to this as "*agency christology*" (Anderson, 1996, pp. 260-216). Perhaps this explains why the Fourth Gospel's prologue begins, "In the beginning was the Word [*logos*] and the Word was with God, and the Word was God" (Jn. 1:1).

The *minimal* claim that the Fourth Gospel makes regarding Jesus' divinity is this. In his role as the divine message (*logos*), Jesus is one with the Father, who is presumably the Source of the message.[2] The question remains as to how far the Fourth Gospel author is willing to bring Jesus along the road toward full omniscience and omnipotence.

Omniscient and Fully Human

Anderson correctly suggests that the Fourth Gospel brings contradictory claims together in perpetual tension, which neither the Fourth Gospel nor Anderson resolves. Anderson thinks it fruitful, nevertheless, to explore the region between the two claims. Clearly, the history of Christian theology has generated numerous speculative theories about the putative relationship between Jesus' humanity and divinity as well as the presumed relationship among the members of the Trinity.

We offer, however, the conjecture that the basic problem was largely swept under the rug from the beginning of Christian theology. Can a human being be genuinely omniscient and at the same time remain genuinely human? In *Fictional Transfigurations of Jesus,* Theodore Ziolkowski recognizes that in

The Idiot, the Christian novelist Dostoevsky "shared Nietzsche's awareness of the problematic psyche of the Savior" (Ziolkowski, 1972, p. 104). Dostoevsky scholar Michael Holquist suggests that no believable novel can portray Jesus as the hero if he is the Jesus as portrayed in the Gospels. Holquist reasons that Jesus of the Gospels lacks sufficient variety of character (Holquist, 1977, p. 111).

The question thus remains as to whether a human being can be truly omniscient and still remain human. We can explore this by asking somewhat similar questions about a duck. Can a duck be raised to engage in an intelligent conversation with a human being? Can it be trained to read and reasonably understand *Tom Sawyer* or *Jane Eyre*? If it could do these things, would it really be a duck? We can make cartoon ducks talk and do all sorts of things uncharacteristic of actual ducks, but we do not confuse the cartoon with reality. If a duck should really converse with us, talk about its future, go to high school or make passing marks in college, we would no longer regard it as a duck. Even if it looked like one, it would not talk and think like a duck.

More fundamentally, neither a duck, nor Balaam's donkey, nor a human being can lead a temporal life if he or she is truly omniscient. The early orthodox Christians apparently did not think through the problem of a person's trying to be a real human being while having complete knowledge of the past, present, and future. Absolutely nothing could come as a surprise to an omniscient individual. She could not even begin to lead a human life. She could never have a human conversation because she would have already heard every word of it. No new thought could occur to an omniscient person because she could have no new thoughts. An omniscient being cannot correct her mistakes because she already knows the correction along with the mistake. Since a mistake has to be made out of ignorance, such a mind could not err.

Those who refer to Jesus as omniscient God on earth have not thoroughly followed their premises to the end. Do they wish to say that Jesus could never misplace anything? He could forget absolutely nothing? He could never make a wrong turn? Never misspell a word? An omniscient being could not be illiterate. He would have to know not only every language that has been spoken everywhere, but also the proper spelling of each word, regardless of the language.

Orthodox Christianity has conceded that its version of Jesus does not portray Jesus as omni*present*. While riding on the donkey into Jerusalem, orthodoxy's Jesus is not simultaneously in India or Japan. Since the Fourth Gospel goes out of its way to portray Jesus as all-knowing, however, orthodoxy is trapped inside the doctrine of Jesus' omni*science*. This serious problem implies that being omniscient requires one to possess infallible thoughts about every person in Japan, all the aborigines in Australia, and all the atoms composing the fish in the Sea of Galilee.

Omnipotence

Orthodoxy has left the omnipotence of the historical Jesus vague. Did he possess all power while asleep? If fully human as well as divine, could he in one grand leap have landed atop Mt. Olympus? It is easier to imagine someone's possessing potential power than potential knowledge. Potential knowledge, a form of temporary ignorance, eats into any version of omniscience worth considering.

At best, orthodoxy has portrayed Jesus as someone switching between a finite human being and the infinite God. This is not so much a theory of the union of deity and humanity as an expedient compromise. The creative tension that the Fourth Gospel allegedly manifests has not proved itself. It was a cognitive cul-de-sac from the beginning. It appears to offer no special moral insights, since moral decisions have to be made by finite mortals. The myth of an ontological, one-time union between deity and humanity seems to satisfy many people emotionally. This factor could likely prove fruitful territory for psychologists to investigate more thoroughly. Given the fact that the Fourth Gospel is the most poetic of the Gospels, perhaps its impact could be compared favorably with the stirring impact of a great musical score performed well.

We suggest that the Fourth Gospel represents, among other things, finite mortals' attempt to believe that their own frailty, mortality, and finitude were somehow transcended for one grand, glorious historical moment, which they dared to think transformed history. The Fourth Gospel will, therefore, always touch the hearts of those who long for supernatural self-transcendence. Its author promises that finitude will one day be a thing of the past. He wants to convince them that by believing in Christ, they can enter at once into eternal life. Though they die, they will not die. Human frailty will, he promises, someday yield to a wondrous new life beyond all expectation. Over the centuries, many mortals have found such a promise a strong temptation.

For all the pretensions of its prologue, however, the Fourth Gospel fails philosophically, and its harsh anti-Jewish tone is morally as primitive as revenge itself. Biblical scholars are doubtless correct when they view the Fourth Gospel as having grown out of a sharp and bitter cleavage between monotheistic Jews and those Christians who tried to deify what they believed was an actual human being.

Christ's Temptations

The Gospel of Mark says very little about the forty days in which Jesus was reputedly tempted. "And the Spirit immediately drove him out into the wilderness. He was in the wilderness forty days, tempted by Satan; and he was with the wild beasts; and the angels waited on him" (Mk. 1:12-13).

Luke and Matthew add details, both picturing Jesus as seated on the pinnacle of the temple as the devil tries to coax him to take the plunge and let the angels rescue him. Luke and Matthew want their readers to know that Jesus did not yield to any of the temptations (Mt. 4:1-11; Lk. 4:1-13).

The Fourth Gospel, however, says nothing of the temptations in the wilderness. If the author knew this story, perhaps he felt that it rendered the divine plan of salvation too precarious a venture. The Fourth Gospel portrays Jesus as in control. He knows everything that will happen, including his arrest and crucifixion. He has no contingency plans because there can be no contingencies. God has arranged every detail. Even when the author strives to make Jesus appear genuinely human, the intense light of his deity renders his humanity suspect. Culpepper notes:

> Unity with the Father colors Jesus' characterization throughout the [Fourth] gospel. He is omniscient, like the Father, and there is apparently nothing that the Father knows that Jesus does not know (in contrast to Mk. 10:40; 13:32). Jesus knows who his betrayer is from the beginning (Jn. 6:64) and speaks not only of his return to the Father but of his past in the history of Israel and his role on "the last day." He knows of his "hour" from the very beginning (Jn. 2:4)....[W]hen the Father speaks to Jesus it is not because Jesus needs confirmation, but for the sake of the crowd (Jn. 12:28-30; contrast the more private experiences of the heavenly voice in Mark). (Culpepper, 1983, pp. 108-109)

In his groundbreaking work on the Fourth Gospel, Alan Culpepper convincingly observes that this Gospel describes Jesus' human emotions as "distant or aloof." He shows a certain coldness toward his mother's words. The terms used to describe Jesus' emotion of anger in Mark 3:5 and 1:41 are not used of Jesus in the Fourth Gospel. To be sure, more than the other Gospels, the Fourth struggles to convince readers that Jesus is truly human. But too many of its other passages undermine this attempt (Culpepper, 1983, pp. 110-112).

Luke and Matthew try to make Jesus' temptation real. Yet, they fail to face the crucial question squarely. Perhaps it did not occur to them. Perhaps they feared facing it for long. Was there a *genuine* possibility he could have yielded to temptation and sinned? Perhaps the whole scene was mere staging, a part in a scripted drama to be played out without any possibility of mishap?

Did the Gospel writers ask themselves what might have happened had Jesus sinned? If the Father's foreknowledge had told him Jesus would fall to temptation, would he have sent him nevertheless? If so, what purpose would this have served? On the other hand, if there was no real possibility that Jesus could have sinned, then in what sense were the temptations anything more than play-acting? According to some first-century Jews and Christians, God could not be tempted by evil (James 1:13). If the Fourth Gospel writer embraced both this position and the view that Jesus Christ was God incarnate, then he or she could not have believed, without self-contradiction, that Christ's being tempted was a possibility.

According to orthodox Jewish and Christian theology, Adam, his temptation, *and* his fall were real. If the Second Adam—Jesus—was presumably chosen to come to earth because the Father foreknew that he would not fall to temptation, then did he send the First Adam because he knew he *would* sin? Or was that particular Adam the only option he had with which to start the human race? No contingency plan?

Furthermore, if the Second Adam (Jesus) had sinned in the wilderness or elsewhere, would the divine "side" of his nature have been involved in his sin? If the divine side had sinned, how could Christ thus become the Savior? Crucial questions similar to these plagued some early Christian Docetists and Gnostics. The First Epistle of John was an attempt to combat the Docetic threat (4:1-3). The Second Epistle of John, written perhaps later than the Fourth Gospel, indicated that the threat might have largely passed (2 Jn. 2:7). We suggest also that much hostility toward "the Jews" in the Gospel of John came because the rabbis and other synagogue members had raised difficult questions about explicitly combining real humanity with the Godhead for even a short time.

Notes

1 In *Conjectures and Refutations*, Karl Popper offers profound insights into the weaknesses of complementarity in physics. His insights could help the exegete of the Fourth Gospel see both the advantages and limits of this principle in understanding the Fourth Gospel.

2 In the section "Of the Son" in his "The Christian Doctrine," the English poet John Milton deals forthrightly with critical problems encountered in making Jesus equal to the Father (Milton, 1933, pp. 944-967).

12 Jesus as King

Who Is the Prince of Peace?

Upon conquering Egypt, the Greek general Alexander the Great was legally declared to be the crowned Pharaoh who owned Egypt by divine right, just as later the Romans claimed ownership of Judea. The religious and political meaning that had become essential elements of the royal pharaonic line now went to Alexander. At his apotheosis, he became a living God, which entailed that he was the highest priest in the Egyptian scheme of things. So that native Egyptians would accept Alexander as their divine pharaoh, a divine kingship biography claimed Alexander to have been the divine seed of the last native Egyptian pharaoh before the Persian invasion. Although this pharaoh had died long ago, Alexander's sacred biography portrays the pharaoh as appearing on earth as a powerful magician. The pharaoh then visited Alexander's mother in the form of the Sun-God and impregnated her. Thus, Alexander's sacred biography tied his bloodline to the last native pharaoh of Egypt before the Persian invasion. The protocol that Alexander used was standard, as all pharaohs had to legitimize their ancestry with a divine kingship biography, which proclaimed them as the virgin-born incarnation of Horus (Morris, 1999).

Regarding the sovereign of the land as deity on the throne continued for another millennium into seventeenth-century England. King James boldly proclaimed himself to be a god.[1] To gain a profound understanding of the emergence of first-century Christianity, scholars must see how thoroughly entrenched emperor worship had become in antiquity. Fortunately, in a 1994 response to his critics, John Dominic Crossan has begun to take very seriously the place and image of Caesar Augustus in the formation of early Christianity. He boldly raises the crucial question of "the pre-Constantinian imperialization that prepared Christianity for that pyrrhic victory" (Crossan, 1994c, p. 144; Crossan, 1994a, p. 21). In the early seventeenth century, Roger Williams raised the penetrating question that Crossan today asks New Testament scholars to ponder. How did a Jewish peasant become an imperial Christ?

Margaret Morris has only recently completed an entire book manuscript on that very question. Although our book provides scarcely more than a hint of the depth and scope of her sweeping theory, we express our profound gratitude to her for permission to read her manuscript "Jesus-Augustus," which is currently in her literary agent's hands. While Morris' conclusion differs greatly from Crossan's, they both raise the critical issue.

> When the Julian (Julius Caesar) calendar was introduced across the Roman Empire under Augustus, inscriptions on the province of Asia, say from Priene in 9 BCE, spoke of Augustus' birth as *good news* about the advent of a *savior* and *a god* who brought *peace* to a war-torn empire. How, against that background, should one judge the angelic annunciation to Mary and the shepherds in Luke 1:28-35 and 2:8-14 where Jesus' birth is *good news* about the advent of a *savior* and *son of God* accompanied by *peace* on earth? (Crossan, 1994c, p. 145)

For understanding early Christianity as a movement, one cannot overestimate the importance of this specific question. What indeed is the connection between the imperial Augustus and the lowly Jesus? Crossan probes further.

> Do you celebrate the daring paradoxical vision that equated or replaced the birth of Caesar Augustus (mentioned in...Luke 2:1 in case one might miss the point) with that of a poor Jewish peasant child? Or do you shudder slightly knowing that Jesus would eventually become Augustus and what once was paradox would then be fact? How early does that cost-accounting with Constantine have to begin? (Crossan, 1994c, p. 145)

Octavianus, the High Priest

Unaware that Crossan had raised the above questions, Margaret Morris sought to answer them (Morris, 1999). She calls attention to the fact that Augustus was not only emperor but also high priest. This union of roles was not a novel phenomenon. The pharaohs were high priests. Ironically, despite the Hasmonaean (Maccabean) rulers' revolt against Greek intrusions into Jewish life and religion, they followed the ancient pagan practice of combining the office of high priest with the kingship. The earlier Hebrew tradition of separating these two powers is graphically explored in the conflict between Saul the king and Samuel the priest-seer. Whereas Saul was fiercely condemned for performing a priestly duty, David sometimes crossed the line with impunity.

In antiquity, the masses often viewed their rulers as something of deity incarnate. For many, Gaius Julius Octavianus (Augustus) was a divine being. As the proclaimed founder of the Roman Empire, he was considered the new or reincarnated Romulus. The poet Virgil in his *Fourth Eclogue* anticipates Augustus' glorious apotheosis. As we will show later in this chapter, Luke's Gospel emphasizes that Jerusalem rejected Jesus Christ as her king. Morris contends that behind the current Gospels were earlier gospel stories about Caesar Augustus. The stories were a part of the ancient king myths about the ruler's serving as a lowly peasant or shepherd who performed wondrous deeds and acts of healing (Morris, 1999).

After Octavianus defeated Antony and Cleopatra at Actium in 31 BCE, the Roman senate showered titles on him, including *imperator* (general) and *augustus* (revered). The commander of the forces that defeated the combined fleets of Antony and Cleopatra was Marcus Vipsanius Agrippa, Octavianus' son-in-law and one of his chief advisors. Soon after becoming Augustus, Octavianus became tribune with the power of proconsul. The title of high priest soon followed, making him not only supreme civil and military ruler, but also the sovereign in religious affairs. He possessed the power to appoint the high priest in Jerusalem. Roman power and influence pervaded all Palestine. Mark Antony, for example, had appointed Herod the Great as King of Judea; and upon Antony's defeat, Herod courted the favor of Augustus to keep his position intact.

Augustus' reputation spread throughout the empire as he brought Pax Romana (Roman peace) to what was considered the civilized world. This was the golden age of Roman literature and architecture. Such noted writers as Virgil, Horace, Ovid, and Livy lived during Augustus' rule. During this time, Rome reached its greatest glory.

Son of God

As Margaret Morris' "Jesus-Augustus: from Emperor Cult to Christianity" shows in depth, belief in the apotheosis of rulers was widespread in antiquity, going far back into Egyptian history. It appeared in the Hebrew tradition. "The Lord said to my lord, 'Sit at my right hand until I make your enemies your footstool'" (Psa. 110.1). Psalm 2 is a coronation psalm in which Yahweh says to the new Hebrew emperor or anointed one, "You are my son; today I have begotten you" (2:7). Yahweh then promises to turn all the nations into the new emperor's heritage and to make the ends of the earth his possession (2:8).

Although he may be twenty-five years of age, the newly anointed one at his coronation becomes God's son. *Today I have begotten you.* "I will be to him a father, and he shall be to me a son" (2 Sam. 7:14; Goulder, 1994, p. 147). Paul's Christ is Lord of not only all things on earth, but also all principalities and powers in heaven. According to Michael Goulder, Paul believed the principalities and powers—that is, the senior angels—were waiting to accuse the human race before the heavenly throne, using the divine Law as the chief weapon of accusation (Goulder, 1994, p. 140). This, of course, is the motif operating in the prologue to the Book of Job, where Satan, as one of the heavenly beings, serves as something of a prosecuting attorney. Christ, then, in Paul's way of thinking, is the unique Son of God who has put the Law in its proper place and, in the process, also defeated the malicious principalities and powers. Like a Roman general, he made a public example of his enemies, especially the heavenly enemies. His weapon was not the mighty Law, but the cross.

The Foolishness of God

On the surface, this entire scenario appears utterly foolish. In Paul's mind, however, this very foolishness and weakness became the unfailing instrument of God's power. Christ crucified is God's Wisdom and power to conquer evil. If Satan tricked the First Adam into introducing sin and evil into earthly creation, the Second Adam turned the tables on the entire kingdom of evil. By obeying the Father, the Son gained victory for at least the elect and at the same time was raised in glory as the triumphant Lord of all. In short, Jesus is Emperor or King of the cosmos! There is none like him on earth or in heaven, save the Father.

Jesus and Caesar

Crossan persists in asking how the Church turned Jesus into an Augustus-like figure concerned with accumulating power on earth. The answer must begin at least with Paul's early conceptions of the humble Jesus' becoming the Emperor of Emperors through the cross. This instrument became his *conquering* weapon, and Constantine is later portrayed as receiving a vision commanding him to conquer in its name.

But is not the road from Jesus the suffering servant to Constantine the manipulator and warrior a long journey morally and religiously? Margaret Morris offers the shocking thesis that behind the image of Jesus Christ of the four Gospels were the mythical stories about Caesar Augustus. The Romans embraced the ancient model of the emperor's becoming the Son of God. King Herod built the city of Caesarea for Caesar Augustan worship and festivals. The New Testament scholars who think a Jesus with apocalyptic visions existed have a strong case, not that Christianity sprang from the activities and teachings of a single Jesus. Rather, some first-century Jewish enthusiasts harbored dreams of a messianic leader's initiating a new age, overthrowing the forces of evil, and establishing a righteous kingdom on earth.

Morris' theory is that many Romans and some Jews had looked upon Augustus as the anointed one (messiah) appointed to bring peace on earth. In a war-weary world, the arrival of peace would have been gospel or good news (*euangelion*) indeed. By no means is this a far-fetched notion. The author of 2 Isaiah (45:1-3) hailed the Babylonian ruler Cyrus II as the anointed one (messiah) of Yahweh. His name appears twenty-five times in the Old Testament. Cyrus' military victory made him ruler of possibly the largest empire that the world had known until then. His reign proved to be one of tolerance and remarkable appreciation of ethnic traditions. The Jews felt enthusiastic toward him because he permitted them to leave their Babylonian captivity and return home to rebuild their Temple (Weisberg, 1985, p. 200).

In many ways, Augustus was the Roman version of Cyrus II. Both proved to be conquering messiahs who brought peace to the land. During Augustus' reign, the magnificent Third Temple of Jerusalem came into being. In 325 BCE, Greek conquerors had desecrated and damaged the Second Temple; and in 63 BCE, the Romans added to the ravage. Later, however, after Octavianus became Augustus the Emperor, he permitted Herod the Great to build what scholars call the Third Temple in Jerusalem. Its dimensions compared closely with those of Solomon's Temple. Since one of Herod's motives was to make the Judean kingdom a significant part of the Roman Empire, the Third Temple became a striking, visual statement to Rome that the Jewish kingdom must be taken seriously. From the perspective of many Jews of Palestine and Alexandria, Augustus' reign of relative religious tolerance doubtless appeared as a providential reign of peace.

The emperors of the first century who followed Augustus would stand at best in his shadow. Caligula and Nero were anti-messiahs, and Nero's successor Vespasian was laying siege to Jerusalem when he was named Roman emperor. His son Titus, continuing the attack on Jerusalem, destroyed the Temple. The Arch of Titus, which still stands at the Roman Forum, commemorated this triumph and displayed the treasures stolen from the Temple. Immediately following Titus' death, the senate deified him.

The King's "Triumphal" Entry?

For centuries, the Christian tradition has celebrated Christ's triumphal entry into Jerusalem. W. Barnes Tatum, a Fellow of the Jesus Seminar, contends that an actual Jesus seated on an ass rode into Jerusalem "to make an ass out of Pilate and the Romans" (Tatum, 1998, p. 141). Like an Old Testament prophet acting out a poignant message, Jesus staged his entrance. His was a deliberate contrast to the triumphal entries of Roman emperors and potentates with their customary display of military force and imperial grandeur (Borg, 1987, pp. 173-174). Tatum's point, which is close to Borg's, is that by this symbolic act, Jesus made a statement, "a declaration about God's rule over against Caesar's rule. God's rule implied a leveling of human authority and submission to God's authority" (Tatum, 1998, p. 141). The majority of the Jesus Seminar scholars concluded that the historical event of Jesus' entry into Jerusalem was a symbolic act. This is not to say they believe all four Gospels treat it that way. In Luke and John, Jesus does not conspicuously make a mere symbolic act but is hailed as "king," an acclamation based on Psa. 118:25-26. Tatum acknowledges that each Gospel evangelist has adapted the story to his or her own special narrative purpose.

In a recent article, Brent Kinman spells out what he takes to be Luke's fundamental purpose in telling the story of Jesus' entry into Jerusalem. Simply stated, Luke stresses the regal element of the entry. Jesus arrives as king, as David's descendent (Lk. 1:32-33). Luke builds the scene to a climax as the royal welcome is anticipated. He shapes his narrative to portray Christ as a royal personage whose followers herald his approach to the city of David. The climax comes at this point, raising the crucial question: What sort of reception will Jerusalem give her King (Kinman, 1999, p. 289)?

Kinman and Tatum agree that while an ass was considered a work animal used by peasants, in the Near East, such an animal was often set aside for special royal use in ceremonies and entry processions (Kinman, 1999, pp. 286-287). Margaret Morris sees no problem with Jesus' being king and, at the same time, riding on a lowly donkey. This image of a king's assuming temporary humble status is a part of the ancient kingly bio-mythology (Morris, 1999). Just before being anointed king, Saul's father had sent him to find the family's donkeys that had strayed.

The image of King David and the royal family, of course, are behind the Zechariah 9:9 passage that Matthew quotes as prophecy (Mt. 21: 4-5). As if to press the connection on the reader's mind, Matthew has the crowds in front of Jesus shouting "Hosanna to the son of David!" Luke again makes it clear that Jesus is arriving as no less than their *king*. As he approaches the path from the Mount of Olives, the whole group of disciples shouts, "Blessed is the king who comes in the name of the Lord!" (Lk. 19:38). Luke alone among the evangelists makes explicit the link between the entry and God's judgment on the city (cf. Mk. 11). The plot takes a radical turn from joy to lament.

Kinman shows in detail how cities and districts in Asia Minor, Egypt, and Palestine organized elaborate greetings and ceremonies for arriving magistrates. Failure to demonstrate respect in greeting rulers could evoke severe consequences. When the Samaritan villagers refused to welcome Jesus because they knew he was heading for their rival city Jerusalem, Luke portrayed the disciples as eager to command fire to come down from heaven and consume the citizens (9:52-54). According to the renowned classicist F. Millar, "A city or an individual might incur serious risks by misjudging the warmth of welcome to which a Roman governor felt himself entitled…." The governor, on the other hand, would have at his disposal several options as to what he would demand or how he would treat those who presented themselves to him (Millar, 1997, p. 28).

In Luke 8:22-56, a collection of four miracle stories demonstrates that Jesus' authority is absolute. This, too, contributes to the narrative's climax. Jerusalem lies ahead. Although Jesus' followers have announced his royal arrival, the city utterly fails to recognize the "time of visitation." When seen against the background of the first century, the rejection appears as an appalling insult. Luke shapes Mark's story to make it clear that this rejection is so serious that divine judgment will follow. In both his Gospel and Acts, Luke stresses the theme of rejection. Just as he charges that Jerusalem rejected Jesus, so he portrays Stephen as accusing Jerusalem of turning away from the prophets and persecuting them. The chief priests, scribes, and leading men prove to be the foremost opponents of Jesus. It is they who will bring disaster on their city because they have rejected their king and the God he represents. Kinman does not miss the irony. *In 70 CE, Jerusalem suffered destruction in return for the city's rejection of the Roman ruler—Caesar* (Kinman, 1999, p. 294).

W. Barns Tatum believes he offers a reasonably accurate description of an actual historical Jesus who literally rode a donkey into Jerusalem for the specific purpose of making a messianic declaration. Far from being about himself as savior, however, the declaration was about "God's rule over against Caesar's rule " (Tatum, 1998, p. 141). In short, Jesus intended to bring about a religious and social revolution that would lead individuals into a new way of thinking and feeling about the rigid hierarchical structure at the heart of Rome's imperial system. In God's rule or kingdom, all human beings would be viewed as on the same level (Tatum, 1998, p. 141).

Kinman differs with Tatum in two important ways. First, instead of raising the question of the historical Jesus, Kinman deals exclusively with the literary Jesus of the Gospel of Luke. This is not to say that Kinman has no view regarding the historical Jesus. He simply does not confront the issue in his significant article. Second, Kinman states clearly that the Jesus of Luke's Gospel accepts claims about *himself*. Heralded as the son of King David, he accepts the title of "king," God's agent or representative. He weeps over Jerusalem just because he knows the city will reject him as king and will thereby bring destruction down upon itself (Luke 19: 41-44).

Our position is that Kinman's interpretation of the Gospel of Luke against its background is on target. Tatum's attempt to work through the Gospels to arrive at a stable description of an actual person is the more ambitious undertaking. Although he may have failed to make his case, Tatum throws considerable light on the thinking of at least one major strain of first-century Christianity. One image of Jesus that emerged and developed early was that of a person standing in sharp contrast to a corrupt and self-aggrandizing Caesar like Caligula. Paul's epistles, the Synoptic Gospels, and the Epistle to the Hebrews portray Jesus as *both* more genuinely humble and more exalted than a Roman ruler like Caligula. Margaret Morris can help us see that the Epistle to the Hebrews and all the Gospels grew out of the attempt to portray a royal savior and Lord more like Augustus than the arrogant Caligula or Nero. If we interlace Kinman's thesis with David Seeley's, we might see that not only the Epistle to the Hebrews and the Gospels, but also the Apostle Paul's epistles reflect the projection of an ideal Redeemer who descended from heaven and eventually conquered the forces of evil, including death. This projection, however, did not come about by spontaneous generation, but drew upon numerous sources that were themselves revisions, redactions, and creative adaptations. By focusing on the mythology that accompanied royalty in ancient Egypt, Greece and Rome, Margaret Morris exposes scholars to two essential facts. First, the emergence of first-century Christianity cannot be profoundly comprehended unless the Jesus figure and Christology are viewed against the background of Caesar worship in all its self-contradiction and ambivalence. Second, in the ancient world, the cosmic myths about their supreme earthly rulers were more than entertaining tales. Ideally, they served to *weave earth and heaven into a seamless whole*. When an actual ruler's earthly life and reputation became a public scandal and a literal disgrace, however, three responses became live alternatives:

1) A sweeping skepticism about the myths.
2) A moderate skepticism that issued into revising the myths in targeted areas only.
3) A skepticism that maintained much of the structure of the mythology while revising it so severely at critical points as to produce either a polar effect or rival myths.

We suggest that Christianity of the first three centuries suffered its own internal polarity. The first pole exemplified the devotion to an ideal profoundly different from the Roman hierarchical system with its quest for power to rule others. At the opposite pole was the drive to emulate the Roman model. Morris and Crossan help us ask the critical question. How deep-seated was the Roman model in first-century Christianity (Morris, 1999; Crossan, 1994b, pp. 1-4, 26-27)?

We contend that this polarity lies at the heart of the apocalyptic literature that influenced early Christianity. Profoundly troubled by the hostile, violent component in the apocalyptic vision, the Jesus Seminar scholars believe they have discovered the original Jesus who taught a new way of life not centered on the power to control unbelievers by force. This is a kind of First-Amendment Jesus whose Kingdom was built on love, mutuality, and goodness rather than political and military power. He is the Jesus whom Dostoevsky's Grand Inquisitor would ban from society.

An Ancient Motif

To arrive at Jesus' identity, one must recognize that, like other sacred texts of antiquity, the Gospels carry the ancient motif of divine kingship. The sacred writings concerning various Gods and their living representatives (the sovereigns of different nations) carry elements of this divine kingship pattern. These sacred biographies of sovereigns include a definite pattern consisting of several stock story elements. The kingship pattern was individualized to create a unique divine biography for each sovereign. These official divine biographies asserted the sovereigns' identity as the heaven-sent king. Despite the individualization of the kingship biographies, elements of the pattern are conspicuous in surviving accounts. Examples of divine kingship accounts include the sacred biographies of Alexander the Great, King Sargon of Akkad, King Cyrus of Persia, and several other real and legendary kings and Gods. Most important, Morris observes that the various renditions of the divine kingship pattern in the Bible apply only to high-ranking members of the power elite.

Savior-Gods

In her work on Jesus, Morris conveys that the Gospels typify the sacred literature genre designed to portray sovereigns as Savior-Gods coming to earth to walk among the people and to live and die for mankind's benefit. The Gospels reflect the divine kingship pattern as told in the pagan passion plays of the gods. The passion plays were festive pageants, conducted at the beginning of every new year for many generations to assure agricultural prosperity by celebrating the epiphany of the Savior-God(s). The passion plays, the forerunners of modern religious holidays, animated events in the lives and deaths of the Savior-Gods. Morris sets out a comparison between the Gospels' stories of Jesus' life and death and the pagan passion plays of the various Gods. In the Gospels, as in other sacred literature, the myth of the God-king, often represented by the reigning sovereign, is set in real historical time and place among historical people and events (Morris, 1999).

When rulers visited cities, people greeted them as Gods. Plutarch described a long procession in which Alexander the Great was carried through the streets on a raised platform drawn by eight horses. He was surrounded by a procession in which people were dressed as Satyrs and Pans. Participants engaged in bacchanalian revelry as though the God were present in the person of Alexander. As noted earlier, a comparable scene occurred in 41 BC and involved Mark Antony. After a stay in Athens, Antony made his entry (*adventus*) into the city of Ephesus, where he was celebrated as the God Dionysus. The crowd escorted Mark Antony through the streets amidst cult festivities. Cult paraphernalia included ivy and thyrsus-wands, and the music of pipes, harps and flutes accompanied the festivity (Morris, 1999).

Morris believes that examples from early Christian art and literature depicting *Christ as a reigning earthly sovereign* bolster her premise that the God-king of the Gospels was a powerful ruler. In Egypt, early Christians worshiped Jesus as the Sun-God Horus, a deity believed to have been embodied by each reigning pharaoh. The early Christian art of Rome shows Jesus worshiped as the Sun-God Apollo (who was identified with the Egyptian Horus). Byzantine art portrays Christ as the Roman emperor sitting on a throne.

Like the early images of Christ in Old Cairo's Coptic Museum, the artwork in early Christian catacombs just outside Rome depict Christ in pagan themes. These various artifacts, which capture images of Christ as the reigning sovereign, allow us to appreciate the vast evolution that Christianity has undergone. Morris raises the question of whether originally no profound difference existed between pagan and Christian forms of art and literature or between the Christian and pagan concept of the supreme deity and the kingdom of heaven.

Augustus Messiah

The powerful ruler Caesar Augustus carried the epithets "Son of God," "Savior of the World," "Prince of Peace," "Firstborn," "Lord," and "Messiah." Art and literature universally portrayed this sovereign as bearded and wearing holy vestments. This ruler ushered in the *Anno Domini* at the time of his apotheosis, i.e., corresponding to his conquering of what was then called "the world." Historians have noted that the *Anno Domini* was also known as "Caesar's day," i.e., alluding to Augustus Caesar, who was heralded as founder of the Roman Empire. It marked the new cycle, initiated by Augustus' empire-wide apotheosis. Augustus was worshiped by the Egyptians as Horus and by the Greeks as Apollo. Virgil's famous *Fourth Eclogue* anticipated Augustus' long-expected, sacrosanct appearance.

> The last Great Era foretold by the Cumaean Sibyl is now arrived; the Cycles begin anew. Now returns the Golden Age of Saturn, now appears the Immaculate Virgin. Now descends from Heaven a divine Nativity. O! Chaste Lucina [God of maternity], speed the Mother's pains, haste the glorious Birth, and usher in the reign of thy Apollo. In thy consulship, O! Pollio, shall happen this glorious Advent, and the great months shall then begin to roll. Thenceforth whatever vestige of Original Sin remains shall be swept away from earth forever, and the Son of God shall be the Prince of Peace!

Today's Christians scarcely view Christ as the Apollo of the Cumaean *Sibylline Oracles*. Such a pagan identity, however, was not foreign to the Church of the late Roman Empire and Middle Ages, which considered Virgil's poem as prophesying the Christ's birth.

The identity of the savior-child of Virgil's *Fourth Eclogue* has become a great puzzle in literature. According to Morris, there should be no mystery. The virgin-born child whose advent was alluded to is specifically named in verses of a similar nature in Virgil's *Aeneid*. In the *Aeneid*, Augustus Caesar, the sovereign who carries the above-mentioned epithets and sacred attributes that Luke attributes to Jesus Christ, is described as the long-expected leader destined to usher in the Golden Age. As such, *Aeneid* verses help identify the deliverer alluded to in the *Fourth Eclogue*.

> Now fix your sight, and stand intent, to see
> Your Roman race, and Julian progeny.
> Impatient for the world, and grasps his promised pow'r.
> But next behold the youth of form divine,
> Caesar himself, exalted in his line;
> Augustus promised oft, and long foretold
> Sent to the realm that Saturn ruled of old.
> Born to restore a better age of gold.

Several examples from classical literature show the worship of Augustus during his lifetime. Ovid addressed the living Augustus as the Son of God, the Great Deity, the Heaven-Born, the Divine, the Omniscient, the Beneficent, the Just, the Long Suffering, and the Merciful God. Ovid prayed to Augustus after the Emperor's *ascension* to heaven. In 69 CE, when the army of the East proclaimed Vespasian as emperor, he received from Serapis a kind of supernatural consecration. On the day of his arrival in Alexander, the Nile flooded, promising bounty. Vespasian was reported to have restored a blind man's sight and healed a cripple. In 70 CE, he spent the night in the temple of Isis on the eve of celebrating in Rome his triumph over Judea (Turcan, 1992, p. 90).

Infancy Stories

Morris holds that the infancy stories in Luke and Matthew reflect Augustus' apotheosis, i.e., his exalted position as sole divine master of the world (the event anticipated in Virgil's *Fourth Eclogue*). At the time of a ruler's apotheosis, *regardless of his actual age*, sacred literature portrays him as a newborn God-king whose life the reigning king seeks.[2] To identify the rulers with the solar deity, their divine biographies portrayed them as newborn infant-Gods. In Egypt, for example, every pharaoh, regardless of his age at coronation, was viewed as the Sun-God Horus, who was always depicted as an infant or young child. This reflects the fact that at the beginning of the new year (which marked the birthday of Horus), the Sun appears comparatively small in the sky.

Despite their demonstrable mythical matrix, the Gospels, Morris contends, have often been taken too literally. Scholarship's complete acceptance of Christ's birth during Augustus Caesar's reign (Lk. 2:1) exemplifies the extent to which myth has been taken literally. The infancy stories in Matthew and Luke are different versions of the classical divine kingship biography. The stories' classical elements include the virgin birth (Lk. 1:26-32, Mt. 1:20-21); the angel naming the child before his birth and then foretelling the infant's future greatness (Lk. 1:26-32; Mt. 1:20-22); the threat to the reigning king obtained through prophecy (Mt. 2:3-5); the king's wrath because of the perceived threat to his throne (Mt. 2:2-3); the threat to the infant-God's life (Mt. 2:13); the infant-God's flight to safety (Mt. 2:13); the preordained position of kingship (expressed as either the child's adoption into the royal palace or inclusion into the royal line) (Lk. 1:32-33). None of these elements belonging to the classical divine kingship pattern can be taken literally.

The Name Jesus

Morris believes even the name Jesus might have been taken into the sacred orbit of Augustus Caesar. Elements of the divine kingship pattern are preserved in the myth of the God Janus-Quirinus (identified by some ancient Italians with Jupiter, the Father in heaven). As founder of the Roman Empire, Augustus was considered the reincarnation of Romulus, the legendary founder of Rome. When Romulus ascended into the sky, according to his divine biography, he was identified with the God Janus-Quirinus. Thus Augustus was the living Janus-Quirinus, a deity Virgil called by the ancient name *Iasius* (perhaps a play on the Greek word *Iasis* ["cure, remedy, or healing"], which is close to the New Testament Greek word *Iesous,* Jesus, Joshua). *Iaso* or the contracted *Iasous* is the Goddess of Healing and Health. In the Acts 17 story of Paul's preaching in Athens, the Athenians might be assuming that in proclaiming *Iesous*, Paul is referring to *Isis* or *Iaso*, the divinity of healing (17:8).

Emperor Worship

Although Augustus initially discouraged his worship, he eventually had to compete with Mark Antony, who heavily promoted his own divinity. According to Plutarch, in his triumphal procession into Ephesus, Antony was acclaimed as a new Dionysus, "bringing of joy and source of peace" (*Antony*, 24, 4). Partly because many foreigners who believed the ruler must be divine had entered Rome, Augustus gradually accepted increasing worship there. In other parts of his Empire, however, the worship of Augustus as God-supreme was mandatory, by decree of the Roman Senate.

Under the Roman Senate's enforcement, the imperial cult was established to promote and maintain Augustus' worship forever. Clearly, the level of Augustus' worship was deemed cosmic and universal in nature. People worshiped Augustus as the Son of the Father in heaven and often considered him synonymous with the Father in heaven (i.e., Jupiter). The Greek world eagerly embraced Augustan worship, erecting numerous temples and even lavishly preparing for a possible *adventus*. When Augustus traveled from Egypt to Syria, he might well have journeyed through Jerusalem. Morris suggests that the story of Jesus' Jerusalem advent (*adventus*) reflects the Roman emperor's *adventus*.

As noted in Chapter 9, some scholars think that the image of a pre-Markan cosmic Jesus Christ emerged from the apocalyptic tradition in response to growing *political disillusionment*. Our point is that the mythical image of the divine Jesus developed at the very least *against the background of the popular worship and deification of Rome's emperors.* Morris contends that the earliest Jesus stories were viewed as about the deified Augustus. By contrast, David Seely argues that the mythical cosmic Christ of Philippians 2 developed as a reaction against Caligula's self-aggrandizement. While these two theories as they stand cannot both be correct, they nevertheless highlight the critical importance of the Roman emperor's image and mythology in shaping the Jesus figure for at least one early stream feeding into Christianity.

Notes

1 King James's contemporary Thomas Hobbes, a Church of England Calvinist, scaled down the English king's divinity by making him the absolute head of "the mortal god," that is, the State (Martinich, 1992, p. 336).

2 First Samuel, an ingeniously crafted story, portrays King Saul as seeking to murder David, who will replace him on the throne.

13 Is Jesus a Legend?

Conjectures and Refutations

In answering questions after his summer 1996 lecture at Texas Christian University, the Jesus Seminar leader, Robert Funk, used the term "conjectures" to refer to the various portrayals of the historical Jesus that scholars and others have set forth. He did not exclude his own version. One of the twentieth-century's most penetrating books in philosophy of science is Karl R. Popper's *Conjectures and Refutations*. In it, he articulates his thesis that science grows not only by bold conjectures carefully articulated, but also by informed attempts to *refute* the conjectures in the hope of generating better ones (Popper, 1991, pp. 253-292). Biblical scholarship operates this way, too, because its goal is to produce the best possible theories to explain the phenomena. By trying to find the holes in a theory or conjecture, scholars hope to improve it or to create one with more depth and scope. Most scholars reject the conjecture that the four canonical Gospels can be "harmonized." Because the putative harmony has undergone numerous qualifications and revisions over the years the very concept of harmony has changed. Proponents of the theory have so tinkered with and qualified their original theory that it has evolved into a strikingly new one.

Following the journey of the more carefully articulated theories about the historical Jesus proves highly instructive. In some cases, new theories develop when scholars solve problems encountered in earlier ones. A mark of true scholarship is the commitment to track the theory's details, leads, and promises. One scholar alone or even a team of scholars can scarcely undertake such an enormous job. Quite often, one team learns to revise and improve its theory by discovering how scholars in other fields articulate and improve theirs. In many cases, one text or piece of literary evidence appears in a different light when seen through the lenses of a rival view. Well-constructed, highly informed rival theories are therefore invaluable. Without them, our pet theory would become cognitively stagnant and more a verbal ritual than a window to new insights and fruitful cognitive advances.

From Augustus to Caligula to Christ

Such scholars as John Dominic Crossan, Robert and Mary Coote, Margaret Morris, and Marcus Borg have made it graphically clear that the major characters of any movement in first-century Palestine would have had to come to terms with Rome's ubiquitous presence and might. To understand better how Christ worship emerged in the first century, scholars cannot afford to lose sight of the critical phenomenon of Caesar worship (Coote and Coote, 1990). During Gaius Caligula's reign, many in Palestine and Alexandria became thoroughly disillusioned with the royal office itself (Cheon, 1997; Winston, 1979). New messianic hopes sprang up amid the disillusionment. We suggest that growing political turmoil helped spawn visions of a ruler altogether *unlike* Caligula. For some, the envisioned ruler would be the Anointed One (Messiah, Christ) possessing divine authority from Heaven itself. Instead of being a self-glorifying Caligula seeking to make himself God, the Anointed One would humble himself. Though in the form and likeness of God, he would leave Heaven to assume a lowly position on earth. Though possessing cosmic power and significance, he would become self-serving Caligula's opposite.

Like early Buddhism, early Christianity spawned creative ideals, models, and options for living meaningfully under political, social, and economic repression. One cannot harmonize all the models into one coherent mosaic. It is unlikely that all sayings attributed to the "original Buddha" came from his mouth or that he performed all the deeds and wonders attached to his name. Christian scholars, of course, strongly divide as to which wonders, deeds, and sayings belong to the original or historical Jesus and which ones belong to the envisioned Jesus. By "the envisioned Jesus," we mean those stories, sayings, teachings, deeds, parables, and claims that evolved from varied sources rather than solely from (or through) one historical individual even though they are attributed to him in the Gospels.

Many biblical scholars have devoted their lives to two difficult goals:

1) Identifying the details of the historical, earthly Jesus.
2) Discovering how the envisioned Jesus emerged and evolved in the first century.

Healthy Competition

Professor G. A. Wells has written five scholarly books specifically on the question of the historical Jesus. At first, some reviewers of his earlier works failed to take him seriously because his thesis was so far removed from their own. A few even suggested that he lacked the proper credentials and, therefore, had no right to enter the debate about the historical Jesus. This argument eventually dissolved when it became obvious that, whatever one may say about his conclusions, Professor Wells thoroughly knew the ins and outs of the New Testament scholarship. Admittedly, his thesis is a minority position, but a careful examination of the current research among biblical scholars reveals a wide diversity of opinion regarding the details of the earthly Jesus. When the various portrayals of Jesus are explicated, no one version gains the support of most New Testament scholars. Agreement increases only as an increasing number of details are eliminated or placed in doubt. Most agree that Jesus existed. But as what? Did he really do this or that, say this or that? At this point, those who have devoted their lives to biblical research follow leads in diverse directions, each scholarly alliance striving not only to make its reconstruction appear plausible, but also to expose the weaknesses in rival reconstructions. Dale C. Allison's *Jesus of Nazareth: Millenarian Prophet* (1998) stands as a splendid example of this two-pronged scholarship. It also shows just how far apart competing theories can be. Scholars of one school seek also to show how the data support their theory better than they support rival theories. In "The 'Messianic' Implications of the Q Material," Edward P. Meadors exemplifies this creative side of biblical scholarship. He attempts to show that the data called upon by the Jesus Seminar scholars to play down Jesus' messianic role might better support those like Meadors who advance the theory that the Q material is messianic both in tone and in the selective use of Old Testament texts (Meadors, 1999, pp. 253-277).

In his profound work on the Sermon on the Mount, Hans Dieter Betz discusses two major strains of first-century Judaism. The particularistic strain is found in the apocalyptic and exclusivistic Qumran community located near the Dead Sea. The universalistic, more represented in the Hellenistic world and Stoic philosophy, can be found also in avant-garde Judaism. Betz believes Paul represents this latter version of Judaism, but he finds both in the Sermon on the Mount. The Gospel of Matthew contains a perspective that looks to the wider world. "To what extent Jesus himself held this position is not clear. But the church in Jerusalem did, because they were involved in mission [activity] when the Sermon on the Mount was presumably formulated. Of course," Betz adds, "*this is all very speculative*" (Betz and Schweiker, 1997, p. 18, italics added; Betz, 1995). By "speculative," he means, not that all interpretations are equally good (or bad), but that on the important matter of biblical interpretation, scholars always make assumptions. Furthermore, they look for well-articulated and carefully reasoned rival interpretations. At present, no contender can decisively overcome its rivals and establish itself without suffering from serious, thoughtful challenges. Betz is one of the world's most respected New Testament scholars largely because he daily struggles to come to terms with this sobering fact.

The Core of G. A. Wells' Theory

Wells sees no reason to hold that either Paul or Peter believed that Jesus lived the life ascribed to him in the four canonical Gospels, which most New Testament scholars think were written after Paul's literary career. Drawing strictly from Paul's own writings, Wells concludes that the apostle thought of Jesus as the cosmic Savior who came to earth and lived an obscure life in perhaps the second century BCE. Josephus reports that both Antiochus Epiphanes (175-164 BCE) and Alexander Jannaeus (103-76 BCE) had crucified Jews in Jerusalem while they were still alive. Jannaeus' crucifixion of 800 Pharisees burned deeply into Jewish consciousness. The Jewish traditions on which the Talmud drew persistently placed Jesus among those ancient victims by dating him somewhere in the second century BCE (Wells, 1982, pp. 40-41; Wells, 1975, pp. 198-199). For Christians like Paul, Wells writes, Jesus was viewed from the beginning as a dying and rising divinity. They knew nothing of his putative human biography. "Two New Testament epistles (James and Jude) say next to nothing about Jesus, and James does not even mention his death and resurrection" (Wells, 1975, pp. 56-57). Paul's epistles fill a hundred pages of the New English Bible and include many references to Jesus' death without once indicating clearly when it occurred.

According to Wells, Christianity grew out of not only Judaism, but also other religious and philosophical traditions. His initial thesis appears to be the opposite of the nineteenth-century liberal Christian one that Jesus lived on earth as something of a remarkable human-like teacher who was later turned into a supernatural being. Wells contends that from the start Christians like Paul envisioned a supernatural being who came to earth to suffer and conquer death. Decades later, when the myth of the return of this Savior-God failed to materialize, Christians began to speculate about his life on earth and to search for details about his death. Specifically, they searched primarily through the Septuagint (LXX), the Greek Translation of the Hebrew Bible. In their view, Jesus (whose name means "Yahweh is salvation") came in fulfillment of Old Testament prophecies. They believed further that God had formed the detailed plan by which to save the righteous believers and that Jesus had been foreordained to carry out the supreme role in that plan. The Old Testament thus became for them the divine script intended for Christian use. By turning to that script, Christians could select passages that, to them, appeared to be the foreordained details of Jesus' life on earth. In *Gospel Fictions,* Randel Helms shows how early Christian writers conscripted the Septuagint to generate events, miracles, sayings, scenes, and minor characters for the construction of Jesus' earthly biography (Helms, 1988).

To be sure, this does not represent the way historians today should carry out their quest for historical accuracy. But long before and after the early Christians, various poets, shamans, prophets, and others believed they received information from supernatural sources, both written and oral. In a highly fruitful pamphlet for the American Historical Association, E. S. Gaustad tells of the ninth-century Bishop of Ravenna, who disclosed the method by which he wrote a series of biographies about certain bishops:

> Where I have not found any history of any of these bishops and have not been able by conversation with aged men, or inspection of the monuments, or from any other authentic source, to obtain information concerning them, in such cases, in order that there might not be a break in the series, *I have composed the life myself, with the help of God and prayers of the brethren.* (Gaustad, 1973, p. 51, italics added)

According to historian Gilbert Murray, the ancient Greek poets believed the divine Muses not only inspired them, but also gave them actual knowledge of facts, since the Muses were presumed to be everywhere and to know all things. Homer consulted the Muses on such subjects as the catalogue of the Greek Army (Murray, 1960, p. 96). Karl Popper notes that the pre-Socratic philosopher Heraclitus believed he was possessed by Zeus who gave him words to speak. Parmenides regarded the goddess Dike, the guardian of truth, to be his inspiration and guiding star. He described her as the keeper of the keys of truth and the source of all his knowledge (Popper, 1991, p. 9). Wells notes that early Christian prophets were believed to receive words from the resurrected Jesus. One of the Christian gifts was that of receiving "a word of knowledge." Paul, of course, insisted that God had foreordained him to receive direct communication from his Son Jesus Christ (Gal. 1:1, 11; 15:22).

Even the most conservative biblical scholars deny the historical claims made by the longer ending of the Gospel of Mark. A critical question naturally arises: how did this admittedly unhistorical "account" come to be written? The King James translation of the Bible contains this ending because the translators at the time relied on ancient Greek manuscripts that contained it. This strange passage promises immunity from lethal poisons and poisonous snakes. Apparently, some Christian believer either *edited or composed* the passage. Other passages in other Christian manuscripts are seen as unauthentic. The key question, therefore, is this: did the Christian authors of the passages regard them as unauthentic? Wells opens the door to the scholarly project of reconstructing the thinking process of various Christian believers who wrote down what they believed to be events and sayings in a historical Jesus' life. He considers it a mistake to assume that the composers of various passages thought they were creating deeds and sayings from their own imaginations. Rather, they drew from the Wisdom literature and a variety of other sources that they, rightly or wrongly, regarded as authoritative content to describe Jesus' life.

The Last Supper

In a detailed analysis of Paul's view of Jesus' alleged last supper before his crucifixion, Professor Wells notes that Paul does not claim that he received the account from Peter or John. Rather, he claims that his knowledge of Jesus' words on that night in question came to him directly from the Lord:

> For I received from the Lord what I also deliver to you, that the Lord Jesus took bread ...broke it, and said, "This is my body which is for you. Do this in remembrance of me." In the same way also the cup, after supper, saying, "This cup is the new covenant in my blood. Do this as often as you drink it, in remembrance of me." (1 Cor. 11:23-25)

According to the overwhelming majority of scholars who believe that Jesus lived as Paul's contemporary in Palestine, Paul did not meet Jesus in the flesh. Hence, the Lord (Jesus) could not have given the Eucharistic words to him then. Wells thinks Paul believed that the resurrected Jesus appeared to him and gave him the "information" or at least ratified a pre-Pauline formula from other Christians. In short, since the Eucharistic meal existed among early Christians, they quite readily came to believe that Jesus had instituted it (Wells, 1975, pp. 25-27; Wells, 1996, pp. 33-36).

While not wishing to rule out the possibility that more than one Jesus figure (real or legendary) underlies earliest Christianity, Wells cautions against supposing that the Pauline tradition and the Q tradition refer to the same person (Wells, 1999, pp. 102-113). Given the fact that the name Jesus, or its Hebrew equivalent, was quite popular among Jews, there is the likelihood that one or more Jesuses early in the first century spoke words of wisdom worth remembering and quoting. Furthermore, Roy C. Amore, may be correct in concluding that Buddhist teaching had woven into Jewish and Gentile teaching in Alexandria, Syria, Judea, and areas around the Sea of Galilee. Galilee spawned cultural inbreeding and in the Old Testament is referred to as Galilee of the Gentiles (Isa. 9:1). In the first century, this significant part of a Jewish nation was known as the district of the Gentiles.

In 104-103 BCE, the Hasmonaean King, Aristobulus, conquered Galilee and forced its inhabitants to either submit to circumcision and the Jewish faith or leave (Songer, 1990, p. 315; Josephus, *Antiquities*, 13.11.3). This ruthless intrusion generated considerable hostility toward orthodox Jews and created a moral crisis for many Jews who disapproved of such cruel treatment of their Gentile neighbors, fellow workers, business partners, and customers. Some material that flowed into the so-called Q document doubtless came from teachers and others whose views of religion and righteousness stood in sharp contrast with the Hasmonaeans. To be sure, the Q material, far from being a wholly self-consistent body of teachings and doctrines, represents several sources, including material from wisdom traditions and, especially in Luke, Buddhist teachings (Amore, 1978; Wells, 1996, pp. 170-171).

A Theological Shaping of Historical "Facts"

Controversy over the details and meaning of Jesus' putative life did not begin in the nineteenth century or even the sixteenth. It began at least in the first century. In 2 Corinthians 11:4-5, Paul already faces rival Christians who, he charges, preach *another Jesus* and another gospel.

> For if some newcomer proclaims another Jesus, not the Jesus whom we proclaim, or if you receive a spirit different from the Spirit already given to you, or a gospel different from the gospel you have already accepted, you put up with that all too willingly. Now, I am not aware of being in the least inferior to the superapostles.

The Gospel of Luke's author evidently believed a Jesus lived who ate his last supper with twelve disciples. Yet, even here, theology shapes the putative facts. In *The Orthodox Corruption of Scripture*, Bart D. Ehrman contends that Luke reworked Mark's version of the Last Supper and other passages to delete the passages advancing the theological view that Christ's death was a vicarious atonement for human sin. According to Mark, the tearing of the curtain in the Temple takes place as a result of Jesus' death. In Luke, it occurs *before* Jesus dies (23:45). "In Luke's account the ripping of the Temple curtain does not show that Jesus' death has opened up the path of God…" (Ehrman, 1993, p. 201). That is Mark's view. Luke's view is that the torn curtain "symbolized God's judgment upon his people who prefer to dwell in darkness" (Ehrman, 1993, p. 201). Rather than serving as a blood sacrifice, the Christ of Luke's version died unjustly, as an innocent victim whom God subsequently vindicated and glorified.

The shorter reading of Luke's account of the Last Supper fits with the rest of his two-volume work (Luke and Acts) in which he goes out of his way to eliminate the theological doctrine of Christ's vicarious atonement. When Luke in Acts 8 brings in the Isaiah 53 text, he "includes not a word about the Servant of the Lord being 'wounded for our transgressions' (Isa. 53:5), being 'bruised for our iniquities' (Isa. 53:5), or making himself 'an offering for sin'" (Isa. 53:10; Ehrman, 1993, p. 200).

Girard's Jesus

René Girard, a French literary critic currently teaching at Stanford University, has generated considerable discussion about sacrifice and violence in the Bible. The author of Luke-Acts may very well be Girard's forerunner. Luke clearly avoids suggesting that Christ's death was a blood payment to God, and he gives no support to those Christians who believed that Christ's crucifixion was a ransom payment to the devil. Rather, his death came, not because God had a plan to make him a scapegoat or substitute atonement, but because human evil converged to kill him. Repentance comes to those who are shocked by the realization of their part in perpetuating evil and violence, including the persecution and death of Jesus and innocent people like Stephen (Acts 7). A large portion of the Book of Acts is devoted to purges and persecution (Chapters 4; 5; 7:51-53, 59; 12:1-3; 13:27-28, 50; 14:5-6, 19; 16:22-24; 17:5-9; 19:16, 29; 20:3; 21:30-36; 23:10, 12, 21; 25:3; 26:15, 21,30). The violence directed against Paul, Stephen, Peter and James comes from human agents. In three cases, however, the deity resorts to violence: killing Herod (12:23), striking the magician Elymas with temporary blindness (13:10-11), and conveniently having Ananias and Sapphira drop dead (5:5, 10).

Girard develops a theory about "the scapegoat mechanism," that is, collective human violence. Briefly stated, human beings over the generations have sought to resolve their mutual hostilities and hatreds by turning their frustration and violence away from each other and onto an innocent, chance victim. In this respect, the scapegoat does function as a substitute. Instead of wholesale slaughter, the community or communities unite against the selected scapegoat, denounce him or her (or the substitute group) as the "evildoer," make the victim an outcast, and kill him or her (or them) (Girard, 1977). This scapegoat mechanism is, of course, a collective transfer of violence to a random victim. In Chapter 8, we dwelt on Romans 7 and Paul's complicated struggle with conflicting desires partly because we felt he had in that passage anticipated some of Girard's thesis. Paul's notion of the "law of sin" gains clarity when seen as evil desires that gain individual strength by a coalition with other evil desires. The evil increases when the coalition succeeds in using righteousness as a front. Seen from the perspective of social psychology, sociology and political science, Paul's notion of the "law of sin" or coalition of evil becomes, then, primarily collective violence that comes in various forms. This evil becomes reinforced in the "members" of the body politic because of the powerful collective pressure.

According to Girard's thesis, the New Testament is in some respects a book of literary and religious criticism. It uses the literary device of reversed point of view to expose critically the collective transfer of violence for what it is. Violence viewed from the victim's perspective is a kind of conversion. If Girard's thesis is correct, the Gospels are narratives of skepticism. This way of reading the Bible brings considerable insight. Girard, nevertheless, seems to play down the fact that the insight does not gain a strong foothold in much of the New Testament, which is still a book of violence toward unbelievers. The unbelievers are, after all, *believers* in other religions, other philosophies, and other Jesuses. Jesus in the New Testament appears as victim *and* as apocalyptic avenger. We suggest that the "Christ" of the New Testament is actually the community's envisioned Christ, the Jesus of the churches with all their wondrous insights and disappointing moral flaws (Schwager, 1987, pp. 153-163).

In his article "In the Beginning Was the Deed: A Neo-Girardian Look at the Passion Narrative," Robert M. Price develops his own version of the earthly Jesus. He acknowledges that René Girard has profoundly influenced his thinking about Jesus. Toward the end of his article, however, he offers a rather astounding conclusion that Wells would applaud.

> I should imagine that for the purposes of Girard's methodology, it hardly matters whether there has been a historical Jesus any more than there has been a historical Oedipus. I am not even sure that Girard's actual views of the gospels as a revelation of the scapegoat mechanism ...would require a historical Jesus, even though Girard everywhere speaks of Jesus himself as the revealer. I suppose a fictional exposé of the scapegoating mechanism would be as genuine a revelation as a historically based one. He says "the revelation of the founding victim [Jesus] was first achieved *in this text*." (Price, 1993, p. 300, citing Girard, 1987, p. 443, Price's italics)

The Cosmic Drama

Paul and other first-century Christians viewed the world as populated with personal, hostile, supernatural beings who victimized human mortals and controlled much of their lives (Via, 1990, pp. 40-44). Because this cosmic view is highly anthropomorphic, any presumed account of it had to be cast as a story or drama of conflict with major characters. Jewish apocalyptic literature had already entered this deep, dark forest. The Epistle of Jude borrows the Jewish legend of conflict between the archangel Michael and the devil over the possession of Moses' body. Michael had already come to be regarded as Israel's supernatural protector against both earthly and cosmic enemies.

The Apostle Paul drew heavily from his Hebrew legacy to articulate a sweeping cosmic drama of conflict. Using God and Christ as the major characters, he contributed major elements to a plot that the Gospels later extended by bringing in subplots and additional characters. The German philosopher G. W. F Hegel (1730-1831) created a worldview in which God is caught up in his own drama of self-alienation, a turbulent process of conflict and dialectic. "Spirit [*Geist*] is at war with itself" (Hegel, 1950, p. 66). As one of the most insightful interpreters of Shakespeare, Hegel viewed all human history as a dimension of God's history moving like a Shakespearean drama of conflict.[1]

The Apostle Paul projected a cosmic battle that he presumed was settled, not by a power-seeking Caligula, but by the supernatural Messiah, who became a slave and thereby conquered through his weakness and crucifixion. This demonstrates that a major social and moral development can occur without a paradigm shift. For although Paul transcended the deification of power politics (an ancient and entrenched practice decried later by Popper), he remained within the highly anthropomorphic and apocalyptic paradigm.

Historical criticism may be seen as a prolonged struggle within the paradigm and the problem of relating the first (divine) cause of events with the second (human and natural) causes. If the pendulum swings toward secondary causes only, the question of meaningless or blind chance threatens to cast its chilling shadow. If it swings toward the divine cause, then the question of divine responsibility for horrors and agonies surfaces.

In *Richard III*, Shakespeare raises the biblical and ancient Greek problem of the divine cosmic plot and makes both Calvinists and Arminians in his audience struggle with the terrifying thought that Richard III is God's agent of wrath and woe. Richard, a reprobate, plays his role in the cosmic drama. He plays the predetermined part just as the Judas character acts according to God's script (Acts 1:16-17). Shakespeare himself contributes mightily to the new self-consciousness that gave birth to modern historical criticism. The far-reaching consequences of this child of the Renaissance continue to this day.

> Once historical criticism developed, the Christian explanation of the past could not maintain its supremacy. It slowly collapsed under criticism, but ...just as surely did the interpretations which replaced it—the concept of progress, the

> manifest destinies of competitive nationalism, social Darwinism, or dialectical materialism. (Plumb, 1971, p. 136; Elton, 1988; Hunter, 1976)

In the next chapter, we inquire whether those eventually called Christians spawned a narrative to counter the bitter reversals of life that the ancient Greek tragedies and the Hebrew tragedies of King Saul and Job had dramatized so graphically. We believe this narrative is the heart and soul of that early gospel.

Note

1 In *The Open Society and Its Enemies*, Karl Popper has severely criticized this theatrical way of subsuming human lives under one staged supernatural plot (Popper, 1950, pp. 453-461).

14 Tragedy and Gospel

Tragedy in the Hebrew Tradition

In her analysis of tragedy in the Hebrew Bible, J. Cheryl Exum acknowledges the difficulty of establishing a single definition of tragedy that most scholars can accept. She wisely turns to those literary works recognized as tragedies to find major ingredients to examine. With many other biblical scholars, she regards the story of King Saul as the most consistent and complete example of tragedy in the Bible. The stories of David, Jephthah, and Samson contain powerful elements of tragedy, but they do not measure up to the story of King Saul (Exum, 1996, pp. 70-119). In his remarkable *The Fate of King Saul*, David Gunn unequivocally rates Saul as the most tragic character in the Old Testament records (Gunn, 1989, p. 27).

W. Lee Humphrey's analysis of Saul's narrative stresses the crucial role of *ambiguity* (Humphrey, 1985, pp. 56-57). Gunn adds that the ambiguity shadows not only the tragic character, but also the reader, who must wrestle both with textual meanings and life's ambiguities (Gunn, 1989, p. 31). Soon, we will look at the God Yahweh's ambiguity toward Saul.

According to Exum, the great tragedies lead us as readers to participate sympathetically in the hero's struggle against fate. Jephthah emerges as a less tragic figure than Saul because nothing draws us into his life to witness and feel his struggle against his nemesis. We live vicariously through Saul as we cannot through Jephthah, for Saul's story lays bare much of his inner life. It teems with strife, heroic defiance against an incomprehensible fate, personal anguish, heartbreaking pleas, and emotional explosions. At the core of Saul's tragedy are the relentless demands of destiny and deity against both him and his house. Saul and his kin are marked for life. Even if we readers grant that Saul lacks total innocence, we judge the wrath poured on him excessive enough to indicate a grudge or vendetta. His efforts to satisfy Yahweh usually evoke, not favorable responses, but the brunt of divine vengeance. Exum goes so far as to speak of the "dangerous, demonic side of God" in 2 Samuel (Exum, 1996, p. 119). Plato complains that the tragedies and Homer's *Iliad* made God a direct cause of evil. According to the *Iliad*, on heaven's palace floor stand two urns filled with the destinies that Zeus has allotted, one containing good things, the other bad. Whereas Second Isaiah insists that Yahweh creates evil or disaster (Isa. 45:7), Plato denies that Zeus puts the urn of evil and disaster to mortal lips (*Republic*, II, 379b-e).

We cannot help asking why Yahweh seems so hostile toward Saul, who did not seek to become king. According to 1 Samuel, Yahweh perceived that in seeking a king, the Israelites were rejecting him as their king. Even though Saul is anointed king with minimal ceremony, Yahweh appears exceedingly resentful, as though Saul had schemed to usurp him. Of course, Samuel, who purports to speak for Yahweh, may be projecting onto Yahweh his own bitter resentment of Saul, who, after all, takes over much power and many roles that Samuel possessed for years. Saul is also exercising the power that Samuel wished his sons to exercise eventually. From the beginning, both Samuel and Yahweh seem ambivalent toward Saul, who gradually becomes Yahweh's scapegoat (Exum and Whedbee, 1984, pp. 31-37).

Irony flows through 1 Samuel. While Yahweh remains at best ambivalent toward both the throne and its first occupant, Saul's life becomes a virtual battleground of opposing loyalties and responsibilities. The external conflicts and Saul's inner emotional conflicts mirror one another. We can see Saul as driven in part by his jealousies, rages, suspicions, terrible confusion, rigidity, loves and vain hopes to the point of becoming a disintegrating character. Still, another crucial factor emerges. First, 1 Samuel's implied author makes it clear that Saul's personal unraveling is the work of Yahweh's left hand. None other than Yahweh sent the evil spirit to torment Saul. The story features a tragic figure, not trapped by impersonal forces, but relentlessly persecuted by the powerful Yahweh. Saul's heroism lies in his not accepting his fate without fighting back. But he is, in the end, no match for Yahweh. Students of tragedy explore the crucial relationship between the tragic hero's free choices and the role of fate and necessity. While Saul often *chooses* to do sometimes horrible evil, *Yahweh causes Saul to make evil choices.* Whereas the incident of Yahweh's inciting David to sin is singled out in David's story (2 Sam. 24:1,10) as though it were an exception, the choices that Saul makes seem to be the consequence of Yahweh's manipulative control. Later in this chapter, we will deal with the existence of a wrathful fate in Paul's worldview.

Guilt, Punishment, and Tragedy

Especially relevant to the question of tragedy in the New Testament is the phenomenon of guilt. In *Elements of Tragedy* Dorothea Krook writes:

> The primary "act of shame" is then seen as shameful and horrible because it is a violation of a moral order which is objectively real and absolutely binding. The "suffering" precipitated by the act of shame is seen to be not merely arbitrary but objectively necessary, and thus necessary because *expiatory*.... [T]his act of violation has to be expiated in order that the moral order may be restored. (Krook, 1969, p. 17)

Can the moral order be restored? If so, how? By whom? Exum insists that tragedy entails an imbalance between guilt and crime or sin because the punishment following the hero's deeds appears *excessive*. Double tragedy emerges when punishment fails to restore balance and order. Later, we will ask whether Archbishop Anselm and the sixteenth-century Reformers were following the Apostle Paul's interpretation of this problem of balance and the restoration of moral order.

The Hebrew Bible is rife with ambivalence about injustice, especially the imbalance between sin and punishment and between sin and suffering. In some ways, the Saul and Job tragedies contain more terror than Aristotle perceived in the Greek tragedies. The dramatic impact of Saul and Job in particular throws open the chilling possibility that the presumed transcendent moral order's upheaval is the work of not only mere mortals, but also the powerful deity. We need not decide whether the author of Job intended agonizing irony or a ferocious literary pun when he portrayed God as responding from a powerful, destructive *wind*. Most certainly, his literary art succeeds in raising the unnerving question, not of human justice, but of *divine* justice. If divine justice is out of balance, who will restore it? How can the God of a *tornado* turn chaos into cosmos? The shots fired in the Saul and Job stories echo in Shakespeare's *Hamlet*, driving us to ask whether a divine Providence's governing and controlling the world makes it a nicer place. Robert G. Hunter goes so far as to say that the world's horrors increase considerably if a divinity really does shape what happens in *Hamlet*. "God's existence does not even make what happens *comprehensible*" (Hunter, 1976, p. 124, italics added). In his last novel, the Christian novelist Dostoevsky has Ivan Karamazov question whether *everything* is equally justifiable in a world without God (Dostoevsky, 1992, I, ii, 6, pp. 87-88, 103). Yet, the horrendous tragedies of Saul, Job, and Prince Hamlet force us to question whether the divinity that shapes his creatures is anything more than raw power. Ivan's question is thus upended. If Yahweh does exist, is everything equally justifiable for him? In short, does Supreme Might make right?

The overriding thesis of our chapters is that the heart of the New Testament is an attempt to respond creatively to tragedy's undeniable horror. Paul and other New Testament writers wrestled with disturbing problems articulated in the Greek and Hebrew tragedies. Keeping in mind that Paul draws heavily from the Hebrew scriptures, we turn to a case of glaring moral imbalances and injustice in the David narrative. Paul could not have failed to note the problem leaping out at him.

David's Guilt and Israel's Punishment

Some great tragedies ask whether a person will knowingly bring about his own doom by intentionally violating the moral order. Over the years, David committed many crimes, cruel deeds, and atrocities. According to 2 Samuel 24, David sinned by taking a census of the Israelites. Shocking as it may appear, the divine punishment did not fall directly upon David, but upon seventy thousand men of Israel, whom Yahweh killed by a plague.

Three severe moral and theological problems emerge in this excerpt from the David narrative. David himself articulates one. "I alone have sinned, and I alone have done wickedly; but these sheep [i.e., the victims of the plague], what have they done? Let your hand, I pray, be against me and against my father's house" (2 Sam. 24:17). Thousands of innocent people died because of one king's sin. The second problem has to do with both David and the God Yahweh. Only *after* David had committed his putative sin of taking a census did Yahweh inform him of the terrible punishment to follow. Why did Yahweh withhold this information until it could not influence David's decision? Even if we assume David knew that his census-taking was a sin, he apparently did not anticipate such a violent and sweeping retaliation. Yahweh lifted his punishment from the people only after David built an altar and extended burnt offerings and peace offerings. Ironically, earlier, in 1 Samuel, the prophet Samuel rebuked the fated King Saul because of his burnt offering.

> Has the LORD [Yahweh] as great delight in burnt offerings and sacrifices, as in obeying the voice of the LORD? Surely, to obey is better than sacrifice, and to heed than the fat of rams. (1 Sam. 15:22)

The third moral problem raised by this excerpt from David's life appears early in the account. Yahweh moved David to take the census in the first place. This seemed so morally problematic to a later redactor of the David story that in retelling this excerpt, he did not have Yahweh inciting David to sin. Rather, the tempter was "the Adversary." The Hebrew text never clarifies whether this adversary is a cosmic figure or an earthly mortal. The Hebrew scholars who translated their Bible into Greek (LXX) rendered it as *diabolos*, which in English can mean "the devil." Most English translations rendered it "Satan." "Satan stood up against Israel, and incited David to number Israel. So David said to Joab and the commanders of the army, 'Go, number Israel...that I may know the number'" (1 Chr. 21:1-2).

According to the earlier version (1 Sam. 24), Joab merely questioned David as to why the king would delight in taking the census. Nothing in the text indicates that Joab was warning of horrible consequences. (Elsewhere in the text, Joab seems quite capable of making himself abundantly clear on matters about which he feels strongly.) The author/redactor of 1 Chronicles changes Joab's words, making him warn David, "Why then should my Lord require this? Why should he *bring guilt on Israel*?" (1 Chr. 21:3 Italics added).

Paul's Solution to Divine Injustice

Paul attempts to resolve the problem of injustice on God's part by advancing the rather clear-cut thesis that God *cannot* be unjust or act unjustly. Plato sets himself against his Greek heritage by insisting that the Homeric portrayal of the gods was so highly inaccurate as to make the gods appear debased and immoral. By contrast, Paul advances the view that God cannot be immoral because no independent moral law binds him. God can do what he chooses solely because he chooses it. No one can call him to account. A Calvinist like Gordon Clark has accurately interpreted this particular thread of Paul's thinking. Clark, himself a careful student of ancient Greek thinkers, succinctly states his interpretation of how Paul viewed God's relationship to the moral law. "*Anything* God does is right, because he does it" (Clark, 1961, p. 189, italics added). Clark elaborates so that no one will misunderstand his position.

> Man is responsible because God called him to account; man is responsible because the supreme power can punish him for disobedience. God, on the contrary, cannot be responsible for the plain reason that there is no power superior to him; no greater being can hold him accountable; no one can punish him; there is no one to whom God is responsible; there are no laws which he could disobey. (Clark, 1961, p. 241)

Using clear language, Clark has explicated the point Paul makes in Romans 9:11-23. Whether Paul clings to this position in all his epistles is another matter. There is reason to think that Paul as a theologian did not remain perfectly consistent. In this Romans 9 passage, he wrestles with whether the God of the Hebrew scriptures is just or can be morally judged. In sharp contrast to the ancient Greek theologians, Paul conceives of God not only as wholly free of all moral judgments against him, but also as bound by no fate or external principle of necessity. These two planks are essential to one early Christian vision of the gospel as anti-tragic theater.

The Source of the Imbalance and Disorder

In *Tragedy as a Critique of Virtue*, John D. Barbour follows Hegel's lead, recognizing in tragedy "a character's goodness wasted." The tragic hero seems lost between a hostile fate and a just moral order.

> Though a character's own choices contribute to his or her downfall, the appalling waste of human goodness may be presented as an indication of an essential flaw in the character or judgement of the person destroyed. When an individual is destroyed because his actions express the only ways his essential dignity or integrity can be affirmed, such an event is profoundly upsetting because it reveals the structure of the world at odds with the deepest needs of human nature. (Barbour, 1984, p. 15)

In Romans, Paul assumes that his readers acknowledge that creation lies in a state of frustration, futility, or temporary defeat. Then he adds the curious comment that creation's own will did not cause this state. Rather, it was imposed "by the will of the one who subjected it" (Rom. 8:20). Traditional interpretation designates this "him" as Adam or Satan. A strict Calvinist might even designate God. Nevertheless, since by definition Paul's God *cannot* be morally culpable, Paul locates the fault in the human race (Rom. 1-3). This does not, however, deny that in the apostle's mind demons and perhaps other putative beings contribute to human corruption and condemnation.

Clearly, Paul cannot rest content with the ambiguity so prevalent in many Greek tragedies, the Book of Job, or the tragedy of King Saul. Since he believes *all* human mortals have sinned and fall short of God's glory (Rom. 3:23), he can ultimately justify any tribulation that befalls any human. Everyone stands under perpetual condemnation. Paul writes that trouble and distress await everyone who does evil (2:9). Does that mean, however, that since everyone does evil, trouble and distress become the lot of everyone? Clearly, it means that *no* trouble or distress for any human is *un*justified? Evidently aware that his argument will appear problematic to some, Paul asks whether "God is unjust to inflict wrath on us." He answers, "By no means! For then [i.e., if God is judged to be unjust] how could God judge the world?" (3:5f). As if uncertain as to whether he has made his point, Paul emphasizes that "none is righteous" and "no one does good, not even one." (3:10,12). Whether Jew or Gentile, "all …are under the power of sin" (3:9).

The eleventh-century archbishop of Canterbury Anselm and the sixteenth-century Reformers explicated what they believed to be the fundamental thrust of Paul's view regarding the human race's universal condemnation. They reasoned as follows. Although human beings are finite, their sin is infinite because it insults the infinite, perfect Creator. Justice thus requires infinite punishment. This means that the only real imbalance between sin and deserved punishment is the delay of the punishment. Presumably, hell is infinite because the punishment must be infinite. Thus, the suffering or death of a finite, sinful mortal such as Oedipus or Socrates *cannot* restore the moral order! Only the suffering and death of an infinite, sinless being can accomplish that. Anselm and the Reformers regarded the infinite, sinless Christ as the only being who could receive the infinite punishment due the human race. Only those finite persons who are "in Christ Jesus" enjoy liberation from the curse of the universal condemnation.

Paul's theology presumably eliminates the ambivalence of guilt and suffering, sin and punishment, found in many Greek tragedies. On the cosmic, metaphysical level on which he purports to write, no finite persons are innocent. In King Saul's tragedy, the implied author certainly gives readers enough twists to the story to lead them to see that Saul is *excessively* condemned and punished. Yet, Samuel and Yahweh lead readers to believe that Yahweh rejects even Saul's relatively innocent moves to do what is right and pleasing. Centuries later, Saul (Paul) of Tarsus may have generalized from King Saul's tragedy by, in effect, arguing that in God's eyes, no innocent members of the human race exist.

Calvinism, which purports to follow Pauline premises to their logical conclusion, appears to reject a critical theme of some major tragedies: that tragic heroes suffer a measure of undeserved agony since they have a measure of *innocence* mingled with their guilt. Calvinist Gordon Clark writes, "No innocent person suffers. To be sure, Calvinism also insists that there are no innocent persons, except Christ of course. All are dead in sin" (Clark, 1961, p. 236).

Ironically, Paul unwittingly opens the door to a theory that follows his theology's grim side and concludes that one portion of the human race becomes a horrifyingly tragic story. The Esaus of the world are categorically doomed before their births (Rom. 9:11-13). Despite everything, does the specter of fate sweep across Paul's theology? He went to great lengths to argue that there exists no force or fate external to God's will. But in the final analysis, has Paul paid too dear a price? Has fate gone underground and appeared subversively as internal to the divine nature itself?

Paul and Fate

The problem of fate appears to have weighed heavily on Paul's mind. With his view that God is the Potter and human creatures the clay, he concludes in Romans 9 that God can harden the heart of whomever he wills. Interestingly, Paul uses Pharaoh as his example rather than his own Hebrew namesake Saul. ("Paul" is the Greek form of "Saul"). Regarding Pharaoh, he quotes from Scripture:

> For the scripture says to Pharaoh, "I have raised you up for the very purpose of showing my power in you, so that my name may be proclaimed in all the earth." So then he has mercy on whomever he chooses, and he hardens the heart of whomever he chooses. (Rom. 9:17-18)

Tragedy as viewed by Paul and other New Testament writers needs examination in light of the fate theory prevalent among those ancient Greeks and Romans who believed *the Fates* controlled every life from beginning to end. The Fates were three sisters whom the Greeks called the *Moirai* and the Romans called the *Parcae*. They controlled the threads of life. Clotho held the distaff while Lachesis spun the thread and Atropos cut the thread to end life. Fatalism asserts that events will follow a certain path with such inevitability that present human actions and choices are merely epiphenomenal. For some Greeks, the *Moirai* assign at birth each person's allotment of suffering. The Romans viewed their Gods, the *Parcae*, as the spinners of human destiny. This leaves open the question of whether the gods themselves are free entities or tools of an impersonal necessity (*ananke*). According to the strictest fatalism, a combination of impersonal forces determines everything that happens in each person's life. Paul holds, not to impersonal determinism, but to personal *pre*determinism. For him, the conscious Creator willingly shapes the destinies of individuals. Since Jacob and Esau were made of "the same lump" of clay, neither had merit over the other. Yet, God selected Jacob over Esau. For Paul, this does not imply that the individual's destiny occurs irrespective of his or her personal choices and actions. At the same time, Paul does not advance a doctrine of floating free will. To the contrary, God causes every human desire, choice, and action. God selects each human destiny. Not only that, he selects each choice and all the other means to bring about each preordained destiny. Strict fatalism suggests that human ends are brought about irrespective of their choices and actions. Paul, however, apparently claims that human ends cannot come about without the appropriate human means (e.g., desires, choices, actions) to bring them about. Thus, the means, too, are predestined, one and all.

By using other New Testament texts that place the Romans passages in different perspective, competent scholars can criticize the above interpretation of Paul. Doubtless, Paul had problems with it himself, as Romans 11 perhaps indicates. Clearly, he advances the broad theory (which includes his apocalyptic conjectures) that God controls *all* events. This leads, however, to the heart of tragedy, the tension between human choice and fate. While Paul replaces impersonal fate with personalized predestination, a philosopher in the tradition of William James might well ask, "What is the practical difference?" At this critical point, we suggest that as storytellers, the authors/redactors of the four canonical Gospels lack some of their Hebrew predecessors' subtlety. In the Gospels, for example, doomed Judas is more a narrow role than a living character. Readers are permitted to see scarcely any of his deepest thoughts and feelings. Luke (22:3) says, "Satan entered into Judas." John (6:70) has Jesus saying, "Did I not choose you, the twelve? Yet one of you is a devil."[1] In contrast to the New Testament's treatment of Judas, Shakespeare's *Othello* gives us unforgettable insight into Iago's vile heart. Shakespeare refuses to reduce Iago to a mere devil or to someone possessed by another being. To the contrary, the terror of the story lies partially in our full realization that Iago is a member of our own species.

Gospel Agendas

Examining Paul and the four Gospels against the background of the tragedies has several advantages. First, it can help scholars in narrative criticism see more clearly that each Gospel author has his or her own agenda. But storytelling has always been a very tricky business. A writer who started with one agenda sometimes developed others in the process. Paradoxical as it may sound, in the process of *creating* a story, the teller or writer often *discovers* new facets of the major characters or plot. New insights emerge. As a comparative study of the four Gospels shows, revisions (including additions, deletions, clarifications, etc.) became necessary. New angles forced each storyteller to reexamine certain plot ingredients. At the same time, the overall agenda often survived all the revisions and discoveries. We think such a revision scenario happened with the four canonical Gospels. Yet, if they have an overall agenda, what is it? The answer we wish to set forth is this. The four Gospels envision a divine being on earth who has many marks of a tragic hero struggling against powerful forces, both terrestrial and cosmic. The life of this divine being ends tragically; his punishment and death are unjustified. Furthermore, this Messiah's death is more than martyrdom. Somehow, for especially Mark, Matthew and John, it effects cosmic redemption. Classicist Paul Woodruff says that Thucydides' *History of the Peloponnesian War*, while profoundly influenced by the ancient tragedies, differs from them in at least one significant way. Although Thucydides has no great reverence for the gods, Woodruff reminds us that actors performed the tragedies as a religious service (Woodruff, 1993, p. ix).

New Testament scholars now think that at least the Gospel of Mark was initially read aloud to the assembled believers as a part of their religious service.

Stephen H. Smith notes that most early Christians could not have afforded a copy of the Gospel. The public readings of it, or of excerpts, would have been central to the community's religious experience. With a little imagination, we can recover some of their sense of the drama. Particularly in the passion narrative, we sense the drama as the reader describes the Last Supper and the steady march of events through Jesus' agony in Gethsemane, Judas' kiss, the disciples' disappearance, Peter's demands, the false witnesses, the accusations and interrogations, the stirred-up crowd, the trial, Jesus' humiliation as his persecutors mock him, his crucifixion, his crying out, the centurion's confession, Jesus' death, his burial by Joseph of Arimathea, and the young man in white telling the women that Jesus of Nazareth has risen.

Beyond Tragedy

While Paul and the Gospel writers incorporated some elements of the tragedies, they nevertheless wrote as if they believed they had a good-news story that transcended the ambivalence that pervaded all genuine tragedies.[2] Paul's doctrine of the resurrection of those "in Christ" placed a new perspective on the grim reversals of fortune portrayed in Job and other great tragedies. A redactor may very well have written the Book of Job's epilogue to place the tragic misfortune in a different perspective. It accomplished this by *reversing the reversal*! We suggest that the good news affirmed by Paul and the Gospel writers in particular was an extension of the epilogue to Job. Apocalyptic literature sometimes extends it with a vengeance. For the believers, all earthly reversals will be reversed, so that the present suffering will not be worth comparing to the glory to be revealed (Rom. 8:18). To the church at Philippi, Paul wrote:

> More than that, I regard everything as loss because of the surpassing value of knowing Christ Jesus my Lord. For his sake I have suffered the loss of all things, and I regard them as rubbish, in order that I may gain Christ and be found in him, not having a righteousness of my own that comes from the law, but one that comes through faith in Christ, the righteousness from God based on faith. I want to know Christ and the power of his resurrection and the sharing of his sufferings by becoming like him in his death, if somehow I may attain the resurrection from the dead. (Phil. 3:8-11)

Paul and the Gospels, including John, must be seen as emerging within the apocalyptic tradition. For Paul, the cosmic culmination, or the great reversal of the reversals, needs to take place soon in order to overcome the intensified reversals associated with "the man of lawlessness" who has perhaps already begun his work (2 Thess. 2:3-11). Whereas Christ is portrayed as giving up power to become the crucified servant, the Lawless One exalts himself to the place and rank of God. In short, he represents the hubris and critical flaw sometimes found in both antagonists and tragic heroes. Without attempting in this book to compare in detail each Gospel's Christ with Paul's Christ to see how each does or does not resemble the tragic hero, we emphasize the point that despite the significant differences between Paul's letters and the Gospels, each is apocalyptic in its special way. Paul believed the elect faced a cosmic crisis. Evil would soon triumph unless Christ completed the saving work he began. In the famous 1 Corinthians 15 passage, he reveals that without the cosmic reversal of life's many reversals (including the last great enemy, death), his life and that of his fellow believers would be the most pitiable (1 Cor. 15:19).

The theater of tragedy evokes in us the experience of pity (Aristotle's *Poetics*). Paul appears to suggest that if the gospel he preached was an empty promise, then the believers were to be pitied as people of tragedy, facing inevitable defeat and ruin, while persisting in a fruitless hope and faith. Paul and the Gospel writers were, however, unwilling to cast themselves in the role of tragic figures who evoke pity. To be sure, the Gospel of Mark comes closest to being a tragedy partly because of its stark ending. Without the spurious longer ending, Mark terminates his narrative with the comment that the women at the empty tomb "were afraid" (16:18). Subsequently, Matthew, Luke, and John made the revisions and additions necessary to distance themselves from both Mark's ambiguity and the theater of tragedy.

The Apocalyptic as Counter to Tragedy

In *Pity and Terror: Christianity and Tragedy*, Ulrich E. Simon notes the extreme complexity behind the Gospels' passion narratives. Reflecting on the flood of monographs that have attempted to identify those responsible for Jesus' crucifixion, Simon made the following observation in 1989: "Nowhere is the death of Jesus simply classed as 'tragic'" (Simon, 1989, p. 147). The death of Jesus cannot be classified as tragic without discounting the fact that both Paul and the Gospel writers were a part of the anti-tragic theater that Plato so eloquently articulated (Kaufmann, 1968, pp. 1-25). As will be shown later, Plato and the New Testament writers took different routes in attempting to meet the challenge of the tragedies. The first-century gospel was a rival theater, the stage of which was the entire cosmos. Like its apocalyptic predecessor, it portrayed God as the drama's director. Heavenly and earthly actors were selected to play their prescribed roles in the cosmic conflict. In the first-century Christian drama, the superstar was Jesus Christ, who came from Heaven to assume the role of a lowly human. All the moves he made and all the words he uttered had profound meaning because on him hinged the entire plot of the triumphant drama. In the Gospel of Matthew and the Gospel of John, there is a kind of Fate. It is, however, a fate that the Supreme Director not only willed, but also controls from beginning to eschatological end.

Paul and the Gospels

Contrary to the scenario created by some of the Jesus Seminar scholars, Paul did not misconstrue the message of a "historical Jesus" behind the distortions of the Gospels. Rather, the Gospels are best viewed as attempts to elaborate on the cosmic Christ whom Paul and others preached. The Gospels represent first-century attempts to provide witness or evidence that the heavenly Messiah did have the power and authority to be the triumphant Lord that Paul and others had earlier proclaimed. Drawing from the Old Testament and other sources, the Gospel writers adopted and composed events to be woven into the life of a Savior who could on earth demonstrate his power and could personally identify with suffering humanity to the point of himself dying on a cross. Whereas Paul spoke of Christ's resurrection, the Gospels portray a resurrected body and an empty tomb. Whereas Paul spoke of Christ as spiritual food and water (Rom. 10:3-4), the Gospels give graphic accounts of Jesus' feeding the multitudes and giving wine or water to the thirsty. Along with the hope of a glorious eschatological end came the growing need in the churches for "accounts" and moving stories about the savior's earthly ministry.

In the recent article "What Did Paul Know about Jesus?" Gregory C. Jenks shows in striking detail that, contrary to James D. G. Dunn and Paul

Barnett, Paul's epistles reveal little interest in the earthly ministry of Jesus (Jenks, 1999, pp. 75-90). Surprisingly, Jenks provides no good explanation for why Paul was either abysmally ignorant of Jesus' ministry or showed no interest in it. Our thesis is that the "accounts" of the putative earthly Jesus of the Gospels had not yet been invented or woven into a narrative. Paul did not go to Jerusalem to glean from Peter and James details of Jesus' earthly life because they had no such details. The Peter referred to in Galatians 1 and 2 would not have recognized either the Jesus or the Peter of the four Gospels.

Notes

1 John Milton could enter the thoughts and feelings of his Satan character and write with such power and beauty as to produce two works of epic poetry that became a part of the functional canon of Christian theology. He accomplished this partly by using the Satan characters to explore the profoundest depths of *human* emotions, especially envy and jealousy.

2 For a useful list of ingredients peculiar to the tragedy, see Barbour, 1984, p. 149. We do not contend that Paul wrote everything in 2 Thessalonians although we think he shared some of its apocalyptic vision.

15 Culturology

A Thin Consensus

The recent scholars' impressive books and articles on the historical Jesus divide into two camps. While each seeks to reconstruct a coherent, viable version of Jesus, they differ as to their primary sources. E. P. Sanders and John Meier represent those who treat the four New Testament Gospels as the key primary sources. Marcus Borg and John Dominic Crossan treat the *Gospel of Thomas*, the *Gospel of the Hebrews*, and certain other non-canonical materials as primary texts, too. To call texts primary is not, however, to take them uncritically. Rather, they regard them as the mother lode of information, content, and clues. As such, they become essential to the credible reconstruction of the historical Jesus. Though rich with clues, they must be sifted, weighed, and vigorously put to the test.

The cold fact remains that after decades of intensive research on the historical Jesus and the emergence of early Christianity, highly competent biblical scholars—some of the best in the world—have yet to arrive at anything beyond a thin, virtually meaningless *consensus*. This in no way implies that their work is meaningless. Far from it. They have often surpassed their predecessors in throwing light on the first-century CE and in providing a richer understanding of its social, cultural, and political forces. Ironically, despite massive and unquestionably brilliant research that now allows readers to enjoy a more profound grasp of first-century Palestine, no clear-cut consensus regarding the Jesus figure has emerged. While the scholarly work sometimes takes one's breath, a genuine in-depth *consensus* about the historical Jesus does not appear on the horizon. This calls attention to the vastness of the canyon of difference among the scholars regarding who Jesus was. According to the meager consensus, someone named Jesus (or the equivalent in Aramaic) existed early in the first century and had a significant influence on the emergence of first-century churches that might or might not have accurately represented the core of his message and intent. The majority of leading scholars hold that first-century believers who purported to guide their lives by his teachings or personal impact failed to understand much of what he was about. Not only that, the believers added their own agendas and revisions with heavy hands. The revisions came, however, not as deliberate misrepresentations or intended distortions, but as earnest attempts to interpret their Jesus in their own historical setting.[1] Not outsiders, but the scholars themselves level the best criticisms of the various current reconstructions of Jesus' identity. Each school of thought expresses in impressive detail severe difficulties inside every rival reconstruction.

C. J. den Heyer's sensitive analysis of the past century and a half of the historical Jesus research concludes:

> Since the last century New Testament scholars have passionately gone in search of the authentic Jesus, but the result of their efforts is no more than a brief biographical sketch of someone who lived long ago in the past. He seems to have been a special person, an attractive and creative personality, a man with an inspiring and liberating message. All this is true, but the reader perhaps gets a feeling of disappointment. Is that all that can be said? The historian will reply 'yes' to this question. By present-day scholarly standards, at present no more can be stated than the minimal biography given above. (den Heyer, 1997, p. 163)

We should distinguish between the historical Jesus and what he called "the real Jesus," den Heyer suggests. Unfortunately, his book ends before offering a helpful clue as to the latter's identity. In fact, he adds that the New Testament "does not know one clear, well-rounded picture of Christ" (den Heyer, 1997, p. 168).

One leading scholar of the reputed Third Quest for the historical Jesus, John Dominic Crossan, examines "seven different images of Jesus that have been proposed by scholars in recent years." He candidly concludes that even under the controlled presupposition that Jesus' proper Jewish background must inform our vision of him, the result is "as many pictures as there are exegetes." The "stunning diversity," Crossan comments, is an "academic embarrassment." He recommends the development of a more "scientific stratigraphy," a new methodology, to get the job done properly (Crossan, 1991, pp. xxvii-xxviii). It would be difficult to exaggerate the truly Herculean work of scholars like Crossan. Nevertheless, thus far, no compelling portrayal of the historical Jesus has successfully overcome its rivals' challenges. The "academic embarrassment" continues. We regard it, not as an embarrassment, but as a testimony to the leading scholars' intellectual integrity. We pay tribute to their combination of intellectual boldness, painstaking rigor, and openness to criticism. It is scholarship at its best.

The Literary Jesus

We may view the new literary criticism (narrative, reader-response, rhetorical criticism, redaction, etc.) as a way to conduct important biblical research without the pressure to solve the difficult historical-Jesus question. For many scholars, the *literary Jesus* has become the center of focus. They throw their energy and training into exploring such matters as each Gospel's plot and subplots, major and minor character development, points of view, implied author, and implied reader.

It may very well turn out that in time this expanding field of criticism focusing on the literary Jesus and the literary disciples will have a powerful and revolutionary impact on historical criticism. For the present, however, it has built a hedge of separation between the two Jesuses. Though important messages pass back and forth, the hedge gives at least the literary critics considerable breathing space and freedom to pursue their discipline without historical-Jesus questions falling perpetually like shadows across their paths.

Culturology

In many ways, literary criticism's success has opened an even broader scholarly approach to historical-Jesus questions. This approach will not only include the literary advances, but also open better ways for social scientists and historians to share the fruit of their research regarding Christianity's emergence. In fact, many New Testament researchers (e.g., Crossan, Wells, Borg, Smith, and Vermes) had already moved in that direction when they strove to mark off and explore in depth early Christianity's sociocultural framework. They have uncovered much about the cultural, social, political and literary motifs of the Greeks, Romans, and Jews of the first centuries BCE and CE. As researchers, they hoped to establish a viable *range* of options as to what sort of person Jesus might have been. This approach provides focus for a more efficient concentration of scholarly energy. In some ways, Leslie A. White could be looked upon as one forerunner of this approach. (Daniel Dennett develops Richard Dawkins' theory of memes, which could have been called "cultural genes" [Dennett, 1995, pp. 361-369]). Trained as an anthropologist who called himself a culturologist, White acknowledged his debt to Émile Durkheim, who insisted on the importance of treating social facts (i.e., cultural traits) as things with a relatively autonomous existence. "[T]hese cultural traits have an existence prior to the birth of any person living" (White, 1971, p. 78). Many themes and motifs in, say, the Apostle Paul's repertoire had played for decades and even centuries before his birth. Some were either created or transmitted by Plato's dialogues and the works of those responding to Plato. Almost in passing, Bernard Brandon Scott reminds us that Plato's works were found in the Nag Hammadi library (Scott, Bernard, 1994, p. 270). We do not suggest that Paul merely played the same arrangement found in Plato's dialogues. Rather, we submit that in creating his own arrangement, he appropriated some of the philosopher's ideas, myths, and theories that had become a fundamental part of the intellectual culture of Paul's world. Paul's older contemporary, Philo, thought so highly of Plato's philosophical doctrines that he spent much of his life creating a new arrangement that includes themes and theories from both Plato and Philo's Hebrew heritage.

We do not claim that Paul actually read Plato's dialogues. Rather, over the centuries many of Plato's theories and poetic images became integral to the early Roman Empire's intellectual life. Thus, it would be surprising if they or their variations and mutants had not influenced Paul. Just as Plato drew heavily from his cultural heritage and in the process created literary and philosophical novelties of incalculable impact, so Paul drew from his cultural heritage and in the process created novelties of astounding and immeasurable impact.

Our thesis is that a Palestinian named Jesus or a missionary named Paul *could not* have founded first-century Christianity. The various streams that flowed in the river called early Christianity were too numerous and deep for the movement to have had a founder.[2]

To be sure, one or more people named Jesus who taught in aphorisms and stories might have lived in the first century. Other Jews and Gentiles in Palestine at the time engaged in various healing rituals and magical practices. Some might have died at the hands of Rome. But none of these figures founded a religious movement like Christianity. To be sure, early Christianity was built around a figure bearing the name Jesus. Did he exist *as presented in the New Testament?* We consider that unlikely, partly because the New Testament has no single, coherent version of Jesus although the ecclesiastical forces in *later* centuries that selected the material to form the canon held to a version of Jesus more or less in common.

Starting at the Other End of the Continuum

Both inside and outside the Jesus Seminar, most New Testament scholars presuppose that Jesus was an actual historical person in the first century who had a group of followers in Palestine. According to this narrative, the followers, coming to believe Jesus was resurrected, began to meet in what soon became churches. Within a decade or two after Jesus' death, some churches referred to him as the Son of God, the Lord of the Universe, and the Savior of humanity. Many expected him to return to earth to conquer finally all evil forces.

Culturology approaches the problem of the historical Jesus from a different angle. It presupposes that the cosmic Lord Jesus Christ figure came *first* in a special social and political setting as the product of many cultural developments. The figure was first conceived of as a cosmic and supernatural being. Only later did believers see and feel the need to fill in earthly details about his life on earth. This approach has the advantage of recognizing *psychology* of religion's important role in explaining Christianity's emergence.[3]

In the next chapter, we will advance an alternative theory of the Jesus figure. It helps explain why neither the apocalyptic Jesus scholars nor the Jesus Seminar scholars have successfully refuted their rival or established the superiority of their own position. This failure does not reflect a faulty methodology in either camp, but suggests that the time has arrived to direct more research energy toward examining an alternative view. We, however, do not regard the orthodox Jesus as a viable configuration, although we have no doubt it will thrive as a popular appeal for generations to come. The alternative we offer explains why belief in the Jesus of orthodoxy survives. It also explains how *both* the Jesus Seminar Jesus and the apocalyptic Jesus became deeply embedded in the Gospels.

New Testament scholars have been avant-garde in methodology by calling upon the research ideas and tools of archaeology, literary criticism's several branches, anthropology, ethnography, linguistic analysis, philosophy of science and epistemology, sociology, psychiatry, psychology, and traditional historical criticism. Dale Allison has launched New Testament research into new waters by demonstrating ways in which his apocalyptic Jesus compares socially, politically, psychologically, and ideologically with apocalyptic movements universally. Although not persuaded that the Jesus mosaic he has methodically constructed corresponds with one actual person of the first century, we think he has explicated an image or archetype that has profoundly moved, and disturbed, various groups over the centuries.

Our image of the Jesus figure is not of a self-consistent, actual person. It has that in common with the Jesus of orthodoxy. Orthodoxy and we portray the image of a Jesus riddled with inconsistencies and impossibilities. The assumption that such an assemblage ever walked on earth in one flesh is, for us, not a credible option. The Jesus of orthodoxy is the accumulation of intense and sustaining hopes for a better, gentler life; cosmic justice; miraculous solutions; and life beyond the grave. It stems also from resentment toward cruel people in power and even from unmitigated rage toward unbelievers. Although the orthodox profess to accept all the New Testament claims about Jesus and to harmonize them in one historical person, in reality they do what believers have done over the centuries. They interpret the seemingly conflicting passages and claims in such a way as to disguise or touch up the troubling ones so that they will fit with their projected portrait of Jesus.

Our own approach is neither to declare some New Testament passages as inauthentic nor to change them to fit a projected image. The conflicting claims about Jesus are firmly entrenched in the New Testament and Church history. We allow them their intensity, self-contradiction, beauty, ugliness, and boldness. Though all the New Testament descriptions cannot apply to one historical person, they can apply to first-century believers, who are not one being. The churches' descriptions tell us about their fears, dreams, visions, hopes, expectations, longings, projections, hostilities, doubts, and theological demands. The first-century image of Jesus was a projected, shifting montage from the very beginning; and it has continued to be so for two thousand years. It has survived with amazing success over the centuries largely because it began as and has remained an image of many faces. One may view much of Church history as perpetual controversy as to which of the many faces is the "true" one.

The scholars of the apocalyptic Jesus stand out because of their intellectual integrity. In their heart of hearts, many of them wish that Jesus had not suffered his apocalyptic delusions and savage invective. As disciplined scholars, however, they have felt compelled to portray Jesus as less than their ideal person. In our view, the apocalyptic Jesus is the personified reflection of intensely apocalyptic, messianic communities that gave creative vent to their combined desperation and will-to-triumph in the face of perceived threats, rival doctrines, corruption, and wickedness.

The Jesus Seminar scholars rightly discover another face, another Jesus in the first-century literature. Like their opponents, they mistake this wondrous projection for a real person in Palestine who somehow initiated a profound socioreligious movement that thrives to this day. They are, we suggest, correct to see this face of Jesus in the New Testament. For it reflects one of the faces of the first-century believers who responded with astounding moral creativity to their world rampant with corruption, abuse of power, and cruelty. Such a model has survived over the centuries largely because it calls out the better qualities active and latent in ourselves. It is the best of our species projected into an ideal image that genuinely inspires many who contemplate it in all its emotional richness and moral power.

Plato's Response to the Tragedies

Earlier, we conjectured that Plato and Paul, as well as the Gospels, contributed to a worldview that purported to move beyond tragedy and the ultimate "fragility of goodness." In her splendid work *The Fragility of Goodness: Luck and Ethics in Greek Tragedy and Philosophy,* Martha C. Nussbaum makes a powerful case that Plato set out to show how the path of philosophy could provide goodness without fragility (Nussbaum, 1986, pp. 85-233). Thoroughly dissatisfied with the tragic theater, Plato's dialogues became his anti-tragic theater. The Greek poet Pindar had pictured the good person as a young plant: slender, fragile, and constantly needing external nourishment. Though enjoying reason, the human race shows no less vulnerability and finitude than the tender plant or the merely sentient creatures of earth. For every human mortal, bad luck and good luck are ubiquitous companions. Each person is both the agent of his destiny and a tender plant, a creature of contingency. According to ancient Greek ethicists, luck simply happens outside the individual's own agency. The Greeks agonized over their sense of luck. On the one hand, they knew that a life void of contingency and its risks (of love, friendship, passion, ambition) was not a human life. Like Socrates, tragic poets challenged the audience to "know thyself." The tragic theater explored the emotional self with its hills and valleys. For the poets, to know themselves meant knowing not only what they thought, where they originated and what values they embraced, but also how they felt, whether joyful, passionate, compassionate, terrified, awed, dejected, elated, in conflict, or inspired.

On the other hand, the tragic poets knew that the passions and compassions that made them human made them more vulnerable. To be human was to make intense commitments that court heartbreak and agony if ill luck struck. In short, the tragic theater reminded its audience of the terrible risk of goodness.

> The great tragic plots explored the gap between our goodness and our good living, between what we are (our character, intentions, aspirations, values) and how humanly well we manage to live. They show us reversals happening to good-charactered but not divine or invulnerable people, exploring the many ways in which being of a certain good character falls short of sufficiency for *eudaimonia* [i.e., living well and behaving well toward oneself and others]. (Nussbaum, 1986, p. 382)

Plato rejected the poets of the theater because, he believed, they turned human beings into the playthings of fates and undisciplined emotions. The Hebrew tradition projected the human race's earthly beginning in an ideal Garden of Eden. Plato's story, by contrast, portrayed the earth's first human mortals as helpless, hungry, speechless creatures with no medical science and few skills worthy of the name. As humans or proto-humans, they suffered vulnerability both from within and without. Threatened by external forces as well as internal needs and desires ceaselessly conflicting, they lived in confusion and under constant danger.

In Plato's myth, Prometheus, the God of foresight and planning, granted to those miserable creatures the gifts of farming, metalworking, hunting, ship building, speech and writing, and the arts of medicine and weather prediction (Nussbaum, 1986, p. 90). Plato came to see his mission as that of helping his fellow citizens find the wisdom (*sophia*), knowledge (*gnome*) and practical judgment (*techne)* to conquer the internal storms as well as the external threats. He believed that philosophy (the love of *sophia*) led humans away from disrupting contingency and toward greater safety, security and fulfillment.

The Apostle Paul's description of his own divided self (Rom. 7) resembles the description Plato gave of the divided and ungovernable soul. Plato believed his teacher Socrates had discovered a simple, comprehensive value that could order both a person's and the community's life. This comprehensive value could also help control the warring internal passions that increase human vulnerability. Irrational desires could become tamed. Instead of giving the passions free reign to battle one another, Plato would place the reins in the hands of the intellect. The dialectic activity of the intellect as exemplified in the Platonic dialogues became the royal road to human salvation.

The Dark Forest of Vulnerability

For Jewish teachers, the Torah became the divinely revealed path of justice and self-control to follow through the forest of vulnerability. The Hebrew Psalms are filled with emotional and intellectual struggles with the human condition of finitude and contingency. Many prophets cried out against those who, by renouncing justice, made the poor and the needy even more vulnerable.

For the Apostle Paul in particular, the Torah as he perceived it had somehow been turned into something that was not a path to salvation, but a burden and hindrance to righteousness, peace, and salvation. The crucial *problem* for Plato, the Jewish teachers, and Paul was the same in many respects. Paul's answer, however, was neither Plato's justice via the path of the intellect, nor righteousness via the Torah, but Christ via faith. With Christ came righteousness and the order required to sustain goodness and righteousness. As noted earlier, Paul's vision and worldview emerged in part through his contemplating human vulnerability (or *weakness,* as he called it). Having suffered weakness internally and having seen its results in the human tragedy, he craved an absolute, total cure. For Paul personally, the gospel meant triumph. Goodness would not suffer ultimate defeat. Goodness only appeared fragile, for in reality—the apocalyptic reality—goodness was imbedded in the righteousness of the everlasting, victorious God who would eventually transform fragile, unstable human history into a more glorious world. For Paul, the supreme revealer and mediator of that longed-for righteousness and victory was not the Torah or the intellect in quest of *Sophia*. Rather, it *was* Sophia (Wisdom) coming as a slave to die and to be resurrected in triumph. In short, for those "in Christ," tragedy was not the last word.

Personified Love

The idea of a personified or personal mediator has ancient roots. Long before Plato, it could be found in Egypt, where the King was seen as the God Horus mediating divine ways to the Egyptian people. In Plato's masterful dialogue *Symposium*, Socrates speaks of Love as a being existing between God and man to establish community, to break down walls of alienation, and to be the purveyor of friendship between Gods and men (188d). Plato regards Love as the universal impulse toward the Good (*Republic* 505e). Where Love exists, community exists (*Gorgias* 507-508). The Greek word *koinonia* translates as "community" or, in the New Testament, as "fellowship." This Love makes possible the whole world's orderliness, community, and beauty. In one of his poetic myths, Plato speaks of this personified Love as the offspring of Father Resource and Mother Poverty, a theme echoed in Philippians 2:6-11. There, Paul speaks of Jesus Christ who, though being in the form of God the Father, came to earth in the form of a human slave.

Although Plato's figure Love dwells with other great spirits (*Symposium* 202e), he operates among the gods and mortals. It is as if Paul, focusing on this Platonic image of Love, exalts him above all the other great elements and spirits of the universe by making him identical with the Wisdom of God, the Lord of Heaven and Earth. Paul presupposes the existence of angels and principalities, but he views Christ as their superior. Christ alone is the Son of God who harbors the power of God. Therefore, Paul concludes:

> [N]either death, nor life, nor angels, nor rulers, nor things present, nor things to come, nor powers, nor height, nor depth, nor anything else in all creation, will be able to separate us from the love of God in Christ Jesus our Lord. (Rom. 8:38-39)

Nerve Points of Human Frailty

We advance the hypothesis that the four Gospels grew out of the cultural images of a supernatural mediator representing God on earth. The good news (gospel, *euangelion*) is that the supernatural Christ is the answer or solution to human frailty. Attempting to understand more clearly how the details of the supernatural Jesus' life on earth came to be composed, we have spelled out basic elements of human vulnerability. The Gospels' details are in response to at least ten points of human vulnerability or finitude.

Table 1 Ten Points of Human Vulnerability or Finitude

1. Disease & Illness	6. Confusion
2. Death	7. Turmoil of Heart & Emotion
3. Hunger	8. Alienation
4. Political & Social Repression	9. Status Anxiety
5. Guilt	10. Demon Intrusion

The various stories, parables, and incidents of the Gospels were created or appropriated to show that Jesus Christ was the answer to these points of human contingency and vulnerability. Robert Funk once referred to Jesus as the *magnet* that attracted stories and sayings. We offer the key to understanding why some stories and sayings attached themselves to Jesus and some did not: Jesus is first and foremost the one who came to be the Divine Solution to human frailty and vulnerability.

Notes

1 Dr. Barclay M. Newman, Senior Translations Officer of the American Bible Society, contends that through the centuries revisions have often been made by means of translations of the Bible. He goes so far as to say that "theological presuppositions determine the historical perspective." With uncommon frankness, he then adds that in some sense Bible translation should give way to "Bible *transformation*." He defines the latter as the *application* of what is known about God through the person and work of Jesus Christ, the Living Word, to the understanding of the Written Word, especially as regards to matters of race, gender, and social status. (Newman, 1997, p. 7).

2 Both Dostoevsky and Tolstoy knew how misleading it could be to ask *who* founded a movement or city (Dostoevsky, 1992, IV, x, 1, p. 651; Tolstoy, 1970, IX, 1, pp. 667-671; X, 1, pp. 761-765; XI, 1, pp. 917-920).

3 Leslie White tended to play down the psychological factor. More precisely, his culturology absorbed the psychological elements as more or less a constant, especially the element of human finitude and contingency (White, 1971, p. 75).

16 Christ and Human Vulnerability

Two Jesuses, One Tragedy?

The scholars of the Jesus Seminar and those who strongly disagree with their characterization of him appear to be referring to two distinct Jesuses. It is fruitful to ask, "Precisely, at what critical point does the Jesus Seminar part company with Dale Allison, E. P. Sanders, and Clayton Sullivan, who think Jesus was an apocalyptic visionary?" The most obvious answer is that the former scholars do not agree that Jesus actually expected an imminent, God-foreordained catastrophe that would radically transform history instantly.

In a deeply moving epilogue to his book *Jesus of Nazareth: Millenarian Prophet*, Allison acknowledges that the millenarian, ascetic prophet called Jesus plainly was a fool in predicting imminent end of human history as we know it. The apocalyptic enthusiast was wrong in his grandiose predictions, and his departure from the scene was anything but a triumphal exit. Yet, like the Jesus Seminar scholars, Allison wants a Jesus who was not a total fool, a Jesus who had (and has) something worthwhile to offer frail mortals in their struggles against the slings and arrows. What Allison comes up with is a two-pronged message from the millenarian Jesus. First, he was a prophet of judgment implying that God sees through the greedy, power-oriented oppressors who have made the lives of the destitute doubly miserable. God judges the corruption of those in high places (Allison, 1998, pp. 217-218).

Second, the apocalyptic Jesus not only predicts severe, catastrophic judgment against evildoers, but also gives hope and consolation. Allison himself asks if it is a false hope. Surprisingly, his apocalyptic Jesus projects an ideal life that markedly resembles some of the values and human relationships that the Jesus Seminar scholars contend Jesus tried to bring about or at least initiate in his lifetime. Did this Jesus succeed? It is double irony that the Jesus Seminar scholars appear to acknowledge that this Jesus, too, failed, not in his predictions, but largely in his mission. As if that defeat were not sufficient, within a short time, his own disciples grossly distorted his message, turning it into an apocalyptic phantasmagoria by twisting the religion *of* Jesus into a religion *about* Jesus (Funk, 1996, pp. 279-296).

In the penultimate paragraph to his books, Allison dares to ask whether Jesus' predictions of an uncorrupted new order will ever come to pass. Having learned a lesson from the mistake of his deluded prophet, Allison makes no predictions. He concludes that despite his misreading of the times, the millenarian prophet projected the only values worth speaking and dreaming about. Some of the values are those that the Jesus Seminar participants believe Jesus actually spoke of and dreamed about during his brief ministry. In a passage worthy of the ancient Greek tragedians, Allison writes:

> If our wounds never heal, if the outrageous spectacle of a history filled with cataclysmic sadness is never undone, if there is nothing more for those who were slaughtered in the death camps or for six-year olds devoured by cancer, then let us eat and drink, for tomorrow we die. If in the end there is no God to calm this sea of troubles, to raise the dead, and to give good news to the poor, then this is indeed a tale told by an idiot, signifying nothing. (Allison, 1998, p. 219)

Curiously, few religions have envisioned an earthly or heavenly kingdom in which *all* wounds are ultimately healed and every turbulent sea calmed. While agreeing with those who regard Jesus as an apocalyptic visionary, Clayton Sullivan calls attention to the disturbing fact that Jesus did not even envision a world in which all estrangements become reconciled, every hostility transformed, and every grief turned to joy. The apocalyptic Jesus speaks of a spatial Kingdom for righteous believers only. Angels will forcibly bind unbelievers and cast them into a furnace of fire where the inmates will weep and gnash their teeth (Mt. 13: 47-50; Sullivan, 1988, p. 94).

Perhaps the Jesus figure somehow mirrors many of our human moral weaknesses, highest ideals, and fevered longings to transcend the precarious human finitude of which the ancient tragedians dared to remind us.

In exploring the following ten human vulnerability nerve points, we explicate our own conjecture about Christianity's first-century emergence as a response to tragic theater. In contrast to those who have conjectured a historical Jesus as Christianity's originating source, we offer an alternative scenario. The "originating revelation" in the first century was the vision of a cosmic supernatural Jesus Christ (Wisdom of God, Savior, Lord, Son of God). Only gradually, as the envisioned Jesus Christ failed to return with sweeping and dramatic changes, did the communities of believers find it necessary to compose again their image of Christ Jesus, so as to individualize and replenish their "originating revelation." The Gospels served to enrich their Savior with human language and concrete earthly existence. The envisioned Messiah had to become more visualized, more conspicuously human. In the Gospels, the Word was made flesh to make graphic and vivid his triumph over all human vulnerability.

Disease and Illness

Unlike Paul, all four Gospels portray Jesus as a healer. He restores sight, heals a withered limb, makes the lame to walk, heals lepers, and vanquishes fever. Plato placed great hope in medical science and skill, but throngs of people in the Mediterranean world lacked easy access to physicians. Furthermore, even in the first century, medical science was not all Plato had hoped. Sickness and weakness of the body continued to plague many. The Gospels portray Jesus as the Great Physician with final power over disease. They offer stories of his cures as testimony to his promise to include health as integral to full salvation.

In an insightful article on Jesus as a healer, John J. Pilch notes that exegetes can serve as "culture brokers" who help others understand foreign cultures. He maps out what he thinks healing meant to people in first-century Palestine (Pilch, 1993, pp. 154-177; Dewey, Joanna, 1993, pp. 78-193).

Acknowledging his indebtedness to Pilch's medical anthropology, John Dominic Crossan draws an important distinction between:

1) *disease* as biological or mental malfunctioning
2) *illness* as the psychological experience and meaning of the disease.

Crossan argues that Jesus did not cure diseases, but intervened in the harmful *social* process that ostracized the diseased individual and labeled him as less than a person. In short, Jesus' real work was the important one of making the social world more humane. Crossan writes movingly of his Jesus as a man of compassion and force who refused to accept traditional and official sanctions against diseased persons (Crossan, 1994, pp. 81-83).

Crossan's version causes at least one problem. The Gospels portray Jesus as making genuinely *physical and biological changes*, i.e., the withered hand's being restored to a whole hand. The author of this pericope does not claim that Jesus changed the neighbors' minds and hearts so that they would no longer discriminate against the man. Rather, all three of the Synoptic Gospels agree that the man's hand changed, not the Pharisees' hearts.

Crossan, Pilch, Ralph Coffman, Joanna Dewey, E. P. Sanders, and Arthur Kleinman successfully throw considerable light on the way first-century Christians dealt with, defined, and related to disease. They show also that *if* a historical Jesus who healed people existed, he would have operated within his era's cultural beliefs and practices. While innovations might well have happened, they would not have dropped from the blue.

In a carefully developed study of first-century healing expectations, E. P. Sanders notes that physicians did not enjoy the high reputation they do today. (Even in the nineteenth century, medical science was still suspect. In *War and Peace*, Natasha's health improves *despite* the doctors.) Sanders makes it clear that the ancient Greeks, Romans, and Jews did not generally draw the line between the incredible and the credible where contemporary medical science would. Today's research scientists emphasize publicly observable tests of claims under carefully controlled conditions. Among the ancients, some assumed that if a deity could cause a longtime barren woman to become pregnant, he or she could cause a man without eyes to see suddenly. While the ancients could draw a line between reality and fantasy, they did not draw it where perhaps most Americans and Europeans would today (Sanders, 1993a, pp. 135-140). Sanders states that just as shrines and miracle stories of healing throughout the Mediterranean world collected around the Greek God Asclepius, so miraculous healing stories and gospel narratives collected around a charismatic historical Jesus in the first century (Sanders, 1993a, pp. 135-136).

Crossan, Sanders, and the other scholars mentioned above do not pretend that they have proved that a historical Jesus stood behind the Gospels and the epistles of Paul. We do not pretend to prove that no such Jesus existed. Rather, we offer an alternative conjecture, namely, that behind the Gospels stood people who desperately needed a Jesus possessing the power and compassion to heal those suffering from real, crippling, debilitating, painful, and intrusive diseases. They had suffered, or had seen their loved ones suffer, diseases and the accompanying social stigma. Their hearts longed for a healer with the supernatural power to challenge the diseases themselves, to reduce the number of slings and arrows, and to deliver them finally from the ravages of human frailty. They longed for a new world with a deal in life far better than their present ordeal.

Death

Nothing can compare with death as a sure manifestation of human contingency and finitude. The Gospels provide stories of Jesus' raising the dead. The Fourth Gospel portrays Lazarus as dead four days, thus showing Jesus as doing more than restoring a victim merely near death. The supernatural Logos of God has power over death. The Lazarus story (likely Egyptian in an earlier version [Helms, 1988, pp. 96-100]) gravitated to the Jesus figure because of the previous assumption that Jesus enjoyed power over death. The story was intended not only to demonstrate this power, but also to foreshadow Jesus' own resurrection in the narrative. Before the writing of the Fourth Gospel, Paul promised victory over "the last enemy"—death (1 Cor. 15:26). The author of the Fourth Gospel has Jesus say that whoever keeps his, Jesus', word will never see death (8:51).

The Jesus Seminar scholars and most of their contemporary rivals do not regard Jesus' resurrection as a publicly observed event even in principle. Marcus Borg writes that "the resurrection was not a historical event in the ordinary sense of the word." In other words, no one could have caught the risen Christ on camera (Borg, 1994, p. 196n2). Crossan contends that the Gospels had a political agenda in presenting stories of Jesus' resurrection. The stories, therefore, were really about the power and authority of specific leaders among the first-century Christians. Stated more positively, the early Christians debated among themselves as to which direction their faith should take. At least one leader represented each direction. The Gospel stories about the witnesses to the resurrected Jesus were to enhance the spiritual authority of this and that leader over his rivals. "Such narratives...are not about trance or ecstatic experiences but are ways of expressing who is in charge.... These are dramatizations of power and visualizations of authority" (Crossan, 1994b, p. 170).

Crossan's theory suggests that the miracle and resurrection stories tell as much about church politics as about a historical Jesus. In our theory, the *belief* in Jesus' resurrection still needs explaining. Granted that the resurrection stories feed into the political agenda, would the political twist on the stories have been meaningful without the prior belief in Christ's resurrection? The solution is that first-century Christians, like many others of the time, longed for a powerful, supernatural agent to conquer death. Paul understood this. He doubtless already believed abstractly in some version of resurrection. What he came to envision in addition was a supernatural Messiah who possessed deity and yet personally, not abstractly, suffered a human death and subsequently removed death's sting through his own resurrection. Paul perceived this resurrection as "the first fruits" of those who would soon, he believed, follow the Messiah in resurrection. In Christ will all be made to live (1 Cor. 15:22f). We suggest that apocalyptic literature had not only influenced Paul, but also stirred him to think more concretely of resurrection from the dead.

Hunger

Pinder, Plato, and many others before them had written of human hunger and the absolute necessity of food and drink. To show that Jesus possessed the power to solve the perpetual problem of hunger, the three Synoptic Gospels portray his transforming two fish and five loaves into food for thousands who came to hear him. In the Fourth Gospel's sixth chapter (often called the spiritual Gospel), Jesus becomes himself food for the soul, thus satisfying another kind of hunger. For some believers in Jerusalem, hunger apparently grew so serious that Paul sought help for them from the other churches. Since the return of Christ to earth was delayed, some kind of interim ethic became necessary—an ethic of both sharing and working for one's food. This practical moral adaptation became necessary since Jesus' power to solve the hunger problem would presumably not go into full effect until the new age took root.

Crossan portrays Jesus as dealing with hunger in a fascinating way. Instead of generating more food for the hungry, Jesus taught by word and example the message of sharing. This cannot be understood as simply one person with food giving some to the needy. Crossan uses the term "commensality" to refer to a shared table. As he articulates his picture, however, the readers come to see that Crossan is talking about sharing *lives*. "Eating is a behavior which symbolizes feelings and relationships, mediates social status and power, and expresses the boundaries of group identity" (Crossan, 1991, p. 341). This way of looking upon a meal quite naturally leads to meaningful "communion," "Eucharist" (good favor, good grace), and "fellowship" (*koinonia*). We suggest that the people behind the Gospels developed *parallel* interests regarding the problem of hunger. First, they conceived of their Messiah as possessing the power to eliminate hunger. "[T]he poor, sad, hungry and persecuted would soon find their lot reversed" (Kraeling, 1951, p. 153). Second, believers meantime had to eat. One alternative was to take meals together. This meant, of course, sharing food. Acts 4:32-5:11 and 6:1-2 suggest that the Jerusalem believers tried this option. Unfortunately, they generated insufficient food, which prompted James and Peter to ask Paul to urge his churches to help the poor of the Jerusalem church.

In Thessalonica, some believers possibly quit working because they expected Christ's return, which they assumed would eliminate hunger once and forever. Paul had to tell them that those who did not work did not eat (2 Thess. 3:10). Paul offers himself as a model. When among the Thessalonian believers, he worked constantly, earning his own bread and paying his own way even though he had a right to receive food from the church (2 Thess. 3:7-9). He made this same point to the Corinthian church (1 Cor. 9:5-12). The problem of how to share food at common meals seemed never to get itself resolved among the believers (1 Cor. 11:28-34). Paul's apocalyptic promises had to come to terms with empty bellies.

Political and Social Repression

In his critical analysis of the Gospel of Mark, Stephen H. Smith writes:

> [W]e are led to believe that the first Christians were poor, on the whole. We do hear of property-owners, it is true (Acts 4:36-37), but we also hear of the sorry plight of the Jerusalem church, and of the need to send aid (Acts 11:29-30; Rom. 15:26; 1 Cor. 16:1-4). One wonders if the situation at Rome (assuming Mark was writing for that community) was very much different. Certainly a large portion of the members there seem to have been slaves, if their names are anything to go by (Rom. 16), whose wealth would have been minimal. (Smith, Stephen, 1996, p. 30)

The power of Rome brought relative peace under the reign of Augustus Caesar. Later rulers, however, did not enjoy Augustus' popularity. After all, Rome's power depended on exploiting a large population of slaves and conquered peoples. No modern-like middle class lived in the empire, although a very large population existed between the poor and the very rich and influential. In 1 Corinthians Paul noticeably ranks himself with those of lesser means. Yet, textual evidence reveals that some early Christians belonged to the establishment (a centurion, a tradeswoman, a civil servant, a ruler of a synagogue), including Stephanas the Corinthian, Crispus, and Gaius. Abraham J. Malherbe doubtless correctly concludes that while Paul apparently baptized only people from the higher social strata, "he knew that the majority of his converts were from among the poor.... Paul lived with his social equals and used their homes as bases for his missionary operation. Nevertheless, the congregation in Corinth soon counted more members from the lower ranks than the upper" (Malherbe, 1977, pp. 77-78).

Doubtless, the dispute in the Corinthian church over eating meat that had been a part of a pagan ritual reflected different social and economic perspectives (Malherbe, 1977, pp. 85-86). Perhaps more important, Roman society was almost vertical, like a steep pyramid. "The sense of high and low pressed heavily on people" (Malherbe, 1977, p. 86). The different classes carried their own tensions. Paul's 1 Thessalonians epistle clearly states that he and his converts await the divine "Son from heaven" who will deliver them "from the wrath to come" (1 Thess. 1:10). On more than one occasion, Paul wrote of his suffering persecution. At Damascus, the guards of the governor under King Aretas tried to seize him, but he escaped in a basket let down through a window in the wall (2 Cor. 11:32-33). He "fought with beasts at Ephesus." Nevertheless, he took hope, believing that at Christ's return, every rule and authority would be destroyed under God's feet (1 Cor. 15:26-32). Thus, Paul saw himself and his fellow believers as existing in a hostile society. In 2 Thessalonians 1:5-6, he (or someone writing in his name) refers to the suffering and affliction that his readers endured in the hope of being worthy of the kingdom of God. Stridently, he asserts that God deems it just to repay the oppressors with an equal punishment. Christ "with his mighty angels in flaming fire" will descend from heaven for the purpose of "inflicting vengeance upon those who do not know God and upon those who do not obey the Gospel of our Lord Jesus" (2 Thess. 1:7-8).

The writer of 2 Thessalonians envisioned violent treatment of those who caused believers to suffer. Evidently, he believed he lacked sufficient political power to restrain his enemies and those who had caused him and other Christians to suffer. Nevertheless, he envisioned the power of righteousness as returning soon to earth to bring "eternal destruction and exclusion from the presence of the Lord..." (1:9). According to John P. Meier, Jesus' equally apocalyptic vision had prevented him from showing any practical interest in political and social issues. Prophesying the end preoccupied him (Meier, 1991, p. 72).

We suggest that people tend to approach governmental power in one of four ways:

1) become a part of the status quo
2) seek to replace those in the political positions
3) change the system of government
4) avoid the government as much as possible.

According to some versions of the apocalyptic Jesus, his chief goal was to replace those in power with himself or someone else as God's righteous representative on earth. A new King David—son of David—would sit on the throne. Few scholars today regard Jesus as the leader of Zealots dedicated to a violent overthrow of Rome, Herod, and the chief priests. Rather, scholars who see him as an apocalyptic prophet believe his goal was to become the proclaimer of the good news that the present world order would soon undergo in a supernatural upheaval. God's recognized rule would then become conspicuous. Righteousness would spread throughout the land or even the world. God's enemies and the unrighteous would be put in their place, the first becoming last, and the last becoming first.

Marcus Borg, John Dominic Crossan, and Burton Mack deny that Jesus was an apocalyptic visionary. Mack goes so far as to portray Jesus as something of a Hellenized Galilean who ignored the government and politics as much as possible. Jesus was more like the wandering Cynics who mocked the government with its pretensions. According to Mack, Jesus employed clever, aphoristic speech to expose the absurdities and ills of many social conventions of his day. A kind of traveling Socrates, Jesus was a challenging teacher and gadfly stinging the religious hypocrisy and repressive social patterns. He sought to liberate individuals from political and social bondage. Liberation would come, not by their taking up arms or expecting God to overthrow the system, but by their learning to live an authentic life without crippling pretensions and false expectations. At times, Jesus was something of a stand-up comic (Robert Funk's phrase) playfully ridiculing society's absurdities and contradictions. Far from being a Jewish apocalyptic dreamer, Jesus was, Mack contends, scarcely involved with the Jewish world. Instead of making a grand show of cosmic transformation, he dined in private homes and talked with small groups, offering them his sage counsel and helping them overcome some of their harmful illusions (Mack, 1988, pp. 54, 73, 125).

According to both Mack and Funk, only after Jesus' death did the Gospel of Mark's author and others before him turn Jesus into a figure fulfilling some of their own needs and expectations. The story of Jesus' overturning the money tables in the temple, for example, is a crucial scene for those who portray Jesus as an apocalyptic figure. For Burton Mack, however, the temple act cannot be historical. Where did it come from? Mark's imagination. This is not to say that Mark knowingly invented a tale out of thin air. Rather, he patterned the entire passion narrative largely after the stock story of the persecuted Righteous One (Mack, 1988, p. 270). Randel Helms thinks the author of Mark inherited the episodes of the passion story and did not know they were structured by a series of Old Testament verses from Zechariah, Isaiah, and the Psalms. For the most part, they were carefully constructed typological fictions, happenings "according to the Scriptures" (Helms, 1988, p. 108). Ingredients going into the scene of Jesus' disruptive activities in the temple likely came from three prophets—Jeremiah 7:1-15; 26:1-15; Malachi 3:1-5; and especially Isaiah 56:1-8.

Agreeing that Jesus was a sage who did much of what Mack says he did, Marcus Borg adds that Jesus was far more than a traveling Cynic sage. Jesus was a subversive Jewish teacher of wisdom, a prophet, and the founder of a renewal movement. Borg contends also that Jesus did indeed set out to transform the social and political system by expounding an "alternative culture" (Borg, 1991). Unlike Mack, Borg believes Jesus was steeped in the Jewish faith and, like Elijah, had ecstatic religious experiences and gained a reputation as an enlightened one, a healer, a social prophet, and someone who challenged the sociopolitical repression implicit in the "purity system" of his time (Borg, 1984; Borg, 1994b, ch. 3). Perhaps Borg's most important contribution lies in his detailed description and analysis of "purity politics." Basically, the elite political powers of Palestine had created a sweet deal for themselves through heavy taxation of the peasants (agriculturists), artisans, and the "unclean" and degraded classes. According to Borg, Jesus as a social prophet attacked the purity system because it was a religious disguise for cruel discrimination against women, the poor, the peasants, the chronically ill, and the maimed. The high priestly families had become large landowners, not by working, but by adopting the political powers' practice of extorting through an outrageously wicked tax system. This official thievery allowed the elite to confiscate the peasants' land and property (Coote and Coote, 1990, p. 15; Borg, 1994a, ch. 5).

Jesus' conflict with the power brokers, Borg argues, centered on elementary fairness and decency, not holiness. To expose the political power that undergirded bigotry, Jesus created controversy over the Sabbath, purity texts, temple, and table fellowship (Borg, 1994a, p. 26).

Borg agrees fundamentally with Elisabeth Schüssler Fiorenza's contention that, contrary to Sanders and Mack, Jesus engaged deeply in exposing the contradictions and cruelty of his era's sociopolitical practices. She argues that Jesus' talk about the kingdom of God had little to do with a future, dramatic reversal of history. Rather, Jesus sought a transformation of this world, a Jewish life based on a different vision of human community and God's graciousness. She points out that women played central roles in the early Christian missionary movement (Fiorenza, 1983, pp. 72-159). While first-century Judaism had deep roots in patriarchy, Fiorenza notes, the "feminist impulse" also existed within Judaism (Fiorenza, 1983, p. 107).

No one can take the leading contemporary scholars' conclusions on the historical Jesus question and weave them into a coherent picture of Jesus' response to the severe first-century social and political repression. If Jesus was a profound social reformer, why were all twelve of his closest disciples males? On the Mount of Transfiguration, only men were presumably present. When an important church conference took place in Antioch sometime before 50 CE, why did Paul mention the key male characters—the pillars—but refer to no women? When Luke in Acts 15 gave, in his own way, the account of the Antioch conference, he talked of men, but did not mention even one woman. If Jesus had made women equals, how could James and Peter have overlooked it? How could Paul and Barnabas have never heard of it, especially when the Antioch conference had been called primarily to deal with discrimination?

Often, people answer that Jesus' followers very quickly fell back into their old patriarchal habits. While a plausible conjecture, it is not a powerful argument. It gives us either a Jesus who could not communicate his most important teachings or disciples who were truly as thickheaded as Mark portrays them. It also implies that somehow Jesus' genuinely revolutionary social teachings were preserved, albeit often garbled and blended with all sorts of actions and teachings having little to do with him or his ministry. In short, Jesus' friends did to his ministry what his cleverest enemies had not even imagined. They used his name to promote their own agendas and ideologies.

By contrast, we suggest that the early Christians *started* with the projected image of the cosmic Savior and *continued* projecting onto this image their own values, hopes, deep-seated prejudices, dearest aspirations, profoundest teachings and deepest longings for a better life and world. They envisioned a Savior who could in their mind come to earth and conquer human vulnerability. The stories attributed to Jesus are their projections, appropriations, and adaptations, which they sincerely believed belonged to their Lord and Savior when he presumably walked on earth. If in the Gospels Jesus becomes a mixture of diverse and often conflicting ingredients, it is because those ingredients represent the conflicts and diversity within the communities that gave birth to the Gospels. Some early Christians expected an apocalyptic end. Others sought a better way to live on earth, striving not only to live within a political system that they did not create, but also to come to terms with the Torah as well as the temptations, pressures, and hardships of daily living. In addition, they strove for a better understanding of the world and their place within it. Political, social, and economic pressures were real factors. When their Lord and Savior failed to return as expected, they had either to live with his absence or come to believe that while on earth he had somehow manifested the glory of God and the triumph of goodness. The early Christians came gradually to believe that during his years on earth, the Son of God actually did give sage counsel and perform many good and marvelous works as testimony to God's presence and his goodness. Despite the repression all around, God in Jesus had shown in signs and wonders that goodness was not a fragile thing but, rather, the manifestation of God's power on earth. In short, his coming was good news, a gospel far superior to the gospel of Augustus the man.

Our theory in no way precludes the possibility, or even the likelihood, that in Palestine of the first century BCE and the early first century CE various individuals had followers who regarded them as either prophets, healers, teachers, sages, miracle workers, social reformers, messiahs, holy men, martyrs, or political radicals. Doubtless, from Galilee to the Dead Sea, some followers viewed their hero as embodying more than one of these roles. Some heroes might well have carried the name "Jesus" or a similar name. *Christ*ianity has cultural and literary sources that provided believers with various images of a supernatural, cosmic figure. Quite possibly, versions of a few putative feats or sayings attributed to some earthly heroes became attached to the literary Jesus of the Gospels. None of the earthly Jesuses or heroes, however, founded early Christianity.

Guilt

A major crisis of human vulnerability is moral failure and accompanying guilt. When people view sin as an insult to the deity, guilt becomes an even heavier burden. Since the eyes of heaven can follow transgressors wherever they go and can read the inmost secrets and evil thoughts, forgiveness and reconciliation become imperative. In Galatians and Romans, Paul dealt directly with the avenues to forgiveness. The Synoptic Gospels in particular included stories of Jesus' power to forgive sin. When challenged—who can forgive sins but God only?—Jesus did not back down. Despite the charge of blasphemy raised against him, he stated plainly that the Son of man had the authority on earth to forgive sins (Mk. 2:7; Mt. 9:6; Lk. 5:21-24). The Fourth Gospel portrayed Jesus as the Lamb of God who bears away the sin of the world (1:29). The implied author of this Gospel went out of his way to portray Jesus as not himself being baptized by John the baptizer although he attended the baptism ritual. Rather, John says that whereas he himself baptized only with water, Christ will baptize with the Holy Spirit. When two of John's disciples see Jesus on the next day, they follow him (Jn. 1:32-37) and presumably forsake John. Later in the Fourth Gospel, all the disciples of Jesus are given the Holy Spirit and the accompanying authority both to forgive sin and to withhold forgiveness (Jn. 20:22). By the time Matthew and the Fourth Gospel came to be written, the question of who *controls* forgiveness had not only emerged, but evidently created controversy.

The question of guilt raises also the problem of identifying the specific violations committed. The Gospels portray Jesus in conflict with certain Jewish leaders over such matters as the Sabbath and purity regulations. Matthew in particular attempts to demonstrate that Jesus does not violate the Torah, but fulfills it. The Fourth Gospel, presumably written later, gives us a Jesus who conspicuously does not identify himself as the Torah's fulfillment. The canyon between the Jewish and Christian communities has grown wider and deeper. In Matthew and Luke, John complains that "this generation" wrongly accused John the baptizer of having a demon. In the Fourth Gospel, however, it is Jesus who levels the charge, not against John, but against those Jews who had once believed in him but did not, says Jesus, "continue in my word" (Jn. 8:31). Not mincing his words, Jesus in John 8:44 tells the Jews that they are of "your father the devil." He says their will is to satisfy the devil's desires. Among such desires, he says, are to lie and commit murder. These Jews return the insult by repeating that Jesus has a demon (Jn. 8:48, 52).

Clearly, the hostility has become bitter, and the drive to heap guilt upon "the Jews" is strong. We suggest that this story reflects the hostility between at least one Christian community and a Jewish community. Apparently, some people felt they had been expelled from the synagogue for believing that Jesus was the Lord and therefore worthy of worship (Jn. 9:22, 34, 38). In the Fourth Gospel, Jesus informs the Pharisees that their *guilt* remains because they see his miracles but refuse to believe in him (Jn. 9:40-41). Evidently, by the time the Fourth Gospel was written, a number of Christians had come to think that not believing in Christ's deity and divine mission was itself a sin incurring utmost guilt.

A chilling irony hangs over this. The early Christians came to believe in a supernatural Savior Jesus Christ because they needed a being with divine authority to bear away their sin. It now turns out that not believing Jesus to be the divine Savior guarantees condemnation. Since the "only Son" is defined as the light of the world (8:12), all who do not believe in him are classified as living in darkness (3:18-21). *Honest* disagreement is not set forth as an option.

According to New Testament scholar Robert Funk, the orthodox view of Jesus as the supernatural Savior whose sacrifice atones for sin is a theological weight added to a Jesus who taught those about him to see forgiveness in a new light. Funk's Jesus forgives because his Father forgives. Jesus requires only that the forgiven person become an agent of forgiveness. Funk's Jesus offers, not a strict bookkeeping religion, but a new level of joyous reciprocity. By removing control of forgiveness from the professed forgiveness brokers, Jesus says in effect that forgiveness comes only when one has both suffered hurt and recognized his or her own role in hurting others. Forgiveness has the power to release the flow of goodness in the community and the world (Funk, 1996, pp. 310-311). This, we contend, comprises the astounding insight that some early Christians explored in depth despite other Christians' tying forgiveness to a theological doctrine about atonement. The truth behind most theories of atonement is that human evil costs dearly. The cruelty behind the so-called objective theory of atonement comes by confusing vicarious suffering with vicarious punishment.

Confusion

The Gospel of Mark portrays Jesus' disciples as terribly confused and slow to grasp the point despite their membership in Jesus' inner circle. To them, he explains the meaning of his parables. Interpreters of Mark have wondered why the disciples appear to have such limited insight and understanding. Whatever the author's intention, one thing is quite clear. In the Gospel of Mark, Jesus both *has* and *is* the Solution to the riddles. Whatever the "secret" is in Mark, Jesus is presented as the one who knows the truth behind it.

Matthew (13:34-35) portrays Jesus as at least a teacher who tells parables to help relieve his hearers of their ignorance and confusion. According to the Synoptic Gospels, the people at Capernaum, of Galilee found his authoritative teaching astonishing. Mark and Matthew add that his teaching was "not as the scribes" (Mt. 7:28f; Mk. 1:22). All Four Gospels have him explaining the scriptures to people who were themselves acknowledged teachers. In Matthew and Luke, Jesus' parables help his hearers understand. He also reasons with his opponents the way a rabbi might with his students. In dialogue, Jesus, like Socrates, appears quite capable of handling his enemies' arguments and tricks. When a few Pharisees and Herodians attempt to trap him with his own words, he so surprises them with his answer that even they marvel at him.

The Jesus of the Fourth Gospel makes long speeches that explicate his claim to be the Way, the Truth, the Life, and the Light of the World (Jn. 8:12 14:6). Woven with his claim to teach only what the Father has taught him (Jn. 7:16, 8:28) are the miracle stories, which often serve as cues for him to assume his role as teacher. If in the Roman Empire confusion arose regarding the path to salvation and God, the Jesus of the Fourth Gospel is portrayed as the light leading to eternal life (Jn. 12:50). Jesus promises also to continue to give light and teaching by sending the Counselor, the Holy Spirit, to teach his followers. In the Fourth Gospel, the Holy Spirit comes after Christ not only to bear witness to Christ's past ministry, but also to make operative what Christ has already effected. More teaching and explaining become necessary as the churches must deal with Christ's failure to return. They feel compelled also to reevaluate, revise their past visions, and satisfy their growing curiosity.

Philosopher Karl Popper correctly states that our species has a thirst for explanations, an insatiable curiosity. We not only create stories and theories, but also often live by them to see how they work (Popper, 1991, p. 95). We even live in the narratives that our forebears have constructed. The wise accept them as their cognitive house, a gift that came, not of their own doing, but by the grace of those who lived before them. Over the years, they make what they hope will be improvements on the narrative, their cognitive inheritance, for their sake and the sake of those who will follow.

Narratology's emergence in biblical criticism has allowed exegetes to see how often biblical stories (including theological follow-up) were modified to answer new questions or improve aspects of older versions. Where external forces or internal fears do not intimidate the human mind, human communities tend to join some of their deepest rituals with narrative explanations. When verbal rituals in religion fall into crises or dead ends, they cry out for a wider and deeper explanatory narrative to save them. Paul's worldview narrates the story of the Son of God, who was incarnated, crucified, and resurrected. In time, however, more narration became necessary. The limited Christian narrative had to expand, enriching itself with many details between the arrival of the Savior and his resurrection. Thus developed the Gospels and the sources that fed into them.

Although each Gospel author or redactor had a distinctive agenda, they all had the concern to provide a cognitive map or narrative guide into the acts and teachings of the cosmic Son of God. Luke, for example, recognized that other narratives had preceded his. His purpose was to start earlier in the story than did Mark and to make the whole narrative more orderly. He saw the need for a more detailed narrative guide that would counter the encroaching forest of confusion.

Later, the Fourth Gospel author could not be content to begin with Jesus' birth, where Luke and Matthew begin. Whereas Luke's beginning (*arches*) was on earth, the Fourth Gospel's beginning (*arche*) was with God and the Logos. The theme of the beginning appears also in 1 John 1:1; 2:7, 13 and Revelation 3:14, the latter referring to Christ as the *arche* of God's creation.

The paradox, however, always waits in the wings. Each new explanatory narrative with its revisions not only satisfies the mind, but also generates new problems. We cannot avoid the threat of new confusion. Augustine described the human heart as restless. Equally restless is the human mind. The Gospels offered astonishing answers and left a legacy of astounding problems. Many see the problems as windows. Where narrative problems abound, the quest for meaningful insights and answers abounds still more.

Turmoil and War

Plato, the Stoics, and others in the ancient world gave counsel on ways to gain peace. In Luke's Gospel, Jesus' birth is accompanied by an angelic multitude announcing glory to God and peace on earth for those who please him. The Gospels and Paul say little or nothing about Jesus' power to bring peace among nations through either political negotiation or the transformation of individuals. Rather, they make the general assumption that governments rule by the sword. In the Gospels, Jesus makes no clear-cut predictions that the nations will lay down their arms for the sake of peace. Matthew and Luke go so far as to have Jesus say he came, not to bring peace, but a sword. Luke 22 provides a curious scene in which Jesus tells his disciples that if anyone has no sword he should sell his mantle and buy a sword. The whole point, however, is to make the swords a part of the fulfillment of Scripture (Isa. 53:12). Hence, when the disciples say they have *two* swords, Jesus indicates that two are enough—apparently for fulfilling the prophecy (Lk. 22:36-38). In the same Luke 22, an armed crowd comes to arrest Jesus. Someone nearby draws a sword, and, apparently to defend Jesus, cuts off the ear of the high priest's slave. Jesus stops the violence, tells the swordsman to return his weapon, and restores the severed ear. Matthew elaborates by having Jesus say that those who take the sword will perish by it. Then Jesus explains that he could have appealed to the Father, who would have immediately dispatched twelve legions of angels (Mt. 26:52-55). The Father does not dispatch them, however, because fulfillment of Scripture demands Jesus' arrest.

Rather than represent Jesus as having the power to eliminate turmoil among nations, the Synoptic Gospels indicate that dramatic and sudden apocalyptic interventions will change the world order at the coming of the Son of man. In 2 Thessalonians, Paul (or someone writing in his name) indicates that the world's turmoil will actually increase just before Christ returns to punish the evildoers and the Man of Lawlessness. Thereafter, believers will enjoy peace. This peaceful environment will, however, presumably be in heaven rather than on earth, after the last trumpet and the resurrection (1 Cor. 15:51-53).

Paul and the Fourth Gospel in particular portray another sort of triumph over turmoil. In John 16:33, Jesus frankly tells his followers they will have turmoil in "this world." He tells them, nevertheless, to take heart because he has overcome the world. Jesus promises to leave his peace with them, but not the kind of peace that the world gives. Then he urges them to be neither troubled nor afraid (Jn. 14:27).

More than any other New Testament writer, Paul talks about peace with God and of the joy and peace that come through believing. Peace is one of the fruits of the Spirit. In Philippians 4:7, Paul affirms that the peace of God passes all comprehension.

The Gospels and Paul's letters reveal that considerable turmoil existed among the early Christians. Life proved difficult for most of them. The hope of peace and tranquility had doubtless drawn many to Paul's preaching about the Savior, to the community of believers, and to the promises of eventual deliverance from all turmoil and war within and without.

Alienation

In some respects, the cold, hard fact of human self-alienation is the most perplexing manifestation of human finitude. Why should this remarkable creature of the earth be so fiercely at war with itself? In addition, why is each individual self divided at times? Paul wrestled with the question of human alienation from the Creator. When writing of reconciliation, he seems to write out of desperation. Yet, he dares to advance the vision that in Christ there is neither Jew nor Greek, freeman nor slave, male nor female. All are one. The Fourth Gospel has Jesus praying that all the believers may be one (Jn. 17:21). They will not be left as orphans (Jn. 14:16). Their oneness will hold in the form of love among the believers. Although alienated from the world (*in* the world but not *of* it), they are bound to one another and to God (Jn. 13:34).

Alienation is so fundamental to human existence, that few religions could even imagine *universal and* total reconciliation. Far from offering a vision of universal reconciliation, the implied author of the Gospel of Matthew assumes that alienation is a *permanent* part of reality. When the Son of man comes in his glory, the unrighteous and the unmerciful will be forever alienated to suffer punishment. The righteous, however, will enjoy eternal life (Mt. 25:31-46). In many respects, Matthew perceives salvation as, in part, deliverance *from* the unrighteous. He offers no hope of universal reconciliation. To be reconciled to God and to other righteous believers is sufficient. When writing of family members alienated from one another, both Matthew and Luke provide insight into conflicts at play in the early Christian churches. They depict Jesus as saying that anyone who loves family members more than they love him is unworthy of being his disciple (Mt. 10:37-38). Surprisingly, Luke has Jesus saying that anyone who cannot *hate* family members and even his own life cannot be his disciple (Lk. 14:26).

Alienation is such a deep-seated condition of human existence that it seems to have what might one might call "trans-species" roots. The ancient amity-enmity complex conspicuously pervades the Book of Revelation. The Paul of the Epistle to the Romans appears to be the only New Testament writer to have been greatly disturbed by the assumption that perhaps most of the human race will suffer permanent estrangement and even endless punishment, forever alienated from God and all righteous believers. For the early Christians, Christ was the solution to Problem A—the crisis of gaining access to salvation for themselves and their fellow believers. They seemed not to focus on Problem B—that most of the human race will suffer damnation. Christ is not projected as the solution to the problem because it perhaps was overwhelming. Humans could scarcely express it in words, thus leaving it isolated to the deepest cavern of the unconscious. Only in later centuries could a few Christians bring the problem to the surface (Clement of Alexander, Oregin, and Gregory of Nyssa).

Status Anxiety

In political theory, equality ranks as one of the more difficult ideals to discuss without falling into contradiction. Two influential voices of the Jesus Seminar—Marcus Borg and John Dominic Crossan—contend that in both deed and word Jesus taught equality. The Seminar's leader, Robert Funk, thinks Jesus deliberately challenged the social gates that closed people off from equality.

> *Jesus kept an open table.* Jesus ate promiscuously with sinners, toll collectors, prostitutes, lepers, and other social misfits and quarantined people during his life. (He also hobnobbed with the affluent and the powerful, but those associations pose less a problem for us.) Yet his followers, in ritualizing the meal Jesus ate periodically with his friends, began to limit participation to those who belonged to the Christian community. (Funk, 1996, p. 310)

According to Funk, Jesus spoke in parables and aphorisms to help his hearers open their hearts and minds to new and better ways to relate to one another. Consequently, Jesus rarely gave a straight answer because in truth he was a nonviolent revolutionist dedicated to moving his audience to ask searching questions of their own. Jesus' parables arrest the hearers' attention by caricature, hyperbole, or even satire. (Funk, 1996, p. 173). His deeds serve to undermine vicious prejudices and ancient grudges. Knowing that some of his fellow Jews despised the Samaritans, Jesus told the Good Samaritan story. In this parable, the Samaritan has so evidently forgiven the Jews that he can forgo his reaction to discrimination by helping someone in need. More important, a person in need could *accept help* from someone of low status. Thus, Jesus intentionally undermined the cruel scheme of reducing the status of whole classes of people—whether Jew or Samaritan. (Funk, 1996, p. 175). Despite honest disagreements, the leading Jesus Seminar figures hold that Jesus openly exposed the evils and hypocrisy of "the domination system." Bernard Brandon Scott explains:

> Jesus' language offered to his audience an alternative to the world in which they were trapped. A world burdened by purity or shame. A world where those on the bottom are imprisoned in unchangeable structures awaiting a divine solution. A world in which enemies threaten at every point. Jesus in his language offers a counter world, a vision, an openness to experience. (Scott, Bernard, 1997, p. 12)

Robert Funk, who believes a historical Jesus existed behind the Gospels, contends that Jesus spent much of his ministry challenging the status scheme of his day. "Jesus steadily privileged those marginalized in his society—the diseased, the infirm, women, children, toll collectors, gentile supplicants, perhaps even Samaritans—precisely because they were regarded as the *enemy*, the outsider, the victim" (Scott, Bernard, 1997, p. 179).

Crossan and Borg speak of Jesus' concern for equality. But equality in *what*? Several Jesus Seminar scholars seem to imply that Jesus placed everyone on the same footing in God's eyes in that all were his children, thus making everyone siblings. The Jesus in the Gospels did not, however, articulate an all-inclusive principle of equality. Rather, if Funk, Borg, and Crossan are right, Jesus affirmed something like a floor of dignity. No one is to be placed below that floor. Jesus' acts, more than his words, teach this. As Funk stated it, "Jesus kept an open table."

The principle of equality may have to give way to the principle of fairness, which is difficult enough. Even here, however, the acts and deeds of Jesus in the Gospels may throw more light on the status problem than would a carefully worded definition. Funk's position is not that Jesus gave the final formulation of equality, fairness, and status. Rather, Jesus' deeds, parables, and sayings challenged his hearers to reevaluate their own formulations.

Our position is that the New Testament discloses severe status anxiety among the early Christian communities. As participants in a heavily anthropomorphic paradigm, they could not help being concerned with their position in the cosmic scheme of things. Where did they stand in God's eyes? Paul and the author of the Epistle of the Hebrews seemed to concern themselves with the question of the position that he and his fellow believers had regarding angels. If believers could be "in Christ," then Paul could conclude that, like Christ, believers will "judge angels" (1 Cor. 6:3). Paul not only accepted the diversity of gifts among believers, but also argued that all the gifts were necessary to the whole body so that no one in the church could reduce another's gift as unnecessary. Yet, Paul doubtless regarded his own status as that of unquestioned authority. Apostles rank first in the list of gifts. Paul believes that the church—the body—cannot function properly without acknowledgement of his apostolic authority and status. Apparently, in the Corinthian church, some of those designated as prophets had developed a measure of competition among themselves. As an apostle, Paul felt he had the authority to instruct them to wait their turn when prophesying and to listen to one another's prophecy rather than to speak all at the same moment. When challenged by other apostles, Paul denounced some of his rivals as false apostles, and they evidently returned the denunciation. As a channel of divine revelation, he took second place to neither James nor Peter. Although he had not seen Jesus in the flesh, he had, he insisted, seen Jesus as the resurrected Christ and had received revelations from him. (We must add that Paul nowhere suggests that Peter or James knew Jesus in the flesh.)

In the past decade and a half, authors have written much about the status of women in early Christianity. In Galatians 3:28, Paul had written that in Christ there was neither Jew nor Greek, neither slave nor free, neither male nor female. In 1 Corinthians 12:13, nevertheless, when writing that all believers are one in body, he leaves out "male or female." This omission is striking because the passage does not leave out "Jews or Greeks" and "slaves or free." They all drink of one Spirit. Why then the omission of "male or female"? Chapter 14 of the same epistle provides perhaps the answer. It contains a passage that reduces the status of women to that of inferior beings.

> As in all the churches of the saints, the women should be silent in the churches. For they are not permitted to speak, but should be subordinate, as the law also says. If there is anything they desire to know, let them ask their husbands at home. For it is shameful for a woman to speak in church. Or did the word of God originate with you? Or are you the only ones it has reached? (1 Cor. 14:33-36)

These words clash so with other words Paul has written that we wonder if a later hand inserted the passage. It reflects the later concerns of the authoritarian, high-handed, status-anxious author of the Pastoral Epistles (1 and 2 Tim. and Titus). Recently, a few scholars have attempted to show that the so-called Pastoral Epistles are really Paul's letters written in his later years. Even if true, an important qualification would have to be added: Paul in his later years became a radically different person, suffering a hardening of the moral categories, perhaps retracing an earlier stage of his life before his conversion-calling.

The question of the status of women in Paul's acknowledged letters and in the Gospels of Mark and Luke as well as Gospels outside the canon offers promise of continuing fruitful research. In her carefully reasoned article "Jesus, Mary Magdalene and Salome," Kathleen E. Corley writes:

> Although it is unlikely that Jesus challenged the inequality between men and women in his culture, the presence of women among the disciples remains a notable characteristic of his movement and one that drew criticism from his contemporaries. That presence further indicates the complexity and diversity of women's religious choices in antiquity. And like the women in the Jesus movement, women were present and criticized for their association with men among the Cynics, Epicureans, Pythagoreans, Stoics, and the Therapeute of Alexandria. (Corley, 1996, p. 15; Corley, 1993; Corley, 1998)

Status anxiety remains perhaps one of the most difficult psychological problems with which the human species must contend. Paul had to deal with it as best he could in the Corinthian church, where believers had divided into factions, some claiming to belong to Apollos, others to Cephas, and some to Paul. One faction claimed to belong to Christ (1 Cor. 1:11-17; 3:22-23). The Gospel of Mark tells the humorous story of Zebedee's two sons approaching Jesus to ask a stupendous favor. When Jesus comes in his glory, they want to flank him, one brother on his right hand, the other on his left. When the other disciples hear of this, they become indignant. Perhaps embarrassed by this story in Mark, Luke omitted it, saying only that a dispute arose as to whom to regard as the greatest among them. Matthew added that the two brothers' mother came to beg on her knees that Jesus give her sons the favored status in his kingdom. Jesus tells all the disciples that whoever wants to be first should be the slave of the others (Mk. 10:35-45; Mt. 20:20-28). Luke has Jesus saying that the greatest should become as the youngest or as the leader who serves (Lk. 22: 24-27).

A thread throughout the Synoptic Gospels counters status anxiety with the counsel to learn to serve others. Greatness comes in service. In some ways, one may see the Golden Rule as another way to counter status anxiety and the envy that often accompanies it. Robert Funk notes Jesus' technique of using paradox to open the heart. His Jesus counsels his followers to gain status by enriching the wholesome status of others. Before the Gospels, Paul had set the stage for this creative paradox by urging the believers at Philippi to have the mind of Christ, who humbled himself by taking on human form (Phil. 2:5-8). This approach has ancient roots in the Socratic principle that the soul's health fares better if one endures harm rather than initiates it. In perhaps the most informative book written on envy, sociologist Helmut Schoeck explains "that the feeling of envy and jealousy is experienced and learned primarily in the sibling group and that these feelings, on reaching a certain intensity, have an exceptionally inhibiting and destructive effect on the personality" (Schoeck, 1996, p. 85).

By allowing many, or perhaps virtually everyone, in the church to have at least one gift, Paul makes it possible for the individual to enjoy the status of being essential to the whole body. Speaking in tongues was one of the gifts. Apparently, in the Corinthian church, some believers used this gift to gain disproportionate status. This may account for Paul's going out of his way to keep it as a gift but, at the same time, to rank it last on the list of gifts.

After giving the list, Paul moves directly to "a more excellent way"—love. The famous 1 Corinthians 13 passage may very well be Paul's response to status anxiety in the church. One mark of envy is that it feeds on resentment and takes pleasure in another's downfall. Paul says love is not resentful and instead of taking pleasure in doing evil, love rejoices in what is right (1 Cor. 13: 5-6). We conjecture that Paul's theory that all members were "in Christ" dealt with status anxiety in two ways. First, oneness with the Son of God gave believers a transcendent status considered unsurpassed in the world. Second, by emphasizing that being "in Christ" entails humility and even suffering (Rom. 6:6, 8:17; 2 Cor. 1:17, 4:11; Phil. 1:29, 3:10; Gal. 2:20), Paul attempted to undermine the assumption that status came by gaining control and power over others.

Demons

Belief in demons and their intrusion into human affairs was widespread in the first-century Mediterranean world. According to the Synoptic Gospels, demons could be aggressive, causing such physical diseases as deafness, loss of speech, paralysis, and other maladies. In Paul's worldview, cosmic evil forces ruled the present age, although even they were somehow under divine control. Paul found the Torah as he understood it ineffectual in countering the supernatural evil forces. The crisis called for a *cosmic* solution, the Son of God's defeating Satan and his demonic forces. Although Paul might not have been the last redactor of the epistle called Ephesians, it is built on Paul's foundation. This epistle portrays Christ as the one who can provide believers with special power to oppose the spiritual hosts of wickedness.

> For our struggle is not against enemies of blood and flesh, but against the rulers, against the authorities, against the cosmic powers of this present darkness, against the spiritual forces of evil in the heavenly places. (Eph. 6:12)

Paul believed that he and others needed power to oppose "the prince of the power of the air, the spirit that is now at work in the sons of disobedience" (Eph. 2:2). A cosmic Savior was needed to conquer cosmic evils. The Synoptic Gospels supplied specific examples of Christ's power over demons on earth. Some demons recognized him as a supernatural force even though the disciples seemed confused about him (Mk. 1:25; 5:7; 8:27-33). Ancient Palestine had no hospitals for the mentally ill, no asylums, and no institutions beyond the family to care for the permanently sick. Family members not willing to put their ailing members out on the street had to contend the best they could. Many families lived in quiet desperation and were very eager to believe that someone could exorcise demons or heal the afflicted of their illnesses (Smith, Morton, 1978, pp. 8-9; Crossan, 1991, p. 319).

Paul and other early Christians inherited the highly anthropomorphic paradigm that populated the universe with angels and demons. They did not question either the existence of such beings or their power to influence human life. Paul's apocalyptic outlook provided him a way to conceive of the ruling evil forces' ending in permanent defeat. Their defeat was a part of the divine plan of salvation.

The Synoptic Gospels had the challenge of showing Jesus on earth as already confronting demons. In one incident, however, Jesus finds himself accused of being possessed by Beelzebul, the prince of demons (Mk. 3:22, Mt. 12:24, Lk. 11:15). Clearly, Jesus turns his enemies' premises on them by arguing that it would make no sense for Satan to work against himself by casting out his own demons. A grim passage follows about the so-called "unpardonable sin." Jesus tells his accusers that in charging that he was possessed by an unclean spirit, they have just committed the sin that can never be forgiven in this world or the next (Mt. 12:31-32; Mk. 3:28-30).

This passage very likely reflects the experience of some early Christians who were themselves accused of demon possession. When two shamans meet in bitter disagreement, how can they reckon with each other's claiming to be in touch with supernatural power to heal the sick and exorcise demons? Each could first acknowledge the opponent to be in contact with supernatural powers, but then call the supernatural power *evil*.

But this is not the only approach. In Acts 14, Luke tells the story of Paul and Barnabas in Lystra encountering a man who had been crippled from birth. Paul heals him instantly, and suddenly a crowd looking on grows excited and proclaims Barnabas to be Zeus and Paul, Hermes. "The Gods have come down to us in the likeness of men," the people shout. The priest of Zeus, instead of denouncing the visitors as demonic, wants to join the crowd in offering a sacrifice to Barnabas and Paul.

People regarded the world in which Paul, Barnabas, and the Gospel writers lived as filled with angels, Gods, and demons. Some early Christians considered the Gentiles' Gods as demons (1 Cor. 10:20-21). Once a paradigm has taken firm hold of whole populations and has been a tradition for centuries, it will not likely be overthrown in one generation. We suggested earlier that Paul and the first Christians did not bring about a paradigm shift in the thinking of their contemporaries. Rather, Paul in particular, either developed a new model or expanded one he had received. This model with the Son of God at the center reformulated some problems of the first century. As a metaphysical or cosmological system, however, it remained solidly within the ancient paradigm of anthropomorphism. We suggest that Christianity's growth in later centuries can be better understood by examining the organizational skills of its leaders and, of course, the political power that came with Emperor Constantine's reputed conversion. The emperor's conversion, however, did not mean that he possessed the power to initiate a paradigm shift. Rather, he accepted the paradigm and made alliances with certain church bishops against their rivals.

David Livingston, the esteemed missionary to the Bakwin Tribe in the 1840s, succeeded in converting only one person, the tribal Chief Sechele. After the conversion, Livingtston persuaded Sechele to give up the rainmaking ritual as a heathen ceremony. Unfortunately, a prolonged drought followed immediately. Eventually, the tribe forced their chief to start the rainmaking ceremony again (Gilles, 1993, p. 229). A symbolic system does not yield easily to a rival system (Geertz, 1973, pp. 212-220, 250-251).

Christianity, both before and after Constantine, has been a process of maneuvering within the anthropomorphic paradigm. We suggest that the Jesus Seminar has continued this process. But it brings with it scholars who fundamentally either reject most of first-century anthropomorphism or have restated it in such a way that the Bible still proves to be a treasure house even after the "demythologizing" process. Marcus Borg states this position clearly.

> [I]t is possible to take this language about another world seriously, even though not literally. To a large extent, it is the language of the "imagination," that part of us that creates and responds to symbols and images. The crucial question is, "What are these images and symbols about?" (Borg, 1994a, p. 135)

Borg does not answer this crucial question—at least not directly. But a careful reading of his works suggests that his image of Jesus reflects a twentieth-century paradigm that addresses human problems within a non-anthropomorphic paradigm. Similarly, Robert Funk's Jesus sounds strikingly like someone whose teachings and style mesh with the best of the twentieth and twenty-first centuries. The heavy supernatural, anthropomorphic passages in the Gospels are stripped away, bringing us to a remarkable Jesus whose central message was love of one's enemies and special love for outsiders (Funk, 1996, p. 200). John Dominic Crossan confronts the charge that scholars tend to portray Jesus as in harmony with their own highest values. He predicts that there will always be divergent historical Jesuses with divergent Christs built upon them. He adds that this process of reconstructing the historical Jesus and developing various interpretations of the reconstructions began with the New Testament itself (Crossan, 1994b, p. 200).

Crossan's conclusion is as candid as his historical research is impressive. We think that no version of a historical Jesus thus far presented could have initiated the Christian movement. Most New Testament scholars regard a great deal of the Gospels to be artistic creations that the writers and redactors believed reflected the life of Jesus on earth. A key question remains. How much is genuine reflection and how much is creative literary work born of passion and the will-to-believe? We are more inclined to say, not that a historical Jesus initiated a movement, but that early Christians created their movement and did so while believing they were telling the true story of Jesus. Thus, they belong to an ancient tradition that includes Homer, Hesiod, Heraclitus and others who regarded themselves the recipients of divine communication. Paul and the Gospels are unique in their drive to present a divine being who triumphs over all human vulnerability and makes his followers a part of his triumph. Like Plato, the early Christians fought with everything within them against the conclusion that tragedy has the final word.

> [H]e said to me, "My grace is sufficient for you, for [my] power is made perfect in weakness." So, I will boast all the more gladly of my weaknesses, so that the power of Christ may dwell in me. Therefore I am content with weaknesses, insults, hardships, persecutions, and calamities for the sake of Christ; for whenever I am weak, then I am strong. (2 Cor. 12:9-10)

Bibliography

Aaron, Daniel (1992), "What Can You Learn from a Historical Novel?" *American Heritage, vol. 43, iss. 6, p. 62.*

Adam, A. K. M. (1995), *What Is Postmodern Biblical Criticism?* Fortress Press, Minneapolis, MN.

Aichele, G. (1992), *The Fantastic in the Discourse of Jesus, Semeis*, vol. 60, pp. 53-64.

Allen, O. Wesley, Jr. (1997), *The Death of Herod: The Narrative and Theological Function of Retribution in Luke-Acts,* Scholars Press, Atlanta, GA.

Allison, Dale C. (1998), *Jesus of Nazareth: Millenarian Prophet,* Fortress Press, Minneapolis, MN.

Amore, Roy C. (1978), *Two Masters, One Message: The Lives and Teachings of Gautama and Jesus*, Abingdon Press, Nashville, TN.

Anderson, Paul N. (1996), *The Christology of the Fourth Gospel: Its Unity and Disunity in Light of John 6*, Trinity Press International, Valley Forge, PA.

Aus, Roger D. (1988), *Caught in the Act, Walking on the Sea, and the Release of Barabas Revisited*, Scholars Press, Atlanta, GA, [Deals with the maniacal Caligula's crossing the Bay of Naples].

Bar-Efrat, Shimeon (1989), *Narrative Art in the Bible*, Sheffield Academic Press, Sheffield, England.

Barbour, John D. (1984), *Tragedy as a Critique of Virtue: The Novel and Ethical Reflection*, Scholars Press, Chico, CA.

Barrett, Anthony. A. (1990). *Caligula: The Corruption of Power*, Yale University Press, New Haven, CT.

Beare, Francis Wright (1973), *The Epistle to the Philippians,* Third Ed., *Black's New Testament Commentaries,* Black, London.

Bellinger, W. H., Jr., and William R. Farmer, eds. (1998), *Jesus and the Suffering Servant: Isaiah 53 and Christian Origins*, Trinity Press International, Harrisburg, PA.

Betz, Hans Dieter (1995), *The Sermon on the Mount*, Fortress Press, Minneapolis, MN.

Betz, Hans Dieter, and W. Schweiker (1997), "Concerning Mountains and Morals: A Conversation about the Sermon on the Mount," *Criterion*, vol. 36, iss. 2, pp. 18-26.

Bloom, Harold (1998), *Shakespeare: The Invention of the Human*, Riverhead Books, New York, NY.

----- (1994), *The Western Canon: the Books and School of the Ages*, Harcourt Brace and Company, New York.

Bock, Darrell L. (1994), *Commentary on Luke 1: 1-9:50*, Baker Book House Co., Grand Rapids, MI.

----- (1995), "The Words of Jesus in the Gospels: Live, Jive, or Memorex?" in *Jesus Under Fire*, M. J. Wilkins and J. P. Moreland, eds., Zondervan Press, Grand Rapids, MI, pp. 77-87.

Bolles, Edmund Blair (1988), *Remembering and Forgetting: Inquiries into the Nature of Memory*, Walker and Company, New York, NY.

Borg, Marcus J. (1984), *Conflict, Holiness and Politics in the Teachings of Jesus*, Edwin Mellen Press, New York.

----- (1985), "The Historical Jesus and Christian Preaching," *Christian Century*, vol. 102, pp. 764-767.

----- (1987), *Jesus: A New Vision: Spirit, Culture, and the Life of Discipleship*, HarperSanFrancisco, San Francisco, CA.

----- (1994a), *Jesus in Contemporary Scholarship*, Trinity Press International, Valley Forge, PA.

----- (1994b), *Meeting Jesus Again for the First Time*, Harper Collins, San Francisco, CA.

-----, ed. (1997). *The Last Gospel Q: The Original Sayings of Jesus*, Trinity Press International, Valley Forge, PA.

Bowersock, G. W. (1994), *Fiction as History: Nero to Julian,* University of California Press, Berkeley, CA.

Bradford, R. W. (May 1998), "Making Sense of a Life," *Liberty*, pp. 64-65.

Bradshaw, Graham (1987), "The Genealogy of Ideals: *Troylus and Cressida,*" in *Shakespeare's Skepticism,* Cornell University Press, Ithaca, NY, pp. 126-163.

----- (1987) "*Hamlet* and the Art of Grafting," in *Shakespeare's Skepticism,* Cornell University Press, Ithaca, NY, pp. 95-125.

Burkert, Walter (1987), *Ancient Mystery Cults*, Harvard University Press, Cambridge, MA.

Carlson, Jeffrey, and Robert A. Ludwig, eds. (1994). *Jesus and Faith: A Conversation on the Work of John Dominic Crossan*., Orbis Books, Maryknoll, NY.

Cartlidge, David R., and David L. Dungan (1980), *Documents for the Study of the Gospels*, Fortress Press, Philadelphia, PA.

Cassidy, Richard J. (1992), *John's Gospel in New Perspective: Christology and the Realities of Roman Power*, Orbis Books, Maryknoll, NY.

Castelli, Elizabeth A., and Hal Taussig (1997), *Reimagining Christian Origins: A Colloquium Honoring Burton L. Mack,* Trinity Press International, Valley Forge, PA.

Chariton (1989), "Chaereas and Callirhoe," B. P. Reardon, ed., trans., *Collected Ancient Greek Novels,* University of California Press, Berkeley, CA.

Charlesworth, James H., ed. (1983-85), *The Old Testament Pseudepigrapha*, vols. 1-2, Doubleday, New York, NY.

Charlesworth, James H., and Walter P. Weaver, eds. (1994), *Images of Jesus Today,* Trinity Press International, Valley Forge, PA.

Cheon, Samuel (1997), *The Exodus Story in the Wisdom of Solomon: A Study in Biblical Interpretation*, Sheffield Press, Sheffield, England.

Clark, Gordon H. (1961), *Religion, Reason, and Revelation*, Presbyterian and Reformed Publishing Company, Phillipsburg, NJ.

Cohn, Norman (1993), *Cosmos, Chaos, and the World to Come: The Ancient Roots of Apocalyptic Faith*, Yale University Press, New Haven, CT.

Conklin, George N. (1949), *Biblical Criticism and Heresy in Milton*, Columbia University Press, *New York, NY*.

Coote, Robert B., and Mary P. Coote (1990), *Power, Politics, and the Making of the Bible*, Fortress Press, Minneapolis, MN.

Corley, Kathleen E. (1993), *Private Women, Public Meals: Social Conflict in the Synoptic Tradition*, Hendrickson Publishers Inc., Peabody, MA.

----- (1996), "Jesus, Mary Magdalene and Salome," *The Fourth R*, vol. 9, p. 15.

----- (1998), *Feminist Myths and Christian Origins: The Historical Jesus, Gender and Gospel Tradition*, Oxford University Press, New York, NY.

Crossan, John Dominic (1988), *The Cross that Spoke: The Origins of the Passion Narrative*, Harper & Row, San Francisco, CA.

----- (1985), *Four Other Gospels: Shadows on the Contours of Canon*, Winston Press, Seabury Books, Minneapolis, MN.

----- (1991), *The Historical Jesus: The Life of a Mediterranean Jewish Peasant*, HarperSanFrancisco, San Francisco, CA.

----- (1994a), "The Historical Jesus in Earliest Christianity," *Jesus and Faith*, Jeffry Carlson and Robert A. Ludwig, eds., Orbis Books, Maryknoll, NY, pp. 1-21.

----- (1994b), *Jesus: A Revolutionary Biography*, HarperSanFrancisco, San Francisco, CA.

----- (1994c), "Responses and Reflections," *Jesus and Faith*, Jeffry Carlson and Robert A. Ludwig, eds., Orbis Books, Maryknoll, NY, pp. 142-164.

----- (1995), *The Essential Jesus: What Jesus Really Taught*, HarperSanFrancisco, San Francisco, CA.

----- (1996), *Who Killed Jesus? Exposing the Roots of Anti-Semitism in the Gospel Story of the Death of Jesus*, HarperSanFrancisco, San Francisco, CA.

Culpepper, R. Alan (1983), *Anatomy of the Fourth Gospel: A Study in Literary Design*, Fortress Press, Philadelphia, PA.

Cuss, D. (1974), *Imperial Cult and Honorary Terms in the New Testament (Paradosis XXIII)*, The University Press, Fribourg, Switzerland.

D'Costa, Gavin, ed. (1996), *Resurrection Reconsidered*, Oneworld Publications, Rockport, MA.

Davies, William David (1955), *Paul and Rabbinic Judaism: Some Rabbinic Elements in Pauline Theology*, S.P.C.K., London.

Dennett, Daniel C. (1995), *Darwin's Dangerous Idea: Evolution and the Meanings of Life*, Simon & Schuster, New York, NY.

den Heyer, C. J. (1997), *Jesus Matters: 150 Years of Research*, Trinity Press International, Valley Forge, PA.

Deutsch, Celia M. (1997), *Lady Wisdom, Jesus, and the Sages: Metaphor and Social Context in Matthew's Gospel*, Trinity Press International, Valley Forge, PA.

Dewey, Joanna (1993), "Jesus' Healing of Women: Conformity and Non-Conformity to Dominant Culture Values as Clues for Historical Reconstruction," *Society of Biblical Literature*, pp. 178-193.

Dewey, John (1955), *Logic: The Theory of Inquiry*, Henry Holt, New York, NY.

Donaldson, Terence L. (1997), *Paul and the Gentiles: Remapping the Apostle's Convictional World*, Fortress Press, Minneapolis, MN.

Dostoevsky, Fyodor (1992), *The Karamazov Brothers*, Ignat Avsey, trans. and commentator, Oxford University Press, New York, NY.

Dowd, Sharyn E. (1990), "Maccabees, Fourth," in *Mercer Dictionary of the Bible*, Watson E. Mills, ed., Mercer University Press, Macon, GA, p. 537.

Downing, F. G. (1998), "Deeper Reflections on the Jewish Cynic Jesus." *Journal of Biblical Literature*, vol. 117, iss. 1, pp. 97-104.

Dungan, David L. (1971), *The Sayings of Jesus in the Churches of Paul: The Use of the Synoptic Tradition in the Regulation of Early Church Life*, Fortress Press, Philadelphia, PA.

Ehrman, Bart D. (1993), *The Orthodox Corruption of Scripture: The Effect of Early Christological Controversies on the Text of the New Testament*, Oxford University Press, New York, NY.

Elton, William R. (1988), ***King Lear** and the gods*, University of Kentucky Press, Lexington, KN.

Elwel, Walter A., ed. (1989), *Evangelical Commentary on the Bible*, Baker Book House, Grand Rapids, MI.

Evans, C. A., and S. E. Porter, eds. (1995), *The Historical Jesus: A Sheffield Reader*, Sheffield Academic Press, Sheffield, England.

Evans, C. A., and J. A. Sanders, eds. (1997), *Early Christian Interpretation of Scriptures of Israel: Investigations and Proposals,* Sheffield Academic Press, Sheffield, England.

Exum, J. Cheryl. (1996), *Tragedy and Biblical Narrative: Arrows of the Almighty,* Cambridge University Press, New York, NY.

Ewert, David (1989), "1-2 Thessalonians," *Evangelical Commentary on the Bible,* Walter A. Elwel, ed., Baker Book House Co., Grand Rapids, MI., pp. 1064-1097.

Exum, J. Cheryl, and J. W. Whedbee (1984), "Isaac, Samson, and Saul," in *Tragedy and Comedy in the Bible, Semeia,* vol. 32, pp. 5-40.

Fanger, Donald (1965), *Dostoevsky and Romantic Realism: A Study of Dostoevsky in Relation to Balzac, Dickens, and Gogol,* Phoenix Books, Chicago, IL.

Farrar, Austin (1948), *The Glass of Vision,* Dacre, London.

Fears, J. R. (1997), *Princeps A Diis Electus: The Divine Election of the Emperor as a Political Concept at Rome, Papers and Monographs of the American Academy in Rome*, vol. 26, p. 216.

Fehrenbacher, Don Edward, and Virginia Ferhrenbacher, eds. (1996), *Recollected Words of Abraham Lincoln*, Stanford University Press, Stanford, CA.

Ferrill, Arthur (1991), *Caligula: Emperor of Rome,* Thames & Hudson Press, New York, NY.

Fiorenza, Elisabeth Schüssler (1983), *In Memory of Her: A Feminist Theological Reconstruction of Christian Origins*, Crossroad Press, New York, NY.

Fredricksen, P. (1988), *From Jesus to Christ: The Origins of the New Testament Images of Jesus*, Yale University Press, New Haven, CT.

Frogley, Kent (1991), "Salting the Truth," *Sunstone: Mormon Experience, Scholarship, Issues, and Art,* vol. 15:3, iss. 81, pp. 47-48.

Frye, Roland M. (1984), *The Renaissance Hamlet: Issues and Responses in 1600*, Princeton University Press, Princeton, NJ.

Funk, Robert W. (1996), *Honest to Jesus: Jesus for a New Millennium*, HarperSanFrancisco Press, San Francisco, CA.

Gaustad, Edwin S. (1973), *Religion in America: History and Historiography*, American Historical Association, Washington, DC.

----- (1993), *Neither King nor Prelate: Religion and the New Nation, 1776-1826,* Wm. B. Eerdman's, Grand Rapids, MI.

Geertz, Clifford (1973), *The Interpretation of Cultures*, Basic Books, New York, NY.

Gilles, Donald (1993), *Philosophy of Science in the Twentieth Century: Four Central Themes*, Blackwell Publishers, Inc., Cambridge, MA.

Girard, René (1977), *Violence and the Sacred*, Patrick Gregory, trans., Johns Hopkins University Press, Baltimore, MD.

---- (1987), *Things Hidden Since the Foundation of the World*, Michael Metteer and Stephan Bann, trans., Stanford University Press, Stanford, CA.

Goulder, Michael (1994), *St. Paul vs. St. Peter: A Tale of Two Missions,* Westminster John Knox Press, Louisville, KY.

Grant, Frederic C. (1957), *Ancient Roman Religion*, Liberal Arts Press, New York, NY.

Graham, Billy (1981), *Till Armageddon: A Perspective on Suffering*, Word Books, Waco, TX.

Guenther, H. O. (1985), *Footprints of Jesus' Twelve in Early Christian Traditions*, Lang Publishers, New York, NY.

Gundry, R. H. (1982), *Matthew: A Commentary on His Literary and Theological Art*, Wm. B. Eerdman's Publishing Co., Grand Rapids, MI.

Gunn, David M. (1989), *The Fate of King Saul: An Interpretation of a Biblical Story*, Sheffield Academic Press, Sheffield, England.

Hankins, J. E. (1941), *The Character of Hamlet and Other Essays*, University of South Carolina Press, Chapel Hill, SC.

Hanson, A. T. (1987), *The Paradox of the Cross and the Thought of St. Paul*, Sheffield Academic Press, Sheffield, England.

----- (1995), "The Midrash in 2 Corinthians 3: A Reconsideration," *The Pauline Writing*, S. E. Porter and C. A. Evans, eds., Sheffield Academic Press, Sheffield, England.

Harvey, V. A. (1981), *The Historian and the Believer: The Morality of Historical Knowledge and Christian Belief*, University of Illinois Press, Champagne, IL.

Hegel, G. W. F. (1950), *The Logic*, in "The Logic of Hegel," William Wallace, trans., *The Encyclopedia of the Philosophical Sciences*, Geoffrey Cambridge, London.

Helms, Randel (1988), *Gospel Fictions*, Prometheus Books, Buffalo, NY.

Hill, Donna (1997), *Joseph Smith: The First Mormon*, Signature Books, Midvale, UT.

Hock, Ronald F., J. Bradley Chance, and Judith Perkins, eds. (1999), *Ancient Fictions and Early Christian Narrative*, Scholars Press, Atlanta, GA.

Holquist, Michael (1997), *Dostoevsky and the Novel*, Northwestern University Press, Evanston, IL.

Horsley, R. A., ed. (1997), *Paul and Empire: Religion and Power in Roman Imperial Society*, Trinity Press International, Harrisburg, PA.

Humphrey, W. L. (1985), *The Tragic Vision and the Hebrew Tradition*, Fortress Press, Philadelphia, PA.

Hunter, Robert G. (1976), *Shakespeare and the Mystery of God's Judgments*, University of Georgia Press, Athens, GA.

Jenks, Gregory C. (1999), "What Did Paul Know about Jesus?," *Westar Institute Seminar Papers*, Westar Institute, Santa Rosa, CA, pp. 75-90.

Johnson, Luke Timothy (1997), *The Real Jesus: The Misguided Quest for the Historical Jesus and the Truth of the Traditional Gospels*, HarperSanFrancisco, San Francisco, CA.

Josephus (1965), *Jewish Antiquities*, Loeb ed., L. H. Fieldman, trans., Harvard University Press, Cambridge, MA.

Kaufmann, Walter (1968), *Tragedy and Philosophy*, Princeton University Press, Princeton, NJ.

Kelley, D. R., ed. (1991), *Versions of History from Antiquity to the Enlightenment*, Yale University Press, New Haven, CT.

Kinman, Brent (1999), "Parousia, Jesus' 'A-Triumphal' Entry, and the Fate of Jerusalem (Luke 19:28-44)," *Journal of Biblical Literature*, vol. 118, iss. 2, pp. 279-294.

Kloppenborg, J. S., ed. (1965), *Conflict and Invention: Literary, Rhetorical, and Social Studies on the Sayings Gospel Q*, Trinity Press International, Valley Forge, PA.

Kraeger, Linda, and Joe E. Barnhart (1992), *Dostoevsky on Evil and Atonement: the Ontology of Personalism in His Major Fiction*, Edwin Mellen Press, Lewiston, NY.

Kraeling, C. H. (1951), *John the Baptist*, Schribner, New York, NY.

Krook, Dorothea (1969), *Elements of Tragedy*, Yale University Press, New Haven, CT.

Kuhn, T. S. (1971), *The Structure of Scientific Revolutions*, 2nd ed., enlarged, University of Chicago Press, Chicago, IL.

Laato, Antti (1998), *A Star Is Rising: The Historical Development of the Old Testament Royal Ideology and the Rise of the Jewish Messianic Expectations*, Scholars Press, Atlanta, GA.

Larue, Gerald A. (1996), *Free Thought across the Centuries*, Humanist Press, Amherst, NY.

Levenson, Jon Douglas (1993), *The Death and Resurrection of the Beloved Son: The Transformation of Child Sacrifice in Judaism and Christianity*, Yale University Press, New Haven, CT.

Lindskoog, Kathryn (1997), *Dante's* **Divine Comedy/Inferno**: *Journey to Joy*, part 1, Mercer University Press, Macon, GA.

Longman, Tremper (1987), *Literary Approaches to Biblical Interpretations, Foundations of Contemporary Interpretation Series,* vol. 3, M. Silva, ed., Academie Books, Grand Rapids, MI.

MacAllister, A. T. (1982), "Introduction," to Dante Alighiere, *The Inferno*, J. Ciardi, trans., New American Library, New York, NY.

Maccoby, Hyam (1991), *Paul and Hellenism*, Trinity Press International, Philadelphia, PA.

Mack, Burton (1985), "The Innocent Transgressor: Jesus in Early Christian Myth and History," *Semeia*: *René Girard and Biblical Studies*, vol. 33, p. 156.

----- (1988), *A Myth of Innocence: Mark and Christian Origins,* Fortress Press, Philadelphia, PA.

----- (1996), *Who Wrote the New Testament? The Making of the Christian Myth*, HarperSanFrancisco, San Francisco, CA.

MacPike, Loralee (1981), *Dostoevsky's Dickens: A Study of Literary Influence,* Barnes & Noble, Totowa, NJ.

Malherbe, Abraham J. (1977), *Social Aspects of Early Christianity*, Louisiana State University Press, Baton Rouge, LA.

Marius, Richard (1985), *Thomas More: A Biography,* Vantage Books, Random House, New York, NY.

Martinich, A. P. (1992), *The Two Gods of Levianthan: Thomas Hobbes on Religion and Politics,* Cambridge University Press, New York, NY.

McKnight, Edgar V., and Elizabeth Struthers Malbon, eds. (1995), *The New Literary Criticism and the New Testament,* Trinity Press International, Valley Forge, PA.

McNicol, Allan J., David B. Peabody, and David L. Dungan, eds. (1996), *Beyond the Q Impasse-Luke's Use of Matthew: A Demonstration by the Research Team of the International Institute for Gospel Studies*, Trinity Press International, Valley Forge, PA.

McPherson, James M. (1996), "Lincoln Speaks," *The Atlantic Monthly*, vol. 278, iss. 6, p. 121.

Meadors, Edward P. (1999), "The 'Messianic' Implications of the Q Material," *Journal of Biblical Literature*, vol.118 iss. 2, pp. 253-277.

Meeks, Wayne A. (1993), *The Origins of Christian Morality: The First Two Centuries*, Yale University Press, New Haven, CT.

Meier, John P. (1991), "Reflections on Jesus-of-History Research Today," *Jesus' Jewishness*, J. Charlesworth, ed., Crossroad Publishing Co., New York, NY.

Meyer, Marvin., ed. (1989), *The Ancient Mysteries: A Sourcebook*, Harper Books, New York, NY.

Millar, F. (1997), *The Emperor in the Roman World (31 BC – AD 337)*, Cornell University Press, Ithaca, NY.

Miller, William (1973), *Fact or Fiction: The Dilemma of the Renaissance Storyteller*, Harvard University Press, Cambridge, MA.

Milton, John (1933), "The Christian Doctrine," in *The Student's Milton*, F. A. Patterson, ed., Appleton-Century-Crafts, Inc., New York, NY, pp. 919-1076.

Moore, Stephen D. (1989), *Literary Criticism and the Gospels: The Theoretical Challenge*, Yale University Press, New Haven , CT.

Morris, Margaret (1999 revision), "Jesus-Augustus: from Imperial Cult to Christianity," unpublished manuscript currently under review.

Murray, Gilbert (1955), *Five Stages of Greek Religion*. Doubleday Anchor Books, Garden City, NY.

---- (1960) *The Rise of The Greek Epic*, 4th ed., Oxford University Press, New York, NY.

Newman, Barclay M. (1997), "Challenging the Curse on the Chosen Ones," *Explorations*, vol. 11, iss. 3, p. 7.

Noll, K. L. (1997), *The Faces of David*, Sheffield Academic Press, Sheffield, England.

Nussbaum, Martha Craven (1986), *The Fragility of Goodness: Luck and Ethics in Greek Tragedy and Philosophy*, Cambridge University Press, New York, NY.

Orwin, Clifford (1997), *The Humanity of Thucydides*, Princeton University Press, Cambridge, MA.

Ovid (1916), *Metamorphoses: The Lives of the Caesars*, 2 vols., F. J. Miller, trans., Harvard University Press, Cambridge, MA.

Packer, Lynn (1991), "Douglas Stringfellow's War Stories," *Sunstone: Mormon Experience, Scholarship, Issues, and Art*, vol. 15:3, iss. 81, p. 40.

---- (1991), "Paul H. Dunn: *Fields of Dreams*," *Sunstone: Mormon Experience, Scholarship, Issues, and Art*, vol. 15:3, iss. 81, pp. 12-15.

Pearson, Birger A. (1997), *The Emergence of the Christian Religion: Essays on Early Christianity*, Trinity Press International, Harrisburg, PA.

Peck, Elbert Eugene (1991), "Casting Out the Spell," *Sunstone: Mormon Experience, Scholarship, Issues, and Art*, vol. 15:3, iss. 81, pp. 12-15.

Pervo, Richard I. (1987), *Profit with Delight: The Literary Genre of the Acts of the Apostles*, Fortress Press, Philadelphia, PA.

----- (1994), "Romancing an Oft-Neglected Stone: The Pastoral Epistles and the Epistolry Novel," *Journal of Higher Criticism*, vol. 1, pp. 25-47.

Peterson, Brian. K. (1998), *Eloquence and the Proclamation of the Gospel in Corinth*, Scholars Press, Atlanta, GA.

Pickett, Raymond (1997), *The Cross in Corinth: The Social Significance of the Death of Jesus*, Sheffield Academic Press, Sheffield, England.

Pilch, John J. (1993), "Insights and Models for Understanding the Healing Activity of the Historical Jesus," *Society for Biblical Literature 1993 Seminar Papers*, Scholars Press, Atlanta, GA, pp. 154-177.

Plothow, Roger D. (1991), "The Unintentional Lessons of Paul H. Dunn," *Sunstone: Mormon Experience, Scholarship, Issues, and Art*, vol. 15:3, iss. 81, pp. 49-50.

Plumb, J. H. (1971), *The Death of History*, Houghton Mifflin, Boston, MA.

Polhill, John B. (1990), "Pastoral Epistles," *Mercer Dictionary of the Bible*, Watson E. Mills, ed., Mercer University Press, Macon, GA, pp. 649-652.

Poll, Richard D. (1991), "Truth, Facts, and Personal Anecdotes," *Sunstone: Mormon Experience, Scholarship, Issues, and Art*, vol. 15:3, iss. 81, pp. 54-55.

Popper, Karl (1950), *The Open Society and Its Enemies*, Princeton University Press, Princeton, NY.

----- (1991), *Conjectures and Refutations: The Growth of Scientific Knowledge*, 5th ed., Routledge, New York, NY.

----- (1992), *In Search of a Better World: Lectures and Essays from Thirty Years*, L. J. Bennett, trans., Routledge, New York, NY.

Porter, Stanley E., and Craig. A. Evans, eds. (1995), *The Pauline Writings*, Sheffield Academic Press, Sheffield, England.

Powell, Mark Allan (1990), *What is Narrative Criticism?* Fortress Press, Minneapolis, MN.

Price, Robert M. (1993), "In the Beginning Was the Deed," *Forum: A Journal of the Foundation & Facts of Western Culture*, vol. 9, iss. 3-4, pp. 257-303.

----- (1994), "Introducing the *Journal of Higher Criticism*," *The Journal of Higher Criticism*, vol. 1, pp. 3-4.

Price, S. R. F. (1984), "Gods and Emperors: The Greek Language of the Roman Imperial Cult," *Journal of Hellenic Studies*, vol. 104, pp. 79-95.

Rabkin, Norman (1967), *Shakespeare and the Common Understanding*, The Free Press, New York, NY.

----- (1981), *Shakespeare and the Problem of Meaning*, University of Chicago Press, Chicago, IL.

Rackin, Phyllis (1990), *Stages of History: Shakespeare's English Chronicles*, Cornell University Press, Ithaca, NY.

Reardon, B. P., ed. (1989), *Collected Ancient Greek Novels*, University of California Press, Berkeley, CA.

-----, (1989), "General Introduction," *Collected Ancient Greek Novels*, B. P. Reardon, ed., University of California Press, Berkeley, CA.

Rée, Jonathan (1987), *Philosophical Tales: An Essay in Philosophy and Literature*, Methuen, New York, NY.

Robert, Louis (1938), *Études epigraphiques et philologiques*, Champion, Paris, France.

Robertson, Richard R. (1991), "Mormon Leader Admits Exaggerating Stories," *Sunstone: Mormon Experience, Scholarship, Issues, and Art*, vol. 15:3, iss. 81, pp. 29-30 in *The Arizona Republic*, 16 Feb 1991.

---- (1991), "Paul Dunn's Comments," *Sunstone: Mormon Experience, Scholarship, Issues, and Art*, vol. 15:3, iss. 81, pp. 44-45.

Rothstein, Arnold M. (1993), *The Jesus Idea*, Prometheus Books, Buffalo, NY.

Rowse, A. L. (1981), *What Shakespeare Read—and Thought*, Coward, McCann & Geoghegan, New York, NY.

Sanders, E. P. (1991), *Paul*, Past Masters Series, Oxford University Press, New York, NY.

----- (1993a), *The Historical Figure of Jesus*, Penguin Books, New York, NY.

----- (1993b), "The Life of Jesus," *Christianity and Rabbinic Judaism,* H. Shanks, ed., Biblical Archaeological Society, Washington, DC, pp. 41-83.

Sanders, J. A., (1969), "Dissenting Deities and Philippians 2:1-11," *Journal of Biblical Literature,* vol. 88, iss. 3, pp. 279-290.

Sayre, Robert F. (1991), "Fiction and Fact in Autobiography," *Sunstone: Mormon Experience, Scholarship, Issues, and Art,* vol. 15:3, iss. 81, pp. 52-53.

Schwager, Raymund (1987), *Must There Be Scapegoats? Violence and Redemption in the Bible*, Maria L. Assad, trans., Harper & Row, San Francisco, CA.

Schweitzer, Albert (1954), *The Quest of the Historical Jesus: A Critical Study of Its Progress from Reimarus to Wrede*, W. Montgomery, trans., 3rd ed., Adam and Charles Black, London.

Scot, Reginald (1973), *Discover of Witchcraft and Discourse upon Devils and Spirits*, 1584 ed., Roman and Littlefield, Totowa, NJ.

Scott, Bernard Brandon (1994), "From Reimarus to Crossan: Stages in a Quest," *Currents in Research*, vol. 2, p. 270.

----- (1997), "Profile of Jesus," Jesus Seminar Paper Presented in Santa Rosa, CA, p. 12.

**Second Esdras.* Suggs, Sackenfeld, and Mueller. 1026-1057.

Seeley, D. (1994), "The Background of the Philippians Hymn (2:6-11)," *Journal of Higher Criticism*, vol. 1, pp. 49-72.

Setzer, C. (1997), "Excellent Women: Female Witness to the Resurrection," *Journal of Biblical Literature,* vol. 116, iss. 2, pp. 259-272.

Shaheen, Naseeb (1987), *Biblical References in Shakespeare's Tragedies*, University of Delaware Press, Newark, DE.

----- (1989), *Biblical References in Shakespeare's History Plays,* University of Delaware Press, Newark, DE.

Shipps, Jan. (1985), *Mormonism: The Story of a New Religious Tradition*, University of Chicago Press, Chicago, IL.

Shoeck, Helmut (1996), *Envy: A Theory of Social Behavior*, Liberty Press, Indianapolis, IN.

Simon, Ulrich E. (1989), *Pity and Terror: Christianity and Tragedy*, San Martin's Press, New York, NY.

Smar, Janet. L., ed. (1993), *Historical Criticism and the Challenge of Theory*, University of Illinois Press, Champagne, IL.

Smith, Morton (1978), *Jesus the Magician*, Harper & Row, San Francisco, CA.

Smith, Stephen. H. (1996), *A Lion with Wings: A Narrative-Critical Approach to Mark's Gospel*, The Biblical Seminar 38, Sheffield Academic Press, Sheffield, England.

Snodgrass, Klyne (1995), "Spheres of Influence," in *The Pauline Writings*, S. E. Porter and C.A. Evans, eds. Sheffield Academic Press, Sheffield, England.

Songer, Harold S. (1990), "Galilee," in *Mercer Dictionary of the Bible*, Watson E. Mills, ed., Mercer University Press, Macon, GA, pp. 315-316.

Steiner, George (1996), *The Death of Tragedy*, Yale University Press, New Haven, CT.

Stendahl, Krister (1976), *Paul among Jews and Gentiles, and Other Essays*, Fortress Press, Philadelphia, PA.

Suggs, M. Jack, Katherine D. Sakenfeld, and James. R. Mueller, eds. (1992), *The Oxford Study Bible: Revised English Bible with the Apocrypha,* Oxford University Press, New York, NY.

Sullivan, Clayton (1988), *Rethinking Realized Eschatology*, Mercer University Press, Macon, GA.

Tatum, W. Barnes (1998), "Jesus' So-called Triumphal Entry," *Forum,* New Series, vol. 1, iss. 1, p. 141.

Theissen, Gerd, and Annette Merz (1998), *The Historical Jesus: A Comprehensive Guide*, John Bowden, trans., Fortress Press, Minneapolis, MN.

Thomas, Keith (1971), *Religion and the Decline of Magic*, Scribner's, New York, NY.

Thucydides (1993), *On Justice, Power, and Human Nature: The Essence of Thucydides' History of the Peloponnesian War*, Paul Woodruff, trans., Hackett Publishing Company, Indianapolis, IN.

Tolstoy, Leo (1970), *War and Peace*, Louise Maude and Aylmer Maude, trans., Simon and Schuster, New York, NY.

Trafton, J. L. (1995), "Introduction to Second Esdras," *Mercer Commentary on the Bible*, W. A. Mills and R. F. Wilson, eds., Mercer University Press, Macon, GA, pp. 915-928.

Turcan, Robert (1992), *The Cults of the Roman Empire*, Antonia Nevill, trans., Blackwell Publishers, Inc., Cambridge, MA.

Vaage, Leif E. (1994), *Galilean Upstarts: Jesus' First Followers According to Q*, Trinity Press International, Valley Forge, PA.

van Buren, Paul N. (1998), *According to the Scriptures: the Origin of the Gospel and of the Church's Old Testament*, William B. Eerdman's, Grand Rapids, MI.

Veyne, Paul (1988), *Did the Greeks Believe in Their Myths? An Essay on the Constitutive Imagination*, Paula Wissing, trans., University of Chicago Press, Chicago, IL.

Via, Dan O. (1990), *Self-Deception and Wholeness in Paul and Matthew*, Fortress Press, Minneapolis, MN.

Warfield, Benjamin B. (1918), *Counterfeit Miracles*, Charles Scribner's Sons, New York, NY.

Weber, Max (1965), *The Sociology of Religion*, E. Fischoff, trans., 4th ed., Beacon Press, Boston, MA.

Wecter, Dixon (1943), *Hero in America*, Scribner's Sons, New York, NY.

Weil, Simone (1976), *Intimations of Christianity among the Ancient Greeks*, Elisabeth C. Geissbuhler, trans., Routledge & Kegan Paul, London.

Weisberg, David B. (1985), "Cyrus II," in *Harper's Bible Dictionary*, Paul J. Achtemeier, ed., Harper & Row, San Francisco, CA, p. 200.

Weisgerber, Jean (1968), *Faulkner and Dostoevsky: Influence and Confluence,* Dean McWilliams, trans., Ohio University Press, Athens, OH.

Wells, George. A. (1971), The Jesus of the Early Christians: A Study in Christian Origins, Prometheus Books, Buffalo, NY.

----- (1975), *Did Jesus Exist?* Prometheus Books, Buffalo, NY.

----- (1982), *The Historical Evidence for Jesus,* Prometheus Books, Buffalo, NY.

----- (1989), *Who Was Jesus? A Critique of the New Testament Record,* Open Court Press, LaSalle, IL.

----- (1996), *The Jesus Legend*, Open Court Press, Chicago, IL.

----- (1998), *The Jesus Myth,* Open Court Press, Chicago, IL.

White, Leslie. A. (1971), *The Science of Culture: A Study of Man and Civilization*, Farrar, Straus and Giroux, New York, NY.

Wicker, Brian (1975), *The Story-Shaped World: Fiction and Metaphysics*, University of Notre Dame Press, Notre Dame, IN.

Wilkins, Michael J., and James P. Moreland, eds. (1995), *Jesus Under Fire*, Zondervan Publishing House, Grand Rapids, MI.

Wilson, J. Dover (1959), *What Happens in Hamlet?* Cambridge University Press, Cambridge, England.

Wilson, William A. (1991), "The Spinners of Tales," *Sunstone: Mormon Experience, Scholarship, Issues, and Art,* vol. 15:3, iss. 81, pp. 50-52.

Wink, Walter (March 1997), "Jesus: as Real as We Can Get Him," *Jesus Seminar Papers, Presented in Santa Rosa, CA,* p. 32.

Winston, David (1979), *The Wisdom of Solomon: A New Translation with Introduction and Commentary*, Anchor Bible, vol. 43, Doubleday, Garden City, NY.

Winter, Bruce W. (1997), *Philo and Paul among the Sophists*, Cambridge University Press, New York, NY.

The Wisdom of Solomon (1992), M. J. Suggs, Katharine Doob Sakenfeld, and James R. Mueller, eds., Oxford University Press, New York, NY.

Wolf, William. J. (1957), *No Cross, No Crown: A Study of the Atonement*, Doubleday, Garden City, NY.

Woodruff, Paul, ed. and trans. (1993), *Thucydides on Justice, Power, and Human Nature: The Essence of [Selections from] Thucydides'* **History of the Peloponnesian War**, Hackett Publishing Company., Indianapolis, IN.

Young, Lawrence (1991), "Truth and Transcendence," *Sunstone: Mormon Experience, Scholarship, Issues, and Art*, vol. 15:3, iss. 81, p. 56.

Ziolkowski, Theodore (1972), *Fictional Transfigurations of Jesus*, Princeton University Press, Princeton, NJ.

Index